T0305147

Bilateral Trade Agreements in the Era of Globalization

This book is dedicated to

Sonakshi Khorana
Graham Rees
Marjorie Kerr

Also

In Memory of

Gerald Yeung

Bilateral Trade Agreements in the Era of Globalization

The EU and India in Search of a Partnership

Sangeeta Khorana
Lecturer, School of Management and Business, Aberystwyth University, UK

Nicholas Perdikis
Director, School of Management and Business, Aberystwyth University, UK

May T. Yeung
Research Associate, Estey Centre for Law and Economics in International Trade, Canada

William A. Kerr
Van Vliet Professor, University of Saskatchewan, Canada

Edward Elgar
Cheltenham, UK • Northampton, MA, USA

Published by
Edward Elgar Publishing Limited
The Lypiatts
15 Lansdown Road
Cheltenham
Glos GL50 2JA
UK

Edward Elgar Publishing, Inc.
William Pratt House
9 Dewey Court
Northampton
Massachusetts 01060
USA

A catalogue record for this book
is available from the British Library

Library of Congress Control Number: 2009937885

ISBN 978 1 84844 795 0

Printed and bound by MPG Books Group, UK

Contents

Figures

Tables

Abbreviations

3PL	third party logistics
ADB	Asian Development Bank
AFTA	ASEAN Free Trade Agreement
ALMP	active labour market programmes
APTA	Asia Pacific Trade Agreement
ASEAN	Association of Southeast Asian Nations
BHC	British High Commission
BIMSTEC	Bay of Bengal Initiative for Multi–sectoral Technical and Economic Cooperation
CAP	Common Agricultural Policy
CARIFORUM	Caribbean Community
CE	Conformité Européenne
CECA	Comprehensive Economic Cooperation Agreement
CECPA	Comprehensive Economic and Cooperation Partnership Agreement
CEFTA	Central European Free Trade Agreement
CEPA	Comprehensive Economic Partnership Agreement
CIS	Commonwealth of Independent States
CLE	Council for Leather Exports
COD	chemical oxygen demand
CUSTA	Canada–US (Free) Trade Agreement
DDA	Doha Development Agenda
EC	European Community
EEA	European Economic Area
EEC	European Economic Community
EFTA	European Free Trade Area
EIA	economic integration agreement

EU	European Union
EXIM	(India's) Export and Import Policy
FDI	foreign direct investment
FIIA	Foreign Investment Implementation Authority
FICCI	Federation of Indian Chambers of Commerce and Industry
FOB	free on board
FTA	free trade agreement
G20	Group of 20
GATS	General Agreement on Trade in Services
GATT	General Agreement on Tariffs and Trade
GCC	Gulf Cooperation Council
GDP	gross domestic product
GSP	Generalised System of Preferences
GSTP	Global System of Trade Preferences
HLTG	High Level Trade Group
HS	Harmonised System
ICT	information and communications technology
ILDP	Integrated Leather Development Programme
ILO	International Labour Organisation
IP	intellectual property
IPR	intellectual property rights
ISO	International Standards Organisation
IT	information technology
LCA	life-cycle analysis
MERCOSUR	Southern Cone Common Market
MFA	Multi-Fibre Agreement
MFN	most favoured nation
MLR	Multinomial Logit Regression
MST	Markenzichen Schadstoffgeprüfte Textilien
MUT	Markenzichen Unweltschonende Textilien
NAFTA	North American Free Trade Agreement
NAMA	non-agricultural market access
NTB	non-tariff barrier
OECD	Organisation for Economic Co-operation and Development
OGL	Open General Licensing System
PCP	pentachlorophenol
PPP	public–private partnership
PSA	partial scope agreement

PTA	preferential trade agreement
REACH	Registration, Evaluation, Authorisation and Restriction of Chemical Substances
ROO	rules of origin
SA	Social Accountability
SAARC	South Asian Association for Regional Cooperation
SACU	Southern African Customs Union
SAFTA	South Asian Free Trade Agreement
SAPTA	SAARC Preferential Trading Arrangement
SITC	Standardised International Trade Classification
SME	small and medium enterprises
SPS	sanitary and phyto-sanitary measures
SSI	small-scale industries
TBT	Agreement on Technical Barriers to Trade and Development
TRIMS	trade–related investment measures
TRIPS	trade–related aspects of intellectual property
TUFS	Technology Upgrade Fund Scheme
UAE	United Arab Emirates
UK	United Kingdom
UN	United Nations
UNCTAD	United Nations Conference on Trade and Development
US	United States
USSR	Union of Soviet Socialist Republics
USTR	US Trade Representative
VER	voluntary export restraints
VOC	volatile organic compound
WRAP	Worldwide Responsible Accredited Production
WTO	World Trade Organization

Preface

While there are a plethora of preferential trade agreements that have been negotiated and then implemented since the multilateral international trade architecture was put in place with the establishment of the General Agreement on Tariffs and Trade in 1947, there has been nothing to rival the ambition of the India–European Union trade agreement that is currently being contemplated. India is a market of a billion–plus people. The 27 member countries of the European Union now comprise a market of five hundred million people. Joining these two markets in a meaningful preferential trade agreement would encompass a fifth of the world's people. That joint market would also contain some of the poorest people to be found on the globe – on the streets of Mumbai or Kolkata – as well as some of the richest – in Mumbai or London. The technology in use in the joint market runs the entire gamut from the futuristic jet engine manufacturing plants of Rolls Royce to agricultural tools that have not changed over three millennia. While the European Union remains a work in process as the twelve new countries that have been added in the last decade are still being fully integrated into the single market, in many ways the Indian federation also remains a work in progress with a constant ebb and flow of influence between the regional focus of the states and the central governments. Hence, while the European Commission and the Indian government will undertake the negotiations, many governments will want their concerns heard. Democracy is an important common trait. English is the lingua franca of modern business in both markets. For all of these reasons, an India–European Union trade agreement will be relatively unique. Any one of these attributes of the prospective joint market could justify the writing of a book.

International trade economists must look beyond the fascination that comes from contemplating such an ambitious endeavour, towards the practicalities of structuring an agreement and the governance institutions that will make it function in a way that will bring the benefits expected from trade liberalization and market integration. Liberalizing trade always imposes costs of adjustment on some individuals and sectors of the economy. There must be benefits that accrue to the societies that can justify imposing those costs. The worst case would be large costs being incurred with little to show for it. The first step is to examine the challenges that are likely to be associated with melding two very large but vastly different economies. The current experience with preferential trade agreements is of only limited assistance in this process. Preferential trade agreements tend not to be entered into by countries with greatly differing economies. The only major preferential trade agreement to include a large developing country is the North American Free Trade Agreement which joins Mexico's developing economy with the developed economies of the United States and Canada – but even the relatively large Mexican market is dwarfed by the combined population of the US and Canada. India is a market that is orders of magnitude larger. The EU has struggled with how to bring the developing Turkish economy into its ranks. Of course, an India–European Union trade agreement will have a much smaller ambition than that associated with full accession to the EU. If the India–European Union trade agreement is, however, to be more than a photo-opportunity, how to deal with the development gap between the two countries must be near to the top of the trade policy agenda.

Further, until recently India was following its third way agenda comprised of heavy doses of socialism, protectionism and Indianization – the latter accomplished through stringent limits on foreign investment. As a result, the Indian economy, as well as developing, has been relatively closed. Hence, an India–European Union trade agreement will have to contemplate particularly severe adjustment costs as the Indian economy opens to European goods, services and investment. On the other hand, the European Union will have to deal with the spectre of low wage competition in some of its most sensitive sectors.

Of course, as with any trade agreement, the devil will be in the details. Hence, we wished to look in more detail at some of the sectors that are likely to be the most difficult to deal with in an agreement. Textiles and clothing as well as footwear and leather will be crucial in the negotiations – they are sectors where India has a comparative advantage, and where countries such as Italy have important industries that are bolstered by protection from international competition. Our book attempts to both look at the big picture – and it is a very big picture – as well as to delve down into selected sectors to provide a snapshot of the complexity of the issues that will arise in the process of negotiating an India–European Union trade agreement. The authors would like to thank David Hutchinson of the Estey Centre for Law and Economics in International Trade for his assistance in the preparation of the manuscript. We would also like to thank the Francine O'Sullivan and all of the people at Edward Elgar for their support and hard work on this project – many hands go into the making of a book.

Sangeeta Khorana and Nicholas Perdikis
Aberystwyth, United Kingdom
May T. Yeung, Calgary, Canada
William A. Kerr, Saskatoon, Canada
May, 2009

Acknowledgements

Authors Khorana and Perdikis would like to acknowledge the funding support they received from the British High Commission, India Office for producing the report titled Convergence towards Regional Integration between the EU and India: Trade Implications for the UK and India. They also acknowledge the valuable contribution of the researchers at ICRIER, their research collaborator in India.

1. Imagine

1.1 INTRODUCTION

An agreement to merge a market of 500 million Europeans with a market of just over a billion Indians is something that fires imaginations. The combined market represents approximately one-fifth of humanity and would be the largest free trade area ever attempted. The diversity of both India – from the tea plantations of Darjeeling to the computer software firms of Bangalore – and the European Union – from the cork groves of central Portugal to Airbus assembly plants in Toulouse, France – provides a range of resources, skills and entrepreneurial flair that is a microcosm of the global marketplace. Much of the benefit of globalization is expected to arise from the specialization stemming from economies of scale (Greenspan, 2007). The possibility of integrating the Indian and European Union (EU) markets, however, raises the question as to whether their joint market is sufficiently large to reap almost all of the potential benefits available from globalization. Would there be any additional benefits from extending the India–EU market to encompass the rest of the world?

This is an important question because, while the European Union is still a collection of individual nation states with a relatively weak collective governance structure and India is a federation where sub-national governments have considerable constitutionally granted authority, both function as relatively unified economic markets. The EU Commission is responsible for developing a common trade policy for the entire European Union. The Government of India also has sole responsibility for trade policy. Thus, trade negotiations pertaining to these two very large markets can be undertaken on a bilateral basis, which considerably reduces the negotiation costs associated with achieving a market with benefits on a global scale. For example, the multilateral World Trade Organization

(WTO) has more than 150 countries as members. The Doha Round of WTO negotiations, which is supposed to achieve a new level of near-global trade liberalization, has been ongoing since 2001 with no successful end in sight – and the possibility of failure is very real. While reaching agreement has proved elusive because some important differences exist among the major players in areas such as agriculture, contingent protection and market access for industrial goods and services (Kerr, 2000b), it has also been difficult because including 150-plus countries in the negotiations in a meaningful way has proved extremely difficult. The WTO negotiation process is both cumbersome and costly. While the Doha Round was launched with an ambitious agenda, if an agreement does eventually arise, it will be only a small step toward a liberal global trading system.

Of course, many of the WTO members' economies are small and would add little in terms of opportunities to achieve global levels of economies of scale, yet they raise the cost of negotiations. In short, the sheer number of WTO members limits the pace of liberalization – meaning that many scale-based benefits cannot be achieved. On the other hand, India and the EU will negotiate bilaterally. If the combined India–EU market is sufficiently large to reap the efficiency gains of world level economies of scale, it will give India and the EU a significant competitive advantage over the remaining countries. Alternative bilateral or regional groupings that include China could reap similar efficiencies from economies of scale, but China has shown little interest in bilateral or regional groupings that it could not dominate. China and Japan have longstanding animosities that inhibit a sufficient degree of trust developing for serious negotiations on economic cooperation to be entered into. It is hard to see a US administration being able to muster sufficient political support in Congress for a bilateral trade deal with China, even if China was interested.

The global economy has suffered through considerable disequilibrium since the 1980s as it has had to accommodate China re-engaging with the world economy after forty years of self-imposed near autarky in the Maoist era and its early successors. While the benefits of trade liberalization accrue in the long run, in the short run there may be considerable economic pain as resources must be moved to better uses – jobs are lost, factories are closed and in some cases local communities are devastated. This disequilibrium is the breeding ground of protectionism. The costs of adjustment associated with China's re-entry into the global market are real (Leger et al., 1999) and have fallen heavily on the US – as the smoking gun of the US trade deficit with China attests. Beyond the trade statistics, it is obvious to the average US consumer that a huge range of manufactured products bearing Made in

China labels is now available – many of those products were until recently produced in the US. The benefits the US receives are less easy to see. As a result, the US Congress has struggled with the China problem. Hence, it is unlikely that Congress would greet a proposed China–US trade agreement with any enthusiasm. After all, they have recently refused to pass trade agreements with small economies in South America such as Colombia. Further, there is a widespread belief (largely unfounded) in the US that Mexico's membership in the North American Free Trade Agreement (NAFTA) has led to a wholesale relocation of US production facilities and jobs to its southern neighbour.

If a China–Japan or China–US agreement is not in the cards, it is hard to see where an agreement to rival the India–EU could be constructed. There are no other developed countries of sufficient size to provide the combination of incomes and technological prowess that the EU will bring to an India–EU agreement. Hence, if an India–EU agreement could be reached, it would likely remain unique and its competitive advantage unrivalled. There is clearly a lot at stake and a great deal to fire the imagination.

1.2 A VAST UNDERTAKING

If the combined Indian and EU economies are a microcosm of the global economy, the bringing together of one-fifth of humanity under a single set of rules for trade is something to inspire the imagination of trade economists at the very least. It is a vast undertaking. Nothing quite like it has ever been attempted. It will be a daunting task for the two teams of trade negotiators. While diversity and complementary resources are what provide the gains from trade, there are also striking differences between India and the EU. There has been rapid growth in India's middle class since the economy began its move toward more openness and engagement with the global economy, but it remains relatively small. India still has a very large percentage of the population that can be considered impoverished. Many are engaged in agriculture. Many are technologically backward. Many, particularly women, are poorly educated. Many remain only tangentially connected to the market economy. Many live in urban slums. All remain vulnerable to economic shocks. Few have savings, most are in debt. Liberalization of trade leads to changes in the use of resources – it creates losers as well as winners.

If one is poor, the cost of being a loser can be great hardship. As a result, the poor fear trade liberalization and will require a great deal of convincing before they will not actively oppose any broad-based attempt at opening markets. By and large, Europeans are well off – rich by Indian standards. While most countries in the European Union have good social safety nets, Europeans understand that their wages are not competitive with those paid in India. Of course, the loss of a job in the EU will not create the absolute hardship that will often be the result in India. It still is likely, however, to lead to a decline in the individual's material wellbeing and status. As a result, one can also expect fierce resistance to an agreement from some quarters in the EU. Fear of low wages in foreign countries is one of the most consistent themes in trade relations since the dawn of the industrial era. While historically the fear of low wage competition was confined largely to labour-intensive manufacturing, in recent times white collar workers have also been faced with low wage competition from offshore. India has been the major source of this competition, particularly in software development and troubleshooting as well as call centre services. Outsourcing has been the protectionist buzzword of the new century. Thus, one can expect fierce resistance to any proposed opening of the European Union market. This will be the first time that white collar workers may feel threatened by a proposed trade agreement and it will be interesting to see how effective they are in putting their protectionist case forward.

While the European Union may be a single market, it is not yet one that is in equilibrium. The expansion of the EU eastward to take in twelve new countries in Central and Eastern Europe, and the Mediterranean, is still a work in progress. Living standards and wages in the acceding countries have not yet reached those in Western Europe, even when differences in productivity are accounted for. As a result, there is disequilibrium. The pressure created by this disequilibrium is manifest in a number of ways. In part, it is reflected in the movement of workers from Central and Eastern Europe to take up jobs in Western Europe. It is also reflected in investment flowing into Central and Eastern Europe to take advantage of lower wages. Slowly this will lead to a convergence in productivity-adjusted wages and living standards. The investments in human capital and evolution of better governance required to level the field in terms of productivity will take much longer. Given that the process of adjustment that will remove disequilibrium in the EU is not yet complete, there may be considerable resistance from the Central and Eastern European member states to what they perceive as lower-wage competition from India. These countries are much more likely to perceive India as a competitor for the lucrative markets in Western Europe, and its investment funds, than as having a complementary set of resources. After all, it was access to the lucrative markets in Western Europe that provided the major incentive for these countries to seek accession to the EU.

In general, labour market adjustment costs in developing countries are expected to be high due to poor education levels – workers with low education have much more difficulty acquiring the skills required to move to a new expanding sector of the economy. Of course, this is the central argument for allowing developing countries to retain border measures and to use safeguards under special and differential treatment provisions in the WTO (Kerr, 2005a). It is also the reason why, with one notable exception, there tend not be comprehensive bilateral or regional trade agreements between developed and developing countries. Trade agreements are much more common between developed countries – the EU itself is one, between Australia and New Zealand, among Western European non-members of the EU – the European Free Trade Area. They are also common among developing countries – MERCOSUR in South America, CARICOM in the Caribbean, ASEAN in Southeast Asia and so on. There are, of course, economic agreements between developed and developing countries but they tend to have narrower mandates and limited ambitions.

The major exception is NAFTA which joins developing Mexico with the developed economies of the US and Canada. While Mexico is a large economy, it is not India, and it is dwarfed by its developed country partners. When the NAFTA was being negotiated, it was viewed as a radical experiment (Clement et al., 1999). Its detractors provided all sorts of doom and gloom scenarios for the future of the Mexican economy. Of course, in Canada and the US protectionists were also making dire predictions for those economies. An agreement was only achieved because: (1) the US feared the threat of illegal immigration if Mexico failed to develop more than the costs of adjustments that would be faced in the US from NAFTA; and (2) the Mexican government perceived NAFTA as a means to justify domestic reforms it saw as fundamental but politically difficult (Gerber and Kerr, 1995). Domestic reforms in Mexico could be justified as being necessary to reap the benefits of NAFTA.

Protectionists tend to make dire predictions in an attempt to bolster their case. They are seldom called to account regarding their predictions. The reasons are that: (1) if they lose the argument and a trade liberalizing agreement is negotiated and put in place, those who were in favour of the agreement have little incentive to study the accuracy of their opponents' positions; and (2) if they win and no agreement comes into force, there is no way to check if their predictions were accurate (Kerr and Foregrave, 2002). The NAFTA experience for all three parties to the agreement has, for the most part, been relatively moderate. Given that, as with all agreements of this nature, there were long phase-in periods for liberalization in sensitive sectors, the changes brought were not particularly dramatic. For the most sensitive sectors, protectionist measures remained in place. Over time, the markets in the three countries have become more integrated (Moodley et al., 2000). While there has been some re-alignment of resource use – as is predicted in the wake of liberalization – there has been no large-scale hollowing out of the US and Canadian manufacturing sector with factories and jobs fleeing to Mexico as a direct result of NAFTA. NAFTA has not propelled Mexico into the ranks of developed economies, and illegal immigration from Mexico is still a major issue in the United States. Trade disputes have not disappeared and the contingent protection mechanisms – anti-dumping and countervailing duty actions – are regularly put into play.

Given the long phase-in periods built into trade agreements and the long-run nature of the resource adjustments they set in motion, it is almost impossible to isolate the effects of a trade agreement such as NAFTA from other economic forces at work at the same time – in economists' terms being able to impose ceteris paribus conditions. Other forces have shaped the economies of all three NAFTA countries (for example, China's rejoining the international economy; the tightening of border security in the wake of the terrorist attacks of 9/11, the lowering of international transaction costs associated with the rapid adoption of the internet, technological improvements in transportation and logistics management, to name only a few). Of course, protectionist vested interests often find it convenient to blame every job lost, every factory closure and every decline in agricultural prices on NAFTA. These arguments, however, seem to carry little weight even if they sometimes garner considerable attention as they did in the campaign comments of Barack Obama and Hillary Clinton in the 2008 US election campaign (Bakhshi and Kerr, 2008).

NAFTA still represents the only major trade agreement that includes both developing and developed economies. The lessons of NAFTA should not be lost on both India and the EU as they seek ways to make their economic partnership work. The first lesson is that gradualism needs to be explicitly built into their agreement. While this means that the benefits that arise from the agreement will accrue more slowly, it spreads the costs of adjustment out over time thus increasing the probability of success. It mutes the appeal of protectionists. An endeavour as vast as an India–EU trade agreement needs to be approached from a long-run perspective. While there will be many entrepreneurs and internationally oriented firms that can see profitable opportunities from rapid liberalization, and will push hard for immediate changes that will allow them to act on those opportunities, prudent policy suggests a more gradual approach.

The first few years of an agreement are crucial to its success. If the changes bring large, and visible, adjustment costs, protectionist demands for cancellation will garner increased support. If, on the other hand, integration is more gradual then, over time, vested interests in the continuation of the agreement will be created. While each partner to the NAFTA has the right to cancel the agreement, it is probably not possible to do so after almost a decade and a half – substantial investments have been made in the integrated North American market. Given the differences between the Indian and EU economies, phase-in periods of 15 or 20 years would seem appropriate for many sectors. The phase-ins should also be gradual rather than front loaded with, for example, a 50 per cent down-payment (that is, 50 per cent of the liberalizations) in the first year as has been demanded by some developing countries in the Doha Round WTO negotiations or back loaded so that the bulk of the liberalization only takes place in the final year of the phase in as was the case in the liberalization of the trade regime for textiles and clothing in the WTO. The primary reason for having phase-ins is to spread out the costs of adjustment.

The second lesson from the NAFTA experience is to have realistic expectations. Trade agreements have only limited impact. Even if the agreement is very successful, it will not fundamentally alter either the Indian or EU economies. Domestic market reforms will still be far more important for India's economic development as will EU initiatives to foster its transition to a knowledge economy. Significant domestic reforms, often politically very difficult reforms, will be required if either India or the EU is to be able to take full advantage of the opportunities that the proposed trade agreement provides. In North America, for example, all three governments have underinvested in such obvious infrastructure as border facilities to accommodate the increased movement of goods and people and transportation links to remove bottlenecks in internal distribution networks (Hobbs and Kerr, 2008). While India and the EU do not share a common border, there will be a host of investments in infrastructure and human capital that will be required to re-orient the respective economies to fully accommodate the provisions of the agreement.

Finally, while the NAFTA example is singular, it does suggest that developing and developed countries can enter into bilateral or regional trade agreements successfully. Of course, NAFTA is not a perfect proxy for the

India–EU agreement because India will carry much more weight in the India–EU market than Mexico does in North America. The NAFTA experience does, however, suggest that neither India nor the EU should be deterred from pursuing an agreement simply because of the differences in their stages of development. It does suggest that any agreement needs to be well thought out beforehand and well managed once implemented. As with the proposed India–EU agreement, NAFTA was a vast undertaking that required a bold political vision. For the most part, the vision has been justified and the dire predictions of the naysayers have not been fulfilled.

1.3   CAN WHAT IS IMAGINED BECOME REALITY?

While the potential of an India–EU trade agreement can fire the imagination of those who see the future writ large, bringing such a vision to fruition will require a great deal of effort by those with a more practical bent. Of course, it is always possible to arrive at an agreement – the real question is whether it will be a substantive one. The trading world is littered with a plethora of trade agreements whose provisions are little more than political window-dressing and/or whose commitments are breached as soon as the photo-op of their signing has concluded. Those types of agreements are easy to reach because, as they have such little ambition, they do not threaten any vested interests. These types of agreement also sometimes arise as a political face saving measure when protectionist vested interests cannot be overcome, but having no agreement would be politically damaging. It is unlikely, however, that any trade agreement between India and the EU would lack ambition – the degree of scrutiny it would be subjected to would quickly dissipate any face-saving value. Hence, the choice is either a substantive agreement or no agreement at all.

Substantive agreements will always encounter stiff opposition from those who perceive that they have a lot to lose. Further, both the EU and India have deep protectionist roots. India, in particular, has a culture of protectionism that will be difficult to overcome. Having protectionism broadly accepted provides excellent cover for vested interests who find it easy to mask their personal gains behind a veil of supposed public interest. In the EU, where the intellectual acceptance of protectionism varies tremendously from member state to member state, protectionism has more practical roots. The difficulties associated with initiating and expanding the European Union's single market have often meant that progress could only be made by pushing costs on to countries outside the EU. One only has to look at the EU's Common Agricultural Policy (CAP) whose single price policy could only be accomplished by heavily protecting the EU market from international prices (Gaisford and Kerr, 2001). As a result, significant costs were imposed on foreign agricultural exporters. Over time, as the high internal CAP prices encouraged expansion of agricultural production, the EU moved from being a net importer to self-sufficiency and eventually to being a net exporter over a range of products. These exports were only accomplished through the extensive use of export subsidies, which drove down international prices of agricultural products, inhibiting the development of exporting developing countries and keeping prices low for farmers in importing developing countries (Gaisford and Kerr, 2001). As the EU expanded to take in new members, CAP levels of protection were extended to new members (Gaisford et al., 2003). Agricultural protectionism in the EU remains a major stumbling block to the conclusion of the Doha Round. While the CAP is the most obvious example of the agenda of the EU project imposing costs on trade partners, many other examples exist.

India's protectionist tendencies have a long history. The colonial experience left a legacy of suspicion of foreign firms and their ability to gain an unfair advantage in the Indian market. India, with its large internal market, was seen as a prime candidate for development being achieved through import substitution industrialization. One of the major criticisms of import substitution as a development strategy is that for many countries, the domestic market would be too small to reap the benefits of economies of scale, meaning that the protected industries would never become internationally competitive. The size of the domestic market was not seen as a constraint in India's case. The post-independence acceptance of socialism as a path to development, with an emphasis on building up the capacity of heavy industry, led to infant industry justifications for protection. Over time, the heavy presence of the state in the economy and the large, inefficient and often corrupt bureaucracy that accompanied it, created a vested interest among the civil service in limiting the disturbing influence of foreign competition. As bureaucratic inefficiency and corruption add to the costs of both state and private sector firms, competition from foreign firms not encumbered with such costs threatens both jobs in the civil service and the corruption income that can be extracted. The international success enjoyed by the Indian software industry arose largely because it was a new industry that only developed after the enthusiasm for socialism had passed, and hence was not subject to the dead hand of the bureaucracy. While considerable progress in opening the Indian economy has been made over the first years of the 21st century, the state still plays a very large role and the bureaucracy has a strong vested interest in perpetuating its role (Perdikis, 2000).

There is, however, a grudging acceptance in India that the economic model used since independence has been a failure – it did not deliver development. Opening the economy is seen as a necessity if development is to take place. China, India's perpetual measuring rod, has had such success with its integration into the global economy that it is impossible to ignore. Partnering with the European Union may be a reasonable option for more conservative India than China's global approach. This is particularly true if the joint India–EU market is of sufficient size to allow all the potential benefits of economies of scale to be realized. There are some other advantages to partnering with the EU. Unlike in China, English is spoken widely in India, especially among those who would be likely to engage in international commerce. While English is the first language in only two EU countries, English has become the de facto language of business in the EU. For India, the widespread use of English is a great advantage relative to a large number of developing countries. It will be an advantage when doing business with Europeans.

India is likely to find many Europeans will be more understanding of the state's role in the economy than, for example, Americans. The US brand of capitalism is as foreign to many Europeans as it is to Indians. Historically, the state has had a large role in the economies of the majority of the member states of the EU and the European Commission reflects that interventionist tradition. Thus, it may be easier to come to agreement on the degree to which the state can intervene when trade flows will be affected. The US, for example, has found it difficult to reconcile the role of Chinese state enterprises in its concerns over unfair competition from Chinese exports.

India and the EU may also have some sectors where they have a mutual interest in not agreeing to liberalization. As suggested above, the EU's agricultural sector is heavily protected. India's agricultural sector receives even higher levels of protection. In the Doha Round negotiations, India has been particularly unrelenting in its unwillingness to open its agricultural markets. Its insistence on structuring the proposed special safeguard for agriculture in a narrowly protectionist way was credited with causing the collapse of the negotiations in 2008. In theory, the WTO has oversight of any trade agreement reached between India and the EU. Bilateral trade agreements are only supposed to be WTO compliant if they include substantially all trade – that they be comprehensive in their coverage. This rule, however, has never been invoked and it is hard to imagine that an India–EU agreement would be challenged if, for example, agricultural trade was not included.

Automobiles may be another sector which might be excluded. India still has the development of a domestic automobile industry as a cherished goal. The transition to an automobile society is just beginning in India and European car makers capturing a significant market share during the car market's future expansion is not something that Indian officials would easily agree to. The EU perpetually struggles with keeping national champions afloat. Further, with considerable automobile manufacturing having recently been located in Central and Eastern Europe due to their lower labour rates, it is unlikely that these countries would look kindly on competition from India at the lower end of the price range. Hence, mutual exclusion of the automobile sector from the trade agreement may be possible. It is more likely that foreign investment may be allowed. For example, Tata Motors already owns Jaguar and Land Rover.

While there may be synergies between India and the EU that raises the probability of a successful agreement being reached, one should not underestimate the difficulties associated with negotiating a deal. While only two parties will be involved in the negotiations, these are two extremely large markets and complex economies. The number of stakeholders that will want to be heard will be enormous. Opposition will be fierce from some quarters. The negotiations are likely to be protracted. Governments will come and go and their positions will shift. While the negotiations will be conducted by the European Commission and the Government of India, many governments will be involved – state governments in India, member state governments in the EU. All will have to be consulted. In both cases, a number of these governments – but probably not all – will have to endorse the agreement if it is to come to fruition. The private sector will weigh in. Negotiating positions will have to be developed and assessed. As with any trade agreement, in the end, the devil will be in the details.

While it is not possible at this stage to discern what the details of a bilateral trade agreement between India and the EU might entail – and hence to assess whether what can be imagined can become a reality – this book provides a guide to both the promise and the pitfalls of such an agreement. It provides a discussion of the place of regional trade agreements within the context of both trade theory and the institutions of international trade. It outlines the major re-orientation of the Indian economy as a result of the reforms put in place over the last two decades.

The evolution of Indian–EU economic relations is described and provides insights into why a bilateral agreement has come to the fore at this time.

This book will focus on two sectors that are likely to be very difficult ones during the negotiations between India and the EU – textiles and clothing, as well as leather and footwear. It draws heavily on the report 'Convergence Towards Regional Integration Between the EU and India: Trade Implications for the UK and India', commissioned by the British High Commission (BHC) to identify existing non-tariff barriers (NTBs) impeding trade in the UK and to evaluate the effects of the proposed EU-India Free Trade Agreement (FTA) on the textiles and clothing and leather and footwear industries in detail (Khorana, et al., 2008).[1] These are industries where India perceives it has a comparative advantage but faces protectionist barriers in the EU. Understanding the perception of these barriers is the key to determining the hurdles that will have to be overcome in the negotiations. Of course, this is the type of analysis that needs to be undertaken for each sector by their stakeholders. The approach used in this book should be useful as a guide for assessing other sectors.

Sector by sector assessment is the painstaking type of work that will be required in turning an idea that fires the imagination into something tangible. Whether an agreement can be successfully negotiated will have to await the results of these endeavours.

NOTE

1. This report was funded by the British High Commission, India office under the GOF program of the Foreign and Commonwealth Office in London.

2. Preferential Trade Agreements and the Global Trading Environment

> The expansion of international commercial relations has been an important and consistent engine of economic growth in the second half of the twentieth century. There has been a general acceptance of the proposition that the liberalisation of international trade and commerce provides economic benefits. (Yeung et al., 1999, p. ix)

2.1 WHY PREFERENTIAL TRADE AGREEMENTS?

Trade liberalization facilitates the capture of benefits arising from trade due to specialization and the more efficient allocation of resources, regardless of the mechanism used to achieve it. Trade liberalization occurs multilaterally and also via preferential trading agreements.[1] Both are effective although historically, multilateral negotiations have been pursued as the preferred means of trade liberalization via the WTO and its predecessor the General Agreement on Tariffs and Trade (GATT), due to acknowledged widespread welfare gains. However, political, cultural and economic realities have ensured that preferential trading agreements (PTA) are still actively pursued (Yeung et al., 1999). These take many forms but two motivations drive countries to pursue PTA – economics and politics.

Although trade liberalization is pursued on a multilateral basis at the WTO, with fewer participants, agreement is easier to reach by pursuing PTAs, providing the parties with 'first off the mark' status in gaining market access for competitive producers, service providers, workers, and investors. That access is also secured with balanced, mutually advantageous rules. In return, nations open their own markets to the same extent, to the benefit of their firms and consumers who gain access to capital, goods and services in greater variety and at world prices (Cameron and Loukine, 2001). PTAs are a means of increasing the national welfare of member nations, thereby increasing economic development and at a far more rapid pace than the multilateral level can provide. For nations whose domestic markets are too small to sustain long-term growth or to take advantage of economies of scale, access to a larger market, as provided by a PTA, can be crucial to their further development. For instance, due to its unique PTA relationship with the United States, Canada engages in six times the level of trade than it would if its trade were proportional to its share in global GDP (Yeung et al., 1999). PTAs also provide a forum for consensus, communications and fostering relationships that encourage international transactions and commerce.

In forming a PTA, countries expect trade expansion amongst the members. Taking down trade barriers between the members causes part of this expansion. However, part is attributed to the increased relative competitiveness of domestic firms, which no longer have to pay tariffs compared to exporters from countries that are not part of the agreement. In short, imports from firms in member states replace imports from non-member states. Non-member states are said to suffer from trade diversion as a result of the establishment of the preferential trade agreement (Kerr and Perdikis, 2003). Members of such agreements therefore, enjoy a special status, in fact a special protected status because they have preferred access to each other's markets. When another country joins an existing PTA, it too will gain the special status, relative to all other non-members, but the existing members will face new competition from products originating in the new member. Existing members will lose some degree of protection from competition when a new member accedes to an agreement (Yeung and Kerr, 2004). 'First off the mark' timing, rapid market access secured by a predictable regulatory regime, wider choice in goods, services and capital, all at lower prices, and special protected status can easily explain the increasing popularity of PTAs. This popularity has increased in recent years as the 150-plus member WTO appears unable to bring its negotiations to a successful conclusion.

PTAs are also political mechanisms, often a multi-purpose tool to achieve a nation's foreign policy goals. PTAs can become a means to address social concerns, security issues, or enhance a country's political or economic credibility. A PTA can be a means of helping developing countries improve welfare and incomes via trade not aid. A PTA can enhance its members' collective clout beyond their individual capabilities because of their combined influence. For example, the Association of South

East Asian Nations (ASEAN) has a larger presence and voice in the global stage than its individual members could achieve on their own. A PTA may also provide a government's economic or political reforms with increased credibility as they are obligated to meet PTA commitments, thereby not being able to back out, and show that the reforms are undertaken with genuine intention (Yeung et al., 1999). This was seen as a major motivation behind Mexico's accession to NAFTA (Gerber and Kerr, 1995). PTAs can also be a mechanism of strategic trade incentives, bargaining power and political clout. The US foreign policy during the Bush Administration is case in point, where the use of PTAs or the promise of PTAs was used to reward nations that helped to advance their foreign policies (Yeung and Kerr, 2004; Kerr and Hobbs, 2006). The Bush Administration has also utilised PTAs to leverage the economic power of the US to influence broader agreements and other countries willingness to negotiate (Van Grasstek, 2004; Yeung and Kerr, 2004; Kerr, 2005b). PTAs can also be a testing ground to address issues of concern to the parties involved that are not yet on the multilateral agenda, thereby breaking ground ahead of the multilateral forum. The NAFTA countries included an investment provision in their agreement prior to the creation of the Agreement on Trade Related Investment Measures (TRIMS) in the GATT/WTO (Yeung et al., 1999). PTAs often become the cornerstones of larger economic and political policy goals; while economic factors are still a means of increasing the national welfare of the parties and of promoting trade, thereby increasing economic development (Yeung et al., 1999), political agendas can often overshadow the intrinsic economic considerations.

2.2 FORMS OF PREFERENTIAL TRADING AGREEMENTS

Preferential trading agreements, regardless of motivation, are a means of regional[2] economic integration where trade liberalization occurs. Regional economic integration is the deepening of intra-regional economic interdependence in a given region, through intra-regional trade, foreign direct investment and harmonization of commercial regulations, standards and practices. Regional economic integration can be achieved through myriad forms, shapes and structures, the extent and depth of which is dependent upon the degree of consideration one trading partner must give to another partner's actions and responses prior to making policy decisions

(Yeung et al., 1999). The mechanisms of regional economic integration exhibit varying degrees of institutionalization, depth and coverage, ranging from loose cooperative arrangements to tightly structured agreements, but are generally known as preferential trade agreements or regional trade agreements.[3]

PTA configurations are becoming increasingly complex, with agreements and networks of agreements scattered across regions, continents and hemispheres. Compounding the complexity exhibited by the geographic reach of PTAs is the often overlapping membership of a single nation in multiple PTAs, requiring the concurrent administration of different trade regimes within a national administration. Multiple memberships means that, depending upon the trading partner concerned, the rules change and firms must navigate between regimes, incurring costs to do so.   Additionally, PTA coverage has expanded far beyond the historical lowering of tariffs between members to address trade-related issues such as standards, safeguard provisions and customs administration, amongst others, as well as providing for a preferential regulatory framework for mutual services trade, and/or rules on investment, competition, environment and labour (WTO, n.d.a.).

The most common and increasingly dominant form of PTA is the free trade agreement (FTA). FTA are:

> Preferential trade organisations which have eliminated internal trade barriers between members for all or groups of goods (and usually services and investment), while member countries maintain individual external trade barriers and commercial policies towards non-member countries. The non-harmonisation of external trade barriers requires an elaborate system of regulations to ensure that imports entering the FTA do not avoid an individual country's tariffs. Tariffs are avoided when imports enter the FTA through the member country with the lowest external barriers and are then transported without encumberment with the FTA, hence avoiding the duties of high external tariff countries. An administrative body is thus usually required to oversee an FTA. (Yeung et al., 1999, p. 18)

FTAs are likely more common and the preferred form of PTA because of their relative ease to negotiate and conclude, given that the parties mutually undertake negotiations to achieve a shared common objective, while maintaining their own external trade and commercial policies towards non-members. Further, FTAs are not limited by geographic considerations, being chiefly concerned with strategic market access. In early 2009, the WTO indicates that 144 FTAs have been notified and in force, with an additional two accessions to existing FTAs. These 146 FTAs[4] account for 60 per cent of the total 243 preferential trading agreements notified to the WTO and in force (WTO, n.d.a.).

A customs union is an FTA with the addition of a common external commercial and trade policy meaning that, regardless of country of entry, all imports are subject to the same barriers to trade. Member states have relinquished some degree of autonomy as the members must have concurrence in order to change external policy. By their nature, customs unions require a high degree of policy coordination and therefore a longer period of negotiation and implementation (Fiorentino et al., 2007). In early 2009, the WTO reported 13 customs unions notified and in force, with an additional 6 accessions,[5] for a total of 19, representing 7.9 per cent of all PTAs (WTO, n.d.a.). Of these, only six have entered into force post-2000.

In a further step towards greater integration, a common market shares the features of a customs union, with the addition of the free movement of labour and capital, with harmonization of taxation and domestic regulations to facilitate equality amongst member countries. Finally, an economic union incorporates a common market with the addition of the complete harmonization of government spending and procurement as well as the coordination of monetary policy. A single currency is not requisite to an economic union as exchange rates can be fixed against one another but a single currency would reduce transactions costs amongst members of the union (Yeung et al., 1999). The European Economic Community (EEC) was an example of a common market while some foresee the EU moving towards becoming an economic union.

Partial scope agreements (PSA; also known as sectoral free-trade areas) are an FTA or customs union covering select traded sectors only and are, according to WTO law, exclusively available to developing countries under the Enabling Clause.[6] Developed countries may conduct sectoral trade negotiations, but they must extend the benefits of sectoral trade liberalization on a most-favoured-nation (MFN) basis (Goode, 2003). The WTO reported that in early 2009, there were 12 PSAs notified and in force, with an additional accession, constituting 5.4 per cent of all PTAs (WTO, n.d.a.).

Economic integration agreements (EIA) are used in Article V[7] of the General Agreement on Trade in Services (GATS) to cover free-trade arrangements in services. The term EIA was chosen because free trade in services requires the possibility of commercial presence in the importing country as well as the free movement of consumers and producers of services. This is seen as involving a greater degree of economic integration than might occur under the conditions of free trade in goods. In order to conform to WTO rules, EIA must have substantial sectoral coverage and provide for the absence or elimination of substantially all discrimination between its members (Goode, 2003). There are 57 EIAs notified and in force at the WTO in early 2009, with an additional six accessions which accounts for 26.4 per cent of all PTAs (WTO, n.d.a.)

PTAs can be negotiated on a bilateral basis. The parties can include countries and/or regions where the region can represent multiple nations. For example, the EC–Chile Free Trade Agreement has 28 members – 27 European Community (EC) members and Chile. PTAs can also be negotiated on a plurilateral basis where more than two parties participate, be they nations and/or regions. NAFTA is an example of a three nation FTA while EC–CARIFORUM States Economic Partnership Agreement has 41 members with the EC representing a PTA of 27 nations. Bilateral PTAs are becoming the dominant configuration, whether as a simple bilateral between two countries or between a country and an existing PTA, such as the EC–Chile Agreement mentioned above. Other bilateral agreements involve two PTAs.

2.3 IMPACTS OF PREFERENTIAL TRADING AGREEMENTS

It should not be assumed that a PTA will automatically provide overall welfare enhancement with the creation of new trade and investment. Entering into a PTA involves a cost-benefit analysis as there will be losers as well as winners based upon trade creation and trade diversion (Viner, 1950). The opportunities created for new trade (trade creation) must be weighed against the incidence of discrimination toward competitive outsiders or the diversion of consumption to goods and services produced within the regional trade organization away from those of more efficient outside sources (trade diversion). If the reduction of trade barriers is non-discriminatory, the welfare enhancement gained from PTAs is clear. Should the PTA utilize discriminatory or sector specific arrangements, the net benefits between trade creation and trade diversion becomes ambiguous. PTAs with high external border protection against non-members have been shown to be 'particularly susceptible to the adverse effects of trade diversion' (Sidgwick, 2004, p. 98). As trade liberalization occurs amongst members of the PTA, internal competition increases thereby benefiting competitive industries in member states. Inefficient industries will, however, face adjustment costs which they may attempt to mitigate by lobbying for import barriers. This is another form of trade diversion.

With some exceptions, it is generally believed that so long as net trade creation is larger than trade diversion, the PTA is beneficial (Kerr and Perdikis, 2003). The greater the degree of trade creation, the greater the welfare enhancing effects of the PTA. Trade creation can be escalated via:

1. A high degree of overlap in economic structure between the PTA members. The higher the level of structural overlap, the greater the inter- and intra-industry trade that will result, and subsequently, the levels of trade creation. The lower the degree of overlap, the higher the probability of trade diversion;
2. A high variation in the production costs of overlapping industries: the higher the variation, the greater the trade creation;
3. High levels of pre-integration tariff levels, meaning that their reduction will provide greater marginal gains (Lipsey, 1960).

Another factor to consider is that the effects of PTAs are dynamic, magnifying and accumulating over time beyond one-off snapshots. Gains in efficiency and cost reduction accrue in the long run as do increases in market size and economies of scale, in turn further affecting investment and output decisions into the future, beyond the initial liberalization period. Productivity improves with better factor utilization including labour mobility and capital movements, facilitating further gains. These dynamic benefits are usually considered of greater value than the static effects in enriching overall gains (Yeung et al., 1999).

If inter-PTA organizations are able to cooperatively reduce barriers between them, they will be a global liberalizing influence. If, instead, they become protectionist trade blocs unable to reduce inter-PTA barriers, they will hinder global trade liberalization (Yeung et al., 1999). Regardless of the theoretical debate over the benefits of PTAs, they have become an essential trade policy tool for virtually all WTO members (Fiorentino et al., 2007). In the past ten years, the number of and the share of overall global trade governed by PTA has been increasing exponentially; given the glacial pace of trade talks at the multilateral level, conditions are highly conducive for the trend to continue.

2.4   THE CURRENT PTA ENVIRONMENT

The WTO reported that there were 243 PTAs notified and in force in March 2009,[8] with an additional 30 early announcements of agreements to be or under negotiation. Virtually every WTO member is active in at least one PTA, with some members active in as many as 20 or more (WTO, n.d.a.). PTAs are becoming the focus of most countries' foreign commercial policy, in a marked shift away from the multilateral forum. Given the moribund state of the Doha negotiations at the multilateral level, that countries would divert resources towards an alternate mechanism effective at achieving their foreign policy goals is not surprising.

The result is that PTAs are spreading throughout the global economy at an unprecedented rate, both in terms of numbers of agreements and the amount of global trade conducted under their auspices. Consider that in the 46-year period between 1948 and1994, the GATT received 124 notifications of PTAs (relating to trade in goods) (WTO, n.d.a.) and since the creation of the WTO in 1995, 119 additional active arrangements[9] covering trade in goods or services have been notified in only 14 years.

The acceleration of PTA proliferation can be attributed to a number of factors. Since 1948, there have been successive waves of 'regionalism' where nations pursued regional trade agreements. The early 1990s featured a crucial 'wave' during which many nations pursued regional PTAs[10] for a variety of geopolitical reasons. Firstly, many nations entered PTAs to hedge against possible failure of the protracted Uruguay Round of multilateral negotiations. Secondly, the dissolution of the USSR created a flurry of PTA activity between and amongst the resulting transition economies, the EU and European Free Trade Association (EFTA). Thirdly, the EU (15) enlargement as well as its dominance in PTA activity spurred nations previously uninterested in PTAs to reconsider their reliance solely on multilateral agreements. They subsequently reacted to the growing number of discriminatory regimes involving major markets, to which they were denied preferential access, in a bandwagon effect by entering into new or acceding to existing PTAs. Chile, Mexico and Singapore are examples (Fiorentino et al., 2007). In a domino effect, more nations have jumped onto the PTA bandwagon partly in fear of being left with multilateralism as their only viable option. The potential failure of the Doha Round of trade negotiations has served to exacerbate the speed at which the dominos fell and PTAs were pursued.

The mechanism of choice in this proliferation has been the FTA because of the relative speed with which an agreement can be reached compared to other forms of PTA and its inherent flexibility and selectivity in scope as well as choice of partners, which in turn facilitates strategic market access or political alliances. The majority of these FTAs are bilateral simply because it easier to negotiate an agreement between two parties.

Bilateral FTAs are also being pursued by parties which are PTAs in themselves. Eleven of the thirty current early announcements being negotiated have a PTA as a negotiating party. The Gulf Cooperation Council (GCC), CARICOM, EU, EFTA, ASEAN are all negotiating bilateral agreements. Presenting a unified voice at such negotiations, such as the EU–Chile with two parties would logistically be easier than the alternative plurilateral negotiation involving 41 parties. The eleven early announcements where PTAs are a negotiating party are all, with the exception of one,[11] cross-regional bilaterals, mostly with a single nation.

Historically, FTAs which include a PTA as a party, have essentially been accessions of neighbouring countries or a consolidation of existing agreements, the latter of which requires a significant amount of policy coordination achieved over longer, more complex negotiations and longer implementation timelines. Agreements of this nature are mostly evidenced by emerging PTA hubs in the developing world,[12] and consolidation of intra-regional PTAs into continent wide blocks.[13]

Another trend in the proliferation of PTAs is a marked lack of geographic continuity. The term regional trade agreement has taken on a new meaning as many of the recent PTAs do not share geographic proximity at all; of the 30 current WTO early announcements, 22 are cross regional. EFTA–Peru, Canada–Jordan, EC–India, Korea–US, Japan–GCC, ASEAN–Korea are just a few examples.

Traditionally, PTAs are formed amongst countries with established trading patterns and usually a shared, contiguous border. NAFTA, ASEAN and MERCOSUR are examples of traditional PTAs within a region. As more regional partners formed or acceded to PTAs,[14] exhausting the neighbourhood of potential partners, cross-regional PTAs are partially the result of countries looking further afield for likely trading partners to provide strategic market access for exports (Yeung and Kerr, 2002). In this context, PTAs are driven less by regional integration than by the desire to open new global market opportunities ((Fiorentino et al., 2007).

Pursuing PTAs for extrinsic geopolitical purposes rather than the intrinsic benefits of economic growth has also been a notable feature in the recent proliferation.[15] Under these circumstances, FTAs have been utilized as a tool to actively foster positive externalities from PTA negotiations. Essentially, FTAs or the promise of FTAs are used as a means of exerting pressure on other governments regarding economic and non-economic issues. It is a strategy that is particularly effective for large economies that can leverage their economic power.[16] The promise of free access to a large lucrative market is a powerful inducement for countries to negotiate or become allies, whether economically, politically or militarily, with the large economy; conversely the withholding of the same can be a significant form of retribution for those that do not.[17] In this manner, PTAs can become an effective means of leveraging economic power to achieve foreign policy goals.

The plethora of PTAs has created a complicated 'spaghetti bowl' of rules and regulations for firms and governments to contend with. For an individual nation, multiple memberships in overlapping PTAs creates a complex regulatory web requiring concurrent administration. Customs officials, bureaucrats and firms must interpret, enforce, navigate and comply with a confounding array of rules and regulations originating from different PTA regimes.

The sheer and increasing number of PTAs, their escalating complexity, the cross-regional trend that is altering traditional trade patterns and the use of PTAs to achieve economically extrinsic objectives has deleterious implications for the multilateral trading system. PTAs were already a contentious issue within the multilateral trade architecture prior to these current trends. The controversy has only intensified with the changing nature and evolving structures of PTAs.

2.5 CONTROVERSY AND CAVEATS FOR PREFERENTIAL TRADE AGREEMENTS AND THE MULTILATERAL TRADING SYSTEM

Prior to the Depression of the 1930s, bilateral agreements were the norm in trade relations, particularly in Europe. These relationships shattered during the Depression; nations reneged on their bilateral obligations. As time passed, they increasingly entered into beggar-thy-neighbour trade wars in futile attempts to prop up their failing economies. The Depression clearly illustrated that the complex web of bilaterals did not facilitate the full realization of the gains from trade, particularly in the case of smaller, less powerful countries. By removing the competitive aspect of bilateral negotiations, widespread welfare gains could be achieved and the best means of doing so was multilateral trade liberalization[18] (Yeung et al., 2004). The depth of the global community's commitment to multilateral trade liberalization up to the completion of the Uruguay Round of negotiations can be credited to the world's Depression-era geopolitical experience (Kerr, 2000a). That same commitment to multilateralism can be credited with the global community's welfare gains since the Depression.

Since the inception of the GATT and multilateral trade liberalization, PTAs have been viewed as a second-best approach to freeing world trade. The WTO has recognized the positive externalities of PTAs such as initiating discussions on issues such as services, intellectual property, environmental standards, investment and competition policies that were later incorporated into the WTO negotiations. That PTAs have also incorporated commitments from countries beyond what was possible at the multilateral level at the time has also been recognized by the WTO (Fiorentino et al., 2007).

However, as more PTAs flourish and overlap, their negative externalities have increasing impact on the multilateral trading system. PTAs are discriminatory instruments that conflict with the WTO's keystone principle of non-discrimination. Their benefits are accepted so long as these benefits are at some point extended multilaterally on an MFN basis, in what is known as open regionalism. Unfortunately, open regionalism does not seem to be as operable in practice as members of a PTA are generally loath to erode their preferential status by sharing their unique PTA preferences with non-members, except in a multilateral liberalization round. Their preferential market access creates a vested interest in preserving that special status and may even translate into multilateral inertia where even in a multilateral liberalization, PTA members fail to meaningfully participate in trade liberalization as such liberalization would also erode their preferential status. PTA-based multilateral inertia erodes the incentive for nations to pursue multilateral trade liberalization at the risk of abandoning multilateralism for regionalism. Given that multilateral negotiations are proving increasingly difficult and slow, extending PTA preferences on an MFN basis is taking longer, if the opportunity for it to occur happens at all as the Doha Round is illustrating.

Notwithstanding multilateral inertia, to some extent, open regionalism must be occurring merely due to the sheer numbers of PTAs and the fact that some trade policies have broad based applicability. Measures to improve customs procedures, speed transactions at borders and ports or open services markets all contribute towards open regionalism, regardless if pursued unilaterally or in a PTA.

With the 243 current PTAs, and another 30 forthcoming, preferential benefits are being extended across a broad spectrum of countries, albeit not to all WTO members as the multilateral negotiations would. Admittedly, those with the least capacity or economic leverage are most likely to be excluded from PTAs. A mitigating factor is the voluntary preference schemes offered by the EU and US such as the Generalized System of Preferences, The Growth and Opportunity Act in the US and the EU's Everything But Arms programme. As these programmes are voluntary and subject to political capriciousness, market access is not guaranteed as it would be under MFN or PTA. Nevertheless, these programmes still offer some means of ameliorating exclusion from PTAs for selected low income countries (Sidgwick, 2004). Some developing countries are also forming regional PTAs with each other and with other regional hubs providing them with some access to the liberalization opportunities and market access offered by PTAs.

Further, given that each PTA has been tailored specifically for the particular partners, preferential benefits vary considerably between nations, in coverage and industries. There exists a high probability that the current state of PTA proliferation is prone towards creating a state of preferential access disparity where those with the capacity and leverage to negotiate PTAs will do so in multiples, while those with less capacity have limited access to PTAs, and the resulting preferential regimes. Much of Africa, for example, has been left out of PTAs.

PTAs that focus on extrinsic objectives lose economic focus with ramifications for economic gain, trade creation and the multilateral trading system. Politically focussed PTAs are driven by forces that have little regard for a coherent economic or trade strategy, and provide less economic gain for the nations involved. The recent flurry of PTA activity by the US is an example where the candidacy for a PTA was determined primarily by compatibility with US interests. Excluding New Zealand from the Australian FTA was not a sound trade policy decision from an economic point of view. Leveraging the promise of PTA to achieve geo-political goals in other fora is similarly a strategy that detracts from sound economic thinking that would enhance trade creation. Such PTAs are susceptible to a considerable degree to the influence of political agendas, misinformation, short-sightedness and poor management.

The spaghetti bowl effect of PTA proliferation can also fragment the multilateral system thereby increasing transactions costs, reducing transparency, increasing the complexity of technical issues[19] and creating logistical problems. For instance, focusing on PTAs diverts scarce negotiating resources from the WTO, an issue particularly germaine to developing countries whose nascent trade policy capacities cannot cope with negotiations at multiple forums. Fragmentation also occurs as PTAs can be highly selective in coverage, addressing relatively painless issues while leaving out contentious issues most relevant to the majority of WTO members. Agriculture is the primary example; best addressed at the multilateral level and the area where developing nations would most benefit, there is no willpower to do so as the arrested state of the Doha Round attests. Nations often exclude agriculture, or have major agricultural exemptions from PTAs. Despite being a major agricultural producer, Australia was not able to secure any preferential market access to the US market for its highly competitive agriculture sector in the US–Australia FTA. Agriculture is essentially excluded from this particular FTA which has become known as a 'manufacturing FTA' (Yeung et al., 2004). Fragmentation also occurs given that selecting partners of like mind (or deliberately not selecting those of opposite disposition) makes PTAs a path of least resistance compared to engaging a far more demanding community of disparate nations. The trade liberalizations created by PTAs can be relatively easy to achieve, but can also be relatively insignificant overall. Engaging the multilateral forum will provide the most direct path towards widespread, substantial trade creation benefits yet the process has become sufficiently mired that nations are turning away from it.

Can PTAs be structured such that they complement the WTO rather than detract from it? Supporting open regionalism to ensure low external MFN tariffs are maintained will facilitate trade creation and support the multilateral trading system. Other measures fostering open regionalism and/or trade creation include a combination of domestic policies and specific PTA traits:

- A sound domestic policy framework that encourages entrepreneurial initiative where the investment climate is supported by macroeconomic stability, adequate infrastructure regulation and basic property rights, including intellectual property, all of which should be appropriate to the level of development;
- Low external MFN tariffs and few sectoral and product exemptions which will minimize the risks of trade diversion;
- Non-restrictive rules of origin that share a framework common to many agreements allowing for increased trade;
- Measures to facilitate trade which increases attention from policymakers when imbedded in PTA and often have widespread trade creation effects across all partners;
- Large ex-post markets;

- Measures to promote new cross-border competition, particularly in services (Sidgwick, 2004).

PTAs should also include provisions for meaningful liberalization in sensitive agricultural sectors, particularly to ensure the inclusion of developing countries in the gains from trade. In general, fewer sectoral and product exemptions will minimize the risks of trade diversion. Non-restrictive rules of origin that share a framework common to multiple PTAs will assist trade creation, particularly in North–South FTAs. Similarly, common regulatory standards across multiple PTAs will help reduce transactions costs and increase transparency. The WTO Agreements provide exclusions to the pillars of non-discrimination and most-favoured-nation treatment to sanction PTAs under the assumption that eventually, the preferential access granted to members of PTAs will be extended to the multilateral stage. Therefore, timely and meaningful progress at the WTO to achieve widespread liberalization is the most effective tool to mitigate the negative externalities of PTAs. Nations must be willing to allow the multilateral negotiations to at some point erode their preferential status to achieve global free trade. There is no sign that this proposition has general acceptance among governments.

2.6 PTAS AND DEVELOPING COUNTRIES

Developing countries have also embraced PTAs for similar reasons as developed nations: advantages gained being first into a market before other competitor nations, permanent preferential status in market access, facilitating domestic reforms, trade-related positive externalities such as facilitation, services or investment and geopolitical motivations. In 2005, the World Bank conducted a series of simulations to examine the benefits of PTAs for developing countries.[20] A benchmark simulation[21] and three global liberalization simulations were conducted.[22]

In the first scenario, it is assumed that all developing countries complete a bilateral PTA with the Quad-plus nations.[23] As a group, and for the most part individually, all developing countries would be better off under a multilateral trade agreement than this type of bilateral PTA. Only the larger developing countries, such as Brazil and China, would gain some benefit from this type of complete hub and spoke agreement system. They are, however, better off under a multilateral liberalization. Most of the Quad-plus countries are also worse off under this scenario, although the degree of trade loss varies. The US and EU benefit more from this type of bilateral deal than from global multilateral reform because despite opening their agricultural markets to some degree, their domestic support programmes remain intact. Therefore, they do not face full competition from each other, particularly in agriculture as they would under a multilateral agreement but still gain market access to previously highly protected developing country markets. Japan gains significantly from this type of bilateral agreement but a multilateral agreement benefits it more. The Quad-plus agricultural exporting nations of Australia, New Zealand and Canada would benefit most from multilateral liberalization due to improvements in access to the EU, US and Japanese markets, as well as the latter group's dismantling of agricultural support programmes.

The second scenario is similar to the first, but with the exclusion of the large developing countries   China, India and Brazil. The results are similar to the first scenario but with dampened results. Compared to a multilateral liberalization, all countries including developing regions are worse off under the exclusion-type bilateral PTA, with developing country losses occurring in absolute terms compared to multilateral reform. Developed nations gain less with the exclusion of the larger developing nations simply because the latters' role in world trade has such significance.

In the third scenario, each individual developing nation or region is assumed to negotiate an individual bilateral agreement with the Quad-plus countries (assuming other developing countries do not sign agreements). By getting there first, developing countries capture some advantages, which are also possible if their PTA is an exclusive one with the developed partners. Under this scenario, roughly 50 per cent of the developing countries would benefit more from this type of bilateral agreement than a multilateral liberalization, and this partially justifies their motivation in pursuing individual PTAs. China, Indonesia and the rest of South Asia benefit more from individual bilaterals than they would compared to a multilateral agreement, while India, Brazil, Vietnam and the rest of Asia gain less from individual bilaterals than they would under multilateral liberalization. PTA proliferation means that many developing countries no longer have opportunities to be first off the mark in a PTA, and the likelihood of any PTA being the only one their partner is involved in is negligible, therefore the benefits of bilateral PTAs, whether individual or as a group or region, are less than those achievable under multilateral liberalization. The conclusions of the World Bank study has clear implications – the most developing-country-friendly option is multilateral liberalization and a 'full-set of bilateral agreements would leave virtually all developing countries worse off than at present' (Sidgwick, 2004, p. 103).

Regardless of the model and scenarios, developing countries are enthusiastically pursuing PTAs, with each other and with developed nations. Generally, developing countries PTAs with developed partners (North–South) achieve greater benefits for the developing partner. Technology transfer, different factor endowments, and access to large post-agreement markets facilitate improved potential for trade creation. However, these gains are balanced by more restrictive rules of origin regimes, exclusions for particular sectors and a lack of orientation towards development needs. Developing country PTAs with themselves (South–South) tend towards partial scope agreements or the exclusion of many key sectors. South–South PTAs have been plagued by a lack of economic diversity, small market size and failure to comply with agreed implementation schedules. There are South–South PTAs that have successfully focused on merchandise trade, minimizing exclusions, adopting less restrictive rules of origin, and reducing border transactions costs (Sidgwick, 2004).

Given that developing nations are unlikely to stop their pursuit of PTAs, how can their trade strategies best take advantage of the benefits of trade as garnered by PTAs? Unilateral liberalization in conjunction with attempts to reform and improve the productivity of the domestic economy has the benefit of helping to integrate the national economy to the global economy. The same process exposes domestic firms to international competition while lowering input costs, contributing to overall productivity gains, regardless of the presence of a PTA or not. The unilateral lowering of barriers in a national economy to the outside also contributes to increased intra-regional trade and the concept of open regionalism such that any potential PTA will contribute to the objectives of the WTO rather than create conditions to detract from it.

Open regionalism in the form of regional collective liberalization may currently be the most effective means to achieve non-discriminatory benefits for developing countries. Open regionalism in the form of PTAs that have low external barriers to trade and few exemptions can help developing nations come together in overcoming political issues, gain economies of scale, garner greater economic leverage as a group (that is, G–20), or reduce regional transactions costs. However, caveats of open regionalism for developing countries include ensuring that PTAs can be leveraged into accomplishing meaningful domestic reforms that foster economic growth. Particularly for South–South PTAs, the fewer the exemptions (the broader, more inclusive coverage, the better), the lower the external border barriers, the greater the services deregulation and competition and the more the trade facilitation combines to foster trade creation, both intra- and extra-regionally (Sidgwick, 2004).

Finally, the best means for developing countries to benefit from trade is liberalization via multilateral negotiations. Leading to market access globally, multilateral liberalization will benefit developing nations the most and is likely the only forum where their case for agricultural liberalization, the control of agricultural subsidies and contingent protection will be discussed. PTAs will provide benefits for some developing nations, but will not achieve the gains for all developing nations that a multilateral liberalization could.

It is with these caveats in mind that the opening of India and its evolution into a global presence in the international economy is developed. As India was a very closed economy, the potential gains, but also the potential adjustment costs, are large. As suggested in Chapter 1, the size of the Indian economy alone makes it a special case.

NOTES

1. Also known as regional trade agreements.
2. Where the term 'regional' may but not necessarily denote geographic proximity, or the relationship between legal entities such as countries or regional groupings.
3. We have chosen to use the term 'preferential trade agreement' rather than 'regional trade agreement' to reflect the current trend in trade agreements where geographic proximity is no longer a prerequisite.
4. As at March 2009, of these, nine are covered by the Enabling Clause, 135 are governed by GATT Art 24, as are the two accessions.
5. All are successive stages of EU Enlargement and each also includes an EIA.
6. The Enabling Clause is the decision by signatories to the General Agreement on Tariffs and Trade (GATT) in 1979 that allows derogations to the most-favoured nation (non-discrimination) treatment in favour of developing countries. In particular, its paragraph 2(c) permits preferential arrangements among developing countries in goods trade. It has continued to apply as part of GATT 1994 under the WTO (WTO, n.d.b.).
7. Article V of the General Agreement on Trade in Services (GATS) reached under the auspices of the Uruguay Round Agreement governs economic integration of trade in services (WTO, n.d.c.)
8. Including accessions to existing agreements as well as new agreements covered by the GATT, the Enabling Clause and GATS.
9. The WTO indicates that in fact over 300 additional notifications have been received, however this number includes inactive agreements as well as those that consolidated prior agreements, thereby reducing the total number of PTAs.
10. NAFTA, ASEAN Free Trade Agreement (AFTA), Commonwealth of Independent States (CIS), EC(15)Enlargement, European Economic Area (EEA), Southern Cone Common Market (MERCOSUR).
11. The Japan–ASEAN negotiations would seem more of a regional accession.

12.	Southern African Customs Union (SACU), Central European Free Trade Agreement (CEFTA), South Asian Free Trade Agreement (SAFTA).
13.	PTAs under negotiations may in fact reduce the final number of PTAs as some will consolidate existing agreements. The EC Enlargement, CEFTA and SACU are examples.
14.	An example was the accession of Mexico to the Canada–US Free Trade Agreement (CUSTA) to form NAFTA, exhausting North America as a source of regional partners – they have all been included. Canada has since been pursuing PTAs with regional neighbours in Central and South America including Chile and Costa Rica, with negotiations undertaken with the Caribbean Community (CARICOM), Columbia/Peru, El Salvador/Guatemala/Honduras/Nicaragua.
15.	Under the Bush Administration, the US utilized a strategy of competitive liberalization where trade negotiations were encouraged at multiple venues. It was believed the fear of being excluded from narrower deals would induce non-member countries to join the group of negotiating countries or accept a broader agreement at other venues to ensure they are not at a competitive disadvantage in gaining market access (Zoellick, 2002). Other than NAFTA, the FTAs entered into or being negotiated by the US account for a small proportion of its exports. Were the US pursuing FTA purely as a means of improving market access for its exports, it would choose larger economies as partners.
16.	The US utilized such a strategy during the Uruguay Round of trade negotiations where it simultaneously initiated FTA negotiations with Canada and proposed an ambitious agenda for the Round, with the implicit threat that if the rest of the world was not as willing to proceed forward, the US would pursue bilateral options with partners of its choice. It has followed a similar strategy during the Doha Round as a method of coalition-building and coalition-busting regarding the Group of 20 (Van Grasstek, 2004).
17.	The US–Australia FTA was in part a reward to Australia for its support during the US war in Iraq. New Zealand, a close partner of Australia, was a logical candidate for a side agreement, increasing total benefits significantly. New Zealand did not support the War on Terror and was not given an FTA. The US–Australia FTA is the first FTA between allies (Yeung et al., 2004).
18.	Via the creation of the GATT.
19.	Such as the need or rules of origin to determine the 'nationality' of products to ensure they are attributed to the correct PTA regime. An apt example is former US trade representative (USTR) Carla Hills' treatment of vehicles manufactured by Japanese car factories in the US. When exporting these vehicles to Japan, the USTR classified them as Japanese and therefore they should not contribute to import quotas the US sought from Japan. Simultaneously, when exporting these cars to the EU, the USTR asserted that these same vehicles should be considered American and not subject to EU quotas for Japanese cars (Yeung et al., 2004).
20.	For the sake of brevity, the discussion of the model and its results are truncated here. For complete details please see World Bank Global Economic Perspectives 2005: Trade, Regionalism and Development.
21.	The benchmark was a scenario in which all merchandise trade distortions were eliminated, domestic distortions dismantled and import quotas in textiles and clothing removed. Services were excluded due to lack of information.
22.	It is important to note that the simulations overstate the effects of PTAs because of their assumptions – full sectoral coverage and non-restrictive rules of origin. The reality of PTAs includes exemptions, phase-in periods and onerous rules of origin tests.
23.	US, EU, Japan Canada plus Australia and New Zealand.

3. India's Engagement with the World Economy

3.1 SOWING THE SEEDS: INDIA'S DEVELOPMENT POLICY

India's unique approach[1] to development, which started in the 1950s and lasted into the 1980s, was founded upon a desire for self-reliance; limiting external influences on domestic issues. Three fundamental strategies were the pillars of this approach:

1. The import substitution paradigm, popular among developing countries during the 1950s and 60s, underpinned the government's industrialization strategy for the economy. In India's large domestic market, import substitution was far more feasible as economic growth was unlikely to be constrained by market saturation. The unlikelihood of market saturation prolonged import substitution's acceptance as a viable policy in India long after other developing countries had abandoned it. Trade restrictions were the unavoidable consequence of import substitution. Philosophically however, in their commitment to its third option[2] of development, India's government, business community and academics did not shun international interactions per se; it was permissible under certain circumstances.
2. An emphasis on domestically owned, heavy industries producing and supplying the Indian economy with heavy capital goods and the Indian consumer with domestic consumer goods. Therefore, industries producing under import substitution were owned and operated by Indian nationals. Strict limits were placed on foreign ownership (up to 40 per cent maximum) throughout the economy, with an accompanying plethora of regulatory controls.

3. Policies of public sector dominance in infrastructure and essential industries such as electric power, transportation and communications as well as heavy industries such as iron and steel (Kerr et al., 2000) ensured that scarce investment resources were channelled to the 'right' industries. Private sector involvement was controlled to ensure consistency with the planning model. Instruments such as licensing of imports and investment as well as controls on the use of foreign exchange, credit allocation and pricing were all utilized to constrain private sector activity (Kochhar et al., 2006). Industries that were not overtly reserved for the public sector operated under the potential threat of nationalization.

Other policies enacted by India during this initial period of development included size restrictions for private firms and groups to avoid undue concentrations of economic power; encouraging production of certain labour-intensive goods by small-scale firms; enacting significant protection for labour, particularly in large firms; and investing in higher education. The latter contrasted sharply with the norms in other developing countries at that time (Kochhar et al., 2006).

India's complex approach to development combined with the emphasis on the public sector had by the 1980s limited India's foreign direct investment (FDI) inflows to less than 0.3 per cent of India's gross fixed capital formation, compared to the 3 per cent averaged by all developing countries. Economic relationships with major sources of FDI were actively discouraged and severely curtailed. The public sector focus on industries that are typically capital-intensive and large scale was consistent with the development approach in planned economies and the antipathy of consumer-led development in market economies. The restrictions on private sector activities and foreign investment as well as limitations on the size of businesses resulted in Indian firms that were smaller than their peers operating in similar industries in other developing countries.

While it enjoyed some initial success in the 1960s and 1970s, India's unconventional development strategy resulted in poor economic performance throughout the 1980s. Moreover, beyond this poor economic performance, India's inward-looking development focus yielded a host of negative consequences. Although import substitution was not constrained by the size of the domestic market, it did restrict meaningful foreign participation in the economy and, as a result, India's economy was deprived of technology transfers, exposure to innovation and knowledge as well as improvements in managerial capability. Import substitution also resulted in a highly self-sufficient, diversified economy but one characterized by high production costs, poor quality and a serious technology lag (Panagariya, 2004). Isolated from any foreign competitive forces, the development India did experience was neither modern nor efficient. The economy became complex without modernizing and the planning outcomes look increasingly chaotic in implementation.

Due to its state sanctioned role in key areas of infrastructure and industry, the public sector became excessively bureaucratic, unresponsive and unable to act as a meaningful instrument of economic growth. State enterprises survived on government subsidies, contributed to ever-increasing budget deficits and never faced the disciplines of market forces (Arun and Nixon, 2000). The public sector grew from roughly 10 per cent of the GDP in 1960–61 to over 25 per cent by the late 1980s. While the public sector's investment to GDP ratio rose, its contribution to the growth of output declined. Over the same period, the private sector's investment to GDP ratio fell (Panagariya, 2004). The private sector was crowded out by the inefficient public sector. Essentially, the public sector was used as an instrument of social policy and planning. Although growth in the Indian economy throughout the 1980s was relatively high, it was variable, fragile and ultimately unsustainable (Panagariya, 2004). The government's inward-oriented development policies effectively shackled any inherent predilection for the economy to move to a sustained development path.

While contentious, policy reforms were begun in the 1980s that had the objective of boosting GDP growth. These reforms included gingerly moving the economy away from bureaucratic control, lessening the repression of the private sector and liberalizing imports especially for capital goods and inputs. Export incentives were expanded through tax exemptions, better access to credit and foreign exchange, relaxation of industrial controls and licensing requirements as well as revamping the price administration mechanism for key intermediate inputs. These changes moved the economy towards a more pro-business stance (Kochhar et al., 2006), but were not guided by a comprehensive reform strategy. Similar to taking a sip of tea to determine if it is scalding, India's initial reforms of the 1980s gave policy makers some confidence in pursuing a broader-based and systematic approach to reform in the 1990s (Panagariya, 2004).

An acute foreign exchange crisis in 1991 prompted Prime Minister P.V. Narasimha Rao to accelerate economic reforms and move to a more comprehensive strategy that included a better thought out approach.[3] The 1991 package of reforms included further policies of liberalization, deregulation and privatization – a pro-market approach as compared to the pro-business reform of the 1980s (Kochhar et al., 2006). Needing to move from an inward focussed, planned, and bureaucratic and interventionist economy toward a more open one that included a dynamic private sector, India's government attempted to shift the country's economic structure.

It liberalized some foreign trade to facilitate a greater role for market signals in determining domestic resource allocation, including the elimination of many import licenses and the progressive reduction of non-tariff barriers (NTBs). Inbound FDI and portfolio investment were encouraged. Tariffs were capped. Reforms also included the abolition of industrial licensing and reducing the number of industries controlled by public sector monopolies. The financial sector regulations were overhauled. Some services were liberalized as well as exchange rate controls. The reform package did not, however, extend to agriculture or the labour market. Small-scale industries retained their preferred treatment (Kochhar et al., 2006).

Heavy industry was to move away from planning-based resource allocation for state enterprises towards privatization, which also included a greater allowance for foreign ownership. The liberalization of FDI included the abolition of the 40 per cent limit on the investment foreigners could make in a firm. Automatic approval for equity investments was introduced (Panagariya, 2004). High priority areas were designated and subsequently benefited from foreign technology agreements; the latter encouraged much needed technology transfers. The priority sectors included electric power, petroleum, food processing, chemicals, electronics, telecommunications, transport and industrial machinery (Kerr et al., 2000). India also initiated FDI promotional events to ease the process of finding domestic partners, negotiating agreements and facilitating investment for multinational corporations, essentially providing one stop shopping for potential foreign investors wishing to enter the Indian market. The government's strategy for economic development changed from import substitution to being one that is export driven. Manufacturing exports were expected to be the means to achieve faster and more efficient GDP growth.

This second wave of liberalization from 1990 to 2000 roughly doubled the ratio of total exports of goods and services to GDP, with imports increasing at a slightly lower rate. Total goods and services trade to GDP increased from 17.2 per cent to 30.6 per cent during the same period.[4] Services grew significantly, particularly in communications and the financial sector, largely attributable to the increase in private sector activity. The industrial sector, however, showed a marked lack of acceleration in its growth rate,[5] likely due to remaining constraints originating from labour laws, the protected status of small-scale industries, a dearth of large-scale firms and insufficient power supplies.

In most development models, as an economy develops, labour shifts from agriculture to be absorbed by industry thereby driving growth.[6] Overall growth in the Indian economy during this period had little to do with industrial growth; rather, the reduction in agriculture's contribution to GDP was absorbed by services. India is unique in the large share services contributed towards overall GDP during this period. It was a trend that continued from the liberalization in the 1980s. Despite the fact that the industrial sector has grown considerably in absolute terms, its overall share of the economy has remained fairly constant – something that was not predicted. As a result, the strategy of manufacturing-led growth did not seem to bear fruit.

Additional reforms were initiated in 1997–99. Their central objective was to eliminate NTBs while reducing and simplifying tariffs. By 2000, the need for additional trade reforms to be accompanied by complementary reforms in domestic policies was clear. Industrial growth and competitiveness continued to be plagued by the structural rigidities caused by the same elements of the economy that were excluded from the 1991 reforms.

During the first decade of the 2000s, India continued to reform and open its economy to competition and foreign trade. The number of industries reserved for very small firms was significantly reduced, and foreign suppliers benefited from a progressive lowering of industrial tariffs to an average of 10 per cent by 2007. The governance of FDI has been further relaxed, notably in the manufacturing sector. The advent of fiscal responsibility laws also significantly improved fiscal discipline in India's central government and the majority of state governments.

The economy continued to benefit significantly from these reforms. By 2006, the average share of imports and exports in GDP rose to 24 per cent, an increase from 6 per cent in 1985. Inflows of foreign direct investment increased to 2 per cent of GDP from less than 0.1 per cent of GDP in 1990. GDP per capita was now improving by 7.5 per cent annually, compared to 1.25 per cent from 1950 to 1980. This faster growth has resulted in India becoming the third largest economy in the world (after the United States and China and just ahead of Japan) in 2006, when measured at purchasing power parities. It accounted for nearly 7 per cent of world GDP. Moreover, with increased openness and rapid growth in exports of merchandise and information technology (IT)-related services, its share in world trade in goods and services had risen to slightly over 1 per cent in 2005, when measured at market exchange rates (OECD, 2007).

3.2 YES TO CHANGE: BUT WHERE TO START?

India's home-grown development strategy of the 1980s is aptly summarized as 'that of a labour rich, capital-poor economy using too little of the former and using the latter very inefficiently' (Kochhar et al., 2006, p. 17), particularly in manufacturing. A developing economy can be expected to follow a logical progression first shifting production and labour away from agriculture into low-skill manufacturing, which will then evolve to higher-skill manufacturing and then, at some later point, services. Productivity and employment increase with each step, boosting overall economic productivity. India has, contrary to the received wisdom, accelerated its development to the services stage, while its progress in the intermediate manufacturing stage has been much slower. One possible conclusion is that India's industrial revolution may still yet occur (Dougherty et al., 2008). This is a pattern unique to India.

Owing to its decision to invest in tertiary education, unique for a developing economy with low per capita income, part of India's labour pool is highly skilled yet inexpensive. This emphasis on higher education in combination with other policy choices prior to the reforms that began in the 1980s appears to have channelled India's development pattern away from the expected norm. Inflexible labour laws may have acted as a disincentive for firms to pursue labour-intensive manufacturing, choosing instead to focus on skills-based sectors such as services.[7] The service industries based in information technology were new industries and, hence, were not inhibited by the dead hand of the bureaucracy and the myriad of vested interests that accompany the regulatory raj.

Additionally, India's policies of reserving industries that generally required large amounts of capital and large scale for public sector enterprises, combined with severe restrictions on large-scale private enterprise have resulted in highly diversified manufacturing industries populated by small-scale firms (Kochhar et al., 2006). Dougherty et al. (2008) state that micro-enterprises of less than ten employees constitute roughly 87 per cent of manufacturing employment, an unrivalled level of 'smallness' and while small firms constitute nearly 90 per cent of manufacturing employment, they only produce roughly one-third of manufacturing output. Manufacturing has, as yet, not been able to benefit from economies of scale and there still exists a high degree of market concentration as well as the dominant presence of public sector firms. The prominence of small-scale enterprises in the manufacturing sector is also a distinctive trait of India's economy resulting from policy manipulation.

Services drove growth in the earlier stages of reform, manufacturing has grown much more slowly. It has benefited sufficiently from liberalization, and in some cases newness, to become more competitive (Ahluwalia, 2007), with output and exports both growing since 2000. The divergence between services and manufacturing output has narrowed significantly in recent years; growth in manufacturing output was, for example, greater than in services in 2007 (Dougherty et al., 2008). Yet manufacturing still maintains a relatively small share of overall production growth in absolute terms and manufacturing's share in total GDP is still not increasing. When consideration is given to the fact that India is a large country, with large factor endowments and a growing labour force, the fact that its manufacturing share of GDP is just over half that of China, Indonesia, Malaysia, Thailand or Korea (Dougherty et al., 2008), the continuing weakness in manufacturing suggests ongoing structural problems.

As a result of the set of policies prior to the reforms of the 1980s, India created capabilities (and constraints) that were and remain atypical in other developing nations. This peculiar economic configuration may, in turn, facilitate a unique development path based upon comparative and competitive advantages that are exclusive to India. It would seem that despite a steady period of reforms, India's unique development features and patterns have not changed. Specializations in high skills and services induced by earlier policy choices have continued. India's economic diversification continues at a greater pace than other developing countries at similar levels of development and the prevalence of services' share in GDP were accentuated with reforms, not reversed. As suggested above, manufacturing, which had been hindered by early policies, is still relatively weak.

Finally, government decentralization has led to a relatively large degree of economic autonomy amongst India's states, and a resulting divergence in their growth rates. States with comparatively well educated populations are growing rapidly and specializing in the skill- intensive manufacturing or services sectors. It would seem probable that the states with less educated populations may not be able to emulate the success of states with better education and, therefore, follow a more traditional pattern of specialization in labour-intensive industries. Kocchar et al. (2006) describe the skill-intensive states with educated populations as being more similar in their development to industrial countries, while the hinterland states' development may pursue a pattern akin to that of the East Asian economies. This divergence in patterns of production, capabilities, specialization and opportunities varies greatly among states and will have important implications to the overall patterns of development and specialization the economy of India develops.

India's economic growth has improved substantially since reforms began. However, the performance is geographically uneven between states, as well as economically between industries and sectors. Some sectors, such as telecommunications and information technologies, have rapidly become globally competitive while others such as manufacturing have had a much slower improvement in performance. Divergence in performance means that some aspects of, and locations in, India's economy will continue to make rapid gains while others fall further behind. As the experience in China has shown, regional disparities are particularly challenging for policy makers.

Regardless of its idiosyncrasies on the path of development, since beginning its unilateral liberalization and reform process, including FDI and trade regimes, India's real GDP has grown at an average annual rate of roughly 6 per cent (WTO, 2007) since the start of the 1990s. Liberalization has benefited services and manufacturing the most – the huge agricultural sector remains a backwater. In order to maintain high growth rates, India will need to continue its reform process.

3.3 PLANNING THE NEXT PHASE OF REFORMS: CONSTRAINTS AND CHALLENGES

Despite ongoing reforms which have significantly improved the dynamism of its economy, India still suffers from barriers to growth. Domestic economic policies and weak institutions are at the root of the problem. Infrastructure is in vital need of investment and reform as it is currently a crucial constraint on growth. Reform of taxation would also assist in reducing constraints in infrastructure by improving incentives and releasing resources. Labour reform is also a major source of structural rigidity. India's overall business environment, characterized by anti-competitive regulations, have restricted the entry of new firms and the growth of existing firms. The absence of effective bankruptcy laws is also a disincentive. The commercial legal system moves at a snail's pace requiring business to be conducted through personal relationships – which are costly to build and which inhibit competition. This environment has acted to limit investment incentives, thereby reducing growth and the creation of employment.

3.3.1 Inadequate Infrastructure

India's inadequate infrastructure arises due to almost total reliance on state provision. Known to be excessively bureaucratic, inefficient and overstaffed, state enterprises used public revenues with little results. As a result of this waste, state enterprises are chronically short of capital. Often, they have difficulty replacing infrastructure as it depreciates. Capital for upgrading and expanding infrastructure is often simply not available. Historically, power generation and distribution, telecommunications, rail and highways, ports, airports, heavy transportation equipment and banking all suffered from political interference in decision making, resulting in consistent underperformance. Their underperformance has also been a major blockage in the growth of India's overall economy. The lack of competition in these state enterprises bred complacency and therefore a lack of innovation and the adoption of new technology. The lack of competition ensured that that modernization could be avoided in the public sector. In many cases, long-run neglect now requires considerable investment to replace existing infrastructure wholesale, rather a gradual modernization to increase capacity.

While India has begun reforming the public sector, state ownership is still pervasive. Continued domination by public sector firms in central industries reduces the potential productivity gains from liberalization over the broader economy. Generally, much of the recent liberalization of the 1990s has benefited manufacturing as the share of public ownership in it has declined significantly. Yet state-owned enterprises still comprise one-seventh of total GDP, and one-fifth of non-farm business sector output (Dougherty et al., 2008). On average, their productivity and profitability is considerably lower than in the private sector (OECD, 2007). Despite some successes, most still act as a bottleneck in India's economic development process.

Telecommunications has evolved from a state enterprise to a dynamic, competitive industry with private and public entities providing improved and cheaper mobile services to consumers – but of course this is a technological fix. Roads or electricity distribution have no such technological fix on the horizon. Highway networks are being built and/or expanded linking major centres in the more advanced areas. New investment is also occurring in railways, ports and airports. Efforts to improve efficiency include initiatives such as a dedicated freight corridor in rail, privatization of rail containers and liberalization for private sector participation in airlines (Ahluwalia, 2007). Infrastructure has also been opened for FDI in varying degrees and conditions, including 100 per cent foreign equity in some sectors. State governments, which are responsible for a considerable portion of infrastructure, vary considerably in their buy in of reforms leading to an infrastructure patchwork.

Power generation and distribution has remained largely in the purview of governments and unreformed. Public enterprise dominates the industry despite the separation of generation, transmission and distribution and the implementation of independent regulators. Pricing, operational efficiency, theft of electricity and collection of revenues remain severe constraints (Ahluwalia, 2007). Demand for electricity far outstrips supply.[8] The inability of the power industry to improve production and efficiency in turn limits the growth of energy intensive industries such as manufacturing. The Organisation for Economic Cooperation and Development (OECD) (2007) suggests that while privatization would seem to offer opportunities for improving productivity in power generation and distribution, the privatization programme has stalled. If there is private investment, either domestic or foreign, only minority holdings are allowed.

3.3.2 Labour

Labour laws remain unreformed and a significant barrier to changing the development path of the Indian economy. The entry, reallocation and exit of workers is highly regulated and gives a strong sense of entitlement to those lucky enough to secure employment in the formal economy. As a result, employment creation, unemployment and underemployment are major issues facing India. Firms, particularly larger ones, are burdened by the inability to renew their labour forces and subsequently exhibit reluctance to hire. As a consequence, they are unable to capture economies of scale. The growth in employment in recent years has been primarily in the smaller, least productive industries as the residual effects of reserving labour-intensive industries for small-scale firms continue. Employment in firms with more than ten employees accounts for less than 4 per cent of total industrial employment (one-quarter of regular employment) and has been falling. This is among the smallest proportion of employment in enterprises with ten or more employees of any OECD country. Full-time employment that comes under the labour market's regulatory regime has been increasing as a share of total employment, but still represents only 15 per cent (OECD, 2007). As a result, India is unable to fully exploit its comparative advantage as a labour-abundant economy.

Employment needs to grow, particularly in larger companies, and firms need the ability to allocate workers to where they are best used. The WTO (2007) estimates 10 million persons are expected to join India's labour market each year. Given that the main driver of recent economic growth is services, characterized as relatively less labour-intensive and more skill-intensive than other sectors, India must create employment opportunities for the less skilled in labour-intensive activities. Reform of labour laws would greatly assist in creating the predicted necessary employment opportunities. It would assist in the process of releasing the vast pool of labour trapped in agricultural production. This trapping of labour in agriculture means that labour rates are low and agriculture has not shared in the recent benefits from growth. The increasing gap in urban–rural incomes leads to resentment, and hence, an increase in the appeal of radical political parties. In turn, this makes pursuing reform in coalition governments, particularly at the state level, much more difficult.

3.3.3 Competitive Environment

Fostering an improved business and investment environment is critically important to changing the path of development. Simply lifting restrictions will not be sufficient to change the public- centred development psychology. Developing a competitive environment requires a conscious effort to overcome tendencies towards bureaucratic planning and allocation. India must reduce the remaining policy-related constraints and excessive transaction costs to support its attempts to improve the operating climate for business and investors.

Without improvements to the business environment, it will not be possible to realize the economy's growth potential. Continuing excessive bureaucratic regulations and market interference raises transactions cost for firms, reduces transparency, acts as a barrier to the diffusion of technology and lowers the rate at which labour productivity can increase. The OECD (2007) indicates there a number of areas where reforms have already lowered regulatory barriers to international best practice but overall, in India, regulation is more restrictive than in Brazil, Chile and all OECD countries. There also exist significant disparities between the Indian states in the extent of regulation, affecting their respective economic performance.

The OECD (2007) further indicates that barriers to competition may be reduced in numerous areas:

1. To encourage innovation and the entry of new firms, India must lower the barriers to entrepreneurship by re-engineering procedures to reduce administrative burdens on new and existing firms. This includes the reduction of the extent of inspections as well as undertaking a regulatory impact analysis of existing and proposed laws.
2. Reservation of specific product areas for small-scale enterprises should be ended in line with the government's timetable
3. A modernized bankruptcy law is necessary to facilitate the restructuring or closing of insolvent or bankrupt businesses.

Competition can also be increased by forcing Indian firms to compete with foreign firms. Although the government has a target of aligning India's tariffs with average ASEAN tariffs by 2010, further cuts should be pursued. Reducing the dispersion of tariff rates would also improve efficiency. India's incoherent tariff rates, which often defy explanation, leads to distortions even at the micro level within industries. Extending the liberalization of FDI into a wider range of service activities would also foster growth, competition and efficiency (OECD, 2007).

3.3.4 Intellectual Property Rights

Developed countries' specialization in the production of goods, as well as the provision of services whose value is comprised of high degrees of intellectual property, is their competitive advantage. These countries are increasingly concerned about the protection of their intellectual property rights (IPRs) in the markets of developing countries. Historically, India's treatment of IPRs is no worse than many others, but its championing of a South view of IPRs at the Uruguay Round negotiations has indicated to foreign investors and firms that their IPRs may be less well protected in India than they would wish. India has also been at the forefront of the battle at the WTO over the right to trade generic drugs used to fight health epidemics such as HIV/AIDS.

The government of India has, however, made efforts to improve IPR protection by increasing training and awareness of IPR enforcement. Training is available to all levels of government, the private sector, the general public and industry. Efforts are also being made through seminars, training and discussions at colleges and universities, to build a culture of intellectual property (IP) protection, particularly in copyright issues. Similar efforts are being made with industry organizations. Of course, part of the reason for this change toward protecting IPRs is a direct result of India's joining the forefront of countries developing information technology and software.

Despite these efforts, much remains to be done to improve IPR enforcement. It is unclear whether the increased number of IPR-related police raids are a sufficient deterrent to further violations of IPRs. It seems there is a need to educate and raise awareness in the judiciary of the role, gravity and importance of IPRs particularly their impact on the economy, innovation and competitiveness. Although IPR legislation and legal provisions exist, whether the judiciary system will enact them properly has not been easily ascertained (WTO, 2007). Intellectual property protection always represents a trade-off between the loss to society associated with the temporary granting of monopoly rights and the need to encourage innovation (Perdikis et al., 2004). Traditionally, India's intellectuals have focussed more on the monopoly distortions than the benefits of innovation. Until this changes, poor effective protection for intellectual property rights may be sufficient to inhibit foreign investment and legitimate technology transfer.

3.3.5 Corruption

Corruption reduces transparency and increases transactions costs for firms. The bribes themselves are only one component of these costs. There are also transactions costs incurred in information gathering to determine the correct official to bribe, the correct amount to bribe with, and assessing whether the good or service purchased by the bribe will actually be received by the official. The power to provide preferential tendering for government contracts or approving licenses for economic activity facilitated the extraction of bribes and during the period when India was utilizing such policies. Corruption is a well recognized fact of doing business in India. Given the widespread dependence of the bureaucracy on corruption income, they have a considerable incentive to resist change that threatens their well-being. Providing a new incentive structure to replace those associated with corruption may be the greatest single challenge to reform of the Indian economy.

Licensing imports and tendering has been removed as a matter of policy thereby limiting bureaucrats' ability to extract bribes. However, this has only displaced the point of rent extraction from bureaucrats at the Ministry of Industries to the actual infrastructure ministries themselves – power, telecommunications, transport, aviation and petroleum (Kerr et al., 2000). Corruption limits the potential from foreign investment as firms are deterred from investing or, if it is made, may not come to fruition.

3.4 WORKING WITH YOUR NEIGHBOURS: TRADE, BILATERAL AND REGIONAL TRADE AGREEMENTS

Since opening its economy to reform and liberalization, including international trade and FDI, India's percentage of trade to GDP has increased steadily. In 2005–2006, the growth rate of merchandise imports was larger than exports, contributing to a trade deficit. Services enjoyed a trade surplus supported by surging exports of software the same period. Software, however, was only the most obvious success. India's most common trading partners are the EU-25, the United States, the United Arab Emirates (UAE) and East Asia. Both the EU-25 and the US are major export destinations as well as sources of imports. In recent years, however, the share of the UAE and East Asia has increased, reflecting an evolving diversification in India's trade.

Inflows of FDI continue to grow as India pursues the opening of additional sectors to inbound investment as well as the raising or elimination of FDI limits. Services and telecommunications have benefited significantly from FDI, as have financial services and the automotive industries. Despite reforms to the FDI regime having increased investment inflows, FDI remains at roughly one per cent of GDP, suggesting that foreign investors are dissuaded by other barriers, including infrastructure and administrative constraints (WTO, 2007).

Exports have become the cornerstone of India's development policy. Ambitious export growth targets set by the government of India[9] have been facilitated by further rationalization of tariffs, tax rebates, reducing border-related transaction costs through trade facilitation, improving export infrastructure, special economic zones, seeking out bilateral/regional trade agreements, and expanding the use of export promotion programmes. Measures also include the further liberalization of controls, simplification of export procedures, and the elimination of tariffs on intermediate inputs used to manufacture exports (WTO, 2007). Imports have an acknowledged role in generating economic growth and subsequently, India's recent policies have called for a simplification of import procedures, the reduction of import barriers, as well as coherence and consistency between trade and other economic policies (WTO, 2007).

Historically, despite its long-standing membership, India had not been a major participant in the WTO or regional trade organizations – of course, trade was not part of its development strategy. Its limited participation had isolated it from the dynamism of the global community, particularly in the Pacific Rim. It is now in the process of playing catch up. As a WTO member, it has submitted proposals on agriculture, non-agriculture market access, services, disputes, competition policy, trade facilitation, rules, Agreement on Trade Related Intellectual Property (TRIPS), as well as special and differential treatment, either as an individual member or jointly with other members, particularly other developing countries.[10] In the era of Doha negotiations, India is an influential member of the G-20 – along with Brazil and China – particularly in relation to agricultural subsidies in rich countries and tariff and non-tariff barriers maintained by these countries on products of export interest to developing countries (WTO, 2007). It has, however, been fiercely protectionist when it has been suggested that it open its agricultural sector to competition.

India has been a firm proponent of the multilateral liberalization process at the WTO but also believes that PTAs can supplement the multilateral gains. It has therefore been pursuing more PTAs recently, mostly with other developing nations and its neighbours. Most of its PTAs are focused upon trade in goods. India is a member of the following PTAs notified to the WTO: Asia Pacific Trade Agreement (APTA) which includes China,[11] a Chile–India agreement, the Global System of Trade Preferences among Developing Countries (GSTP), an India–Bhutan agreement, an India–Singapore agreement, and an India–Sri Lanka agreement. It also is a participant in the more regional South Asian Free Trade Agreement (SAFTA) and the South Asian Preferential Trade Arrangement (SAPTA) (WTO, n.d.a.). Early announcements have been made at the WTO by India for the following PTAs: EU–India, EFTA–India, Japan–India[12] and South Korea–India[13] (WTO, n.d.a.).

India is also a member of the Bay of Bengal Initiative for Multisectoral Technical and Economic Cooperation (BIMSTEC) which was intended to become an FTA by 2012, after cooperating first in goods by 2005, then in services and investment by 2007. None of BIMSTEC's set negotiating deadlines have been met (WTO, 2007). India also extends tariff preferences for certain imports (Special Areas) from Mauritius, the Seychelles and Tonga. Afghanistan, Nepal and Bangladesh have bilateral trade agreements with India with coverage in goods only (WTO, 2007).

Currently, India's Comprehensive Economic Cooperation Agreement (CECA) with Singapore is its only PTA with coverage broader than goods. It includes services and investment but given the small size of Singapore this degree of liberalization did not face any serious opposition. CECA commitments to liberalize services go beyond India's GATS commitments. India is negotiating a Comprehensive Economic Partnership Agreement (CEPA) with Sri Lanka, intending to move beyond its existing FTA in goods to include services and other areas. India's framework for an FTA with Thailand will provide coverage in goods, services and investment, but at this point commitments have only been made regarding goods. As with many Asian economies, India struggles with opening services such as banking and insurance. India also has a CECA framework with ASEAN with coverage in goods, services and investment. Initial tariff concession exchanges were to begin in 2007. India signed an Agreement to Promote Economic Cooperation with MERCOSUR with the objective of identifying potential cooperative opportunities in goods, services, investment and other areas. Commitments have been made regarding goods thus far. Beyond those officially notified as early announcements to the WTO, India is also negotiating PTAs with Mauritius and the Gulf Cooperation Council while exploring the possibilities of PTAs with China, Indonesia, Malaysia, Australia, Russia and Southern African Customs Union (WTO, 2007).

In terms of foreign investment, India continues to liberalize its FDI regime. Inbound FDI has not, however, responded to the degree expected. Constraints including the plethora of procedural requirements in the complex jurisdictions of India's regulatory structure, as well as lack of transparency in the approval procedures, have been cited as explanations. In response, the government created the Foreign Investment Implementation Authority (FIIA) to provide assistance to foreign investors encountering approval or operational difficulties (WTO, 2007). The government continues to simplify investment regulations as well as to reduce or remove equity restrictions in different sectors. FDI can occur in the automatic or approval modes. The majority of FDI, however, can occur automatically. Exceptions remain in particular industries, types of ventures or in activities reserved for the small-scale sector.

India's efforts at PTAs have yet to make a large impact upon its share of global trade. India's share is just above one per cent. In 2007, India's share in total world exports was 1.04 per cent, and its share in total world imports was 1.52 per cent (WTO, n.d.d.). India's efforts at PTAs have generally occurred intra-regionally, none of which have a significant impact upon world trade flows. With the exception of APTA which holds promise due to the recent accession of China, India's other existing PTA's have not contributed to its trade expansion. Political tensions in SAFTA (with Pakistan as a member), or a limited export bundle such as with BIMSTEC, help to explain the limited impact. SAFTA and BIMSTEC combined account for roughly 4.5 per cent of world trade (Nataraj, 2007). Hence, India's relationship with them has not made much of an impact on its overall participation in global trade flows. The implication then is that roughly 96 per cent of India's trade occurs without preferential treatment. In 2007, the EU-27 absorbed 21.7 per cent of India's exports and supplied over 14.8 per cent of its imports. That same year, India's second largest export market was the United States, with 13.8 per cent, followed by the UAE at 9.9 per cent. China was India's second most important source of imports, with Saudi Arabia third at 11.2 and 7.6 per cent respectively (WTO, n.d.d.) in 2007. The potential in trade expansion as provided by China's accession to APTA is clear. It is also apparent that the majority of India's most important trading partners are members of at least one strong well-established PTA with large shares of global trade.[14]

India's motivations then in exploring PTAs with the EU are clear. Given that the EU is India's largest trading partner, that India would want to protect and solidify this market access with a PTA is not surprising. As the EU remains a more regulated economic entity, India is probably more comfortable with an arrangement with it than with the less restrictive alternative of the United States.

NOTES

1. 'A curious combination of simultaneously favouring and disfavouring domestic entrepreneurship with a rich overlay of arcane rules and procedures' (Kochhar et al., 2006).
2. India made a conscious effort to not be classified as either capitalist (the West) or communist (the East) during the Cold War Era. It sought to be the leader (with some success) of a fluid group of 'non-aligned developing countries'. This was called the third way or option. Economically, the third way included socialism with the emphasis on state enterprises and regulation of the private sector. It did not preclude trade but the Indian third option included a strong role for import substitution industrialization (behind high trade barriers). Socialism would not necessarily preclude foreign investment in the private sector but India severely limited foreign investment to promote 'Indianization' of the economy. Therefore, the Indian third way was a combination of socialism, high barriers to trade and severe limits on foreign investment.
3. Panagariya (2004) indicates that the reforms of the 1980s were instituted on a positive list basis whereby restrictions were the norm and their reform meant selective removal (i.e. restrictions had to be specifically listed in order to be removed). With the July 1991 package of reforms, the absence of restrictions became the norm and a negative list

approach was taken in order to retain them (that is, restrictions had to be specifically listed in order to be kept).

4. The exports to GDP ratio increased from 7.3 per cent in 1990 to 14 per cent in 2000, imports increased from 9.9 per cent to 16.6 per cent during the same period (Panagariya, 2004).

5. Average annual industrial growth rate was 6.8 per cent from 1981–91 and 6.4 per cent from 1991–2000 (Panagariya, 2004).

6. Where developing countries can generally increase trade if a sufficient amount of their overall output originates in industry, there are more opportunities to expand labour-intensive manufactures, but it also requires greater inputs (often imported), which increases imports overall.

7. The public sector dominated industries were unable to take advantage of this labour specialization given their legislated penchant for over-staffing, inability to shed inefficient labour, and resulting hesitancy to hire.

8. The OECD (2007) states that India's current plans to increase electricity generating capacity by 6 per cent annually between 2007 and 2012, is still well below the likely growth rate of GDP, despite being double the rate of the past five years and the second largest absolute increase in capacity in the world. Underinvestment in power generation is caused by low profitability. Due to poor management of distribution enterprises and a failure to eradicate theft, in 2000 as much as 40 per cent of electricity was not paid for. Pricing policies at the state level such as extensive cross-subsidization in favour of farmers and households at the cost of industrial and commercial firms further constrains revenues.

9. Such as the doubling of India's share of global merchandise trade by 2009.

10. G-20, G-33 and Non-Agricultural Market Access (NAMA)-11 group.

11. The Asia Pacific Trade Agreement (APTA) including Bangladesh, Republic of Korea, Sri Lanka, China, Lao PDR and India had three rounds of negotiations and implemented the third round concessions from September 1, 2006. The Second Session of the Ministerial Conference was held in Goa in October 2007, and the ministers declared launching of the fourth round of trade negotiations.

12. Negotiations are being held in goods, services, investment and other areas of cooperation. Five rounds of talks have been held.

13. India and Korea are negotiating a Comprehensive Economic and Cooperation Partnership Agreement (CECPA) covering goods, services and investment and nine rounds of negotiations have been held.

14. Nataraj (2007) indicates that NAFTA and EU constitute 50 per cent of India's exports, 10 per cent is destined for ASEAN, and another 10 per cent to Japan and South Asia. Therefore, roughly 70 per cent of India's trade is with countries that are part of strong and well established PTAs.

4. The Evolution of EU–India Trade Relations

4.1 HISTORY OF EU–INDIA RELATIONS

Since 1962, when India established diplomatic relations with the then fledgling European Economic Community (EEC), the evolving relationship has been characterized by increasing levels of cooperation and dialogue across a spectrum of issues including political interaction, trade and investment, economic cooperation, development collaboration, joint civil society activities and cultural exchanges. Initial relations between India and the EEC were particularly easy because the United Kingdom, India's former colonial power, had not yet joined. The UK acceded to the EEC in 1973.

In 1971, the six-member EEC extended to India (as well as other developing countries), preferential tariffs under the Generalised System of Preferences (GSP). From 1973 to 1985, the EEC and India established a series of commercial cooperation agreements which culminated in the formalization of their ongoing dialogues into the first Joint Commission meeting in 1988. In 1991, the partners launched the European Community Investment Partners scheme in India to facilitate financing and joint ventures among small and medium-sized enterprises. The Indian and European private sectors follow suit by launching the Joint Business Forum in 1992. The EC–India Cooperation Agreement on Partnership and Development came into force in 1994, further institutionalizing the parties' regular consultations and other aspects of their relationship. The partners began to hold annual Summit meetings involving high-profile, high-level officials and participants. The relationship solidified further in 1999 when the EU–India Round Table was formally launched, creating a forum for meetings to be held twice annually, beginning in 2001. The meetings culminated in the decision to forge a Strategic Partnership in 2004. By 2005, the EU and India agreed to a joint action plan upon which to base the strategic partnership. The plan is founded upon strengthening dialogue and consultation mechanisms, deepening political dialogue and cooperation, bringing together people and cultures, enhancing economic policy dialogue and cooperation and developing trade and investment opportunities (European Commission, 2006).

A significant component of the strategic partnership is dialogue and consultation in order to define and achieve common objectives in a changing global environment. Issues where India and the EU share common perspectives are viewed as opportunities to work together. Countering international terrorism or strengthening the international legal order, including the role of the United Nations (UN) are examples. Both India and the EU believe that, in addition to sharing common values and policies, they share similar threats and opportunities in the current global environment. Due to these similarities, a shared approach to addressing these issues has been a goal. The value of the strategic partnership is to discover and capitalize on the synergies based upon these commonalities.

Partners and allies created via strategic partnerships are a cornerstone of the EU's geopolitical goal of improving security[1] and India is viewed as a critical partner in Asia. The strategic partnership also recognizes the important regional roles that India and the EU each play and the similarities in values and approach to addressing regional issues such as counter-terrorism, democracy, human rights and freedoms, the environment and reducing the global economic disparity between developing and developed nations.

The strategic partnership utilizes cultural and socio-political forums, dialogues, discussion, initiatives and exchanges. These efforts contribute towards cooperation in building civil society, development of cooperation programmes, health, family welfare, education, rural and natural resources, environment, human rights, and humanitarian aid programmes and are all formalized into the partnership.

The economic incentives associated with the strategic partnership between India and the EU are however, significant. The EU is India's most important trading partner, source of investment inflows and development assistance. The strategic partnership is intended to build a relationship between the two economies that allow their respective competitive advantages, based upon existing economic complementarities, to be more fully exploited. The partnership makes provisions for bilateral cooperative programmes in essential sectors such as environment and climate change, energy, customs procedures, civil aviation, maritime transport, science and technology, the space industry, and information technology and telecommunications (European Commission, 2006b). These programmes ensure formalized regular meetings via Joint Commissions to ensure areas with possible cooperative action are identified. In order to maximize any potential opportunities, the bilateral programmes are expected to expand their activities as their relative importance grows. For example, the EU–India Trade and Investment Development Program provides technical assistance to facilitate the practical aspects of trade and investment including sanitary and phtyosanitary standards, intellectual property rights, investment facilitation and customs facilitation (European Commission, 2006b).

India's emerging prominence in the high-tech industry, particularly information and communications technology (ICT), software, information processing and services provided at a distance are areas that offer significant opportunities for India–EU business opportunities. Outsourcing to India combines technical capacity with low labour costs. The EU sees substantial growth potential for its firms in financial services (especially banking and insurance), power and energy supply, telecommunications (land lines, cellular and internet), mechanical engineering, particularly in infrastructure, biotechnology, and textiles and clothing design. Bilateral trade in services also represents a large growth opportunity for both Indian and EU firms.

Substantial growth opportunities exist for bilateral flows in investment as well. The EU is India's largest source of inbound investment funds, and is also the primary destination for India's investors. Given the potential growth in goods, services and investment, India and the EU have, through the strategic partnership initiatives, committed to improving the overall bilateral trading environment. Specific products will also be targeted. In addition, market irritants that currently inhibit trade flows can also be tackled under the auspices of the partnership. The natural evolution of the Strategic Partnership is to move towards a preferential trade agreement. The PTA has been listed as an Early Announcement to the WTO and is currently under negotiation.

4.2 INDIA–EU TRADE PATTERNS

As suggested in previous chapters, India represents a growing market with more than one billion people. Annual economic activity is valued at roughly US$1 trillion. When India abandoned its policy of import substitution in exchange for an export-oriented development strategy, average per capita incomes increased substantially. The economic gains, however, have not been equally distributed. The Indian economy grew an average of 6 per cent per annum between 1992 and 2002. In more recent years, this rate has accelerated. India's share of world trade increased from 0.5 per cent in 1992 to 1.26 per cent in 2004.

In 2007, India's merchandise exports[2] were valued at roughly US$150 billion, while imports[3] totalled roughly US$216 billion. In 2007–08, India's per capita income growth was 7.2 per cent while inflation grew at 4.4 per cent with fuel and power as its main contributors. The industrial sector grew by 9 per cent but agricultural growth declined to 2.6 per cent, down from 3.8 per cent in 2006–07. Between 2000 and 2007, India's percentage change in merchandise exports was 19 per cent, while imports grew by 23 per cent. Figure 4.1 illustrates the growth of India's international trade. India's major trading partners are the EU, the US and China.

India is the EU's ninth most important trading partner accounting for 1.8 per cent of EU exports and imports in 2006. In turn, the EU constituted 21 per cent and 18 per cent of India's exports and imports respectively during 2006–07. It is India's largest trading partner after developing countries. Figure 4.2 provides a breakdown of India's global trading partners.

The growth rate of trade between the EU and India reached nearly 16 per cent in 2006. In 2007, India's exports to the EU were valued at roughly US$77 billion, comprised mainly of industry and manufactures (48 per cent), textiles (20 per cent) and services (18 per cent); the EU is India's most important export market, absorbing US$21 billion, mostly in these three main categories (Decreux and Mitaritonna, 2007). The EU is also India's most important source of imports, providing nearly 15 per cent of India's total imports. Since India began its programme of economic reforms in 1991, the growth in trade between the EU and India has been gradually but steadily increasing, as has the importance of the trade relationship between them.

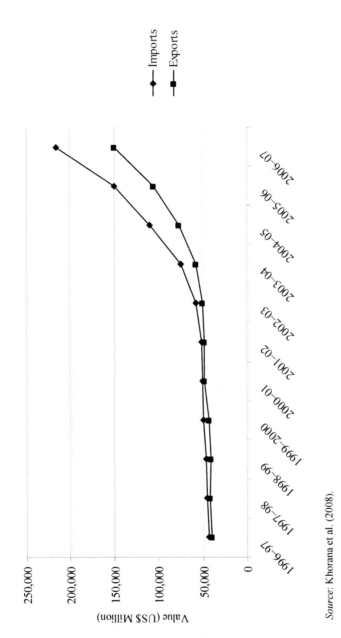

Source: Khorana et al. (2008).

Figure 4.1 India's total trade with the World, US$ millions

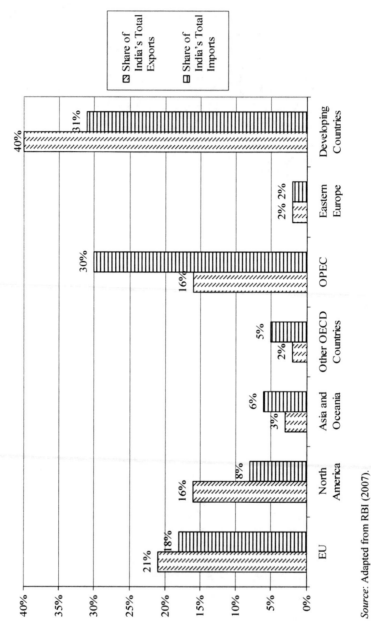

Source: Adapted from RBI (2007).

Figure 4.2 India's main trading partners, percentage share of exports and imports, 2006–07

Between 2000 and 2004, the annual growth rate of EU exports to India was nearly double that of its exports to the rest of world – averaging 5.7 per cent and 3 per cent respectively. The annual growth of EU imports from India for the same period has been even more pronounced, averaging 6.1 per cent compared to the 0.8 per cent average for EU imports sourced from the rest of the world. Essentially, India's importance to the EU as both a supplier of imports and a destination for exports has been increasing more rapidly than that of the EU's other trade partners.

Trade between the EU and India has more than quadrupled from US$72,602 million in 1996–97 to US$316,897 million in 2006–07 with India incurring a trade deficit of US$64,235 million in 2006–07. EU investment flows to India have more than tripled since 2003, from €759million to €2.4billion in 2006, while trade in commercial services has more than doubled from €5.2billion in 2002 to €12.2billion in 2006.

In 2006, India's exports to the EU amounted to €22.4 billion, mainly in textiles and clothing, agricultural products and chemicals, while EU exports to India amounted to €24 billion, consisting mainly of machinery and chemical products. Table 4.1 shows the evolution of EU trade with India and illustrates that although overall EU trade to India has increased both in terms of value and in growth rate, India remains a small trading partner for the EU. India supplies the EU with 1.66 per cent of its imports and accounts for a 2.06 per cent share of the EU's export markets.

Table 4.1 Evolution of EU–India Trade

Year	EU Imports from India (€ billions)	Yearly per cent change	Share of total EU imports (%)	EU Exports to India (€ billions)	Yearly per cent change	Share of total EU exports (%)
2002	13.608		1.44	14.271		1.58
2003	13.975	2.7	1.49	14.517	1.7	1.65
2004	16.234	16.2	1.57	17.031	17.3	1.77
2005	18.915	16.5	1.60	21.092	23.8	1.98
2006	22.361	18.2	1.66	24.061	14.1	2.06
Average annual growth		13.2			14.0	

Source: Eurostat (2007).

Textiles and clothing is the main product category exported by India to the EU in terms of value. Generally, India's exports to the EU consist of both primary products and finished consumer goods. Chemicals, machinery and transport equipment are important components of India's exports. Figure 4.3 presents the product structure of India's exports to the EU during 2002–2006 while Table 4.2 provides a more detailed breakdown by SITC code.

The EU's merchandise exports to India consist primarily of intermediary products for further manufacturing. The EU's most important exports to India in terms of value are precious stones and gems, machinery and electrical equipment, base metals, chemical products and vehicles (Decreux and Mitaritonna, 2007). The EU experienced a substantial trade deficit with India from 2002 to 2006 in exports of agricultural products, energy, and textiles and clothing as illustrated by Figure 4.4. This is, however, not the case in machinery and transport equipment for which the EU enjoyed a trade surplus during the same period. Table 4.3 provides a detailed breakdown of EU exports to India by SITC code.

Despite the impressive growth rates in trade, given the size of the Indian economy and its large production base, India in fact trades very little. Table 4.4 illustrates the share of exports relative to production for both India and the EU. The EU clearly exports a significant amount of its output, while India, with the exception of textiles, leather and wearing apparel, exports very little of its overall output.

Only 13.6 per cent of the India's total manufacturing output is exported, but this sector dominates India's overall exports, constituting nearly half of total exports. Conversely, 28.6 per cent of textiles, leather and wearing apparel output is exported, but this sector only comprises 20 per cent of India's total exports. Table 4.5 indicates the share per industry of India's overall exports and also shows the importance of the EU as India's primary export market, particularly in transportation and trade, other services, vehicles and textiles, leather and wearing apparel.

Services are a large component of the trade between India and the EU. Services comprise 11per cent of India's total exports. The EU25, however, absorbs 43.4 per cent of India's total services exports. India's key services sectors include transport, travel and business services. India's increasingly dominant position in information technology, medical services, tourism and some financial services make these sectors likely candidates to contribute to growth in services exports. Conversely, the EU's expertise in accounting and legal services, financial services, postal and courier services and telecommunication services can be drivers of EU services exports to India.

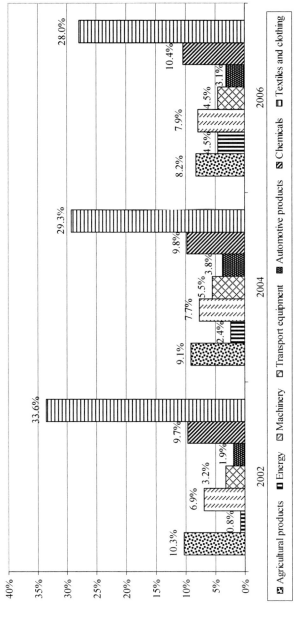

Source: Eurostat (2007).

Figure 4.3 Primary composition of EU imports from India, 2002–06 (%)

Table 4.2 EU imports from India by SITC code, 2002–06

SITC Rev.3 Product Groups	2002 (€ 000,000s)	%	2004 (€ 000,000s)	%	2006 (€ 000,000s)	%
TOTAL	13,608	100	16,234	100	22,361	100
Primary products	1,799	13.2	2,201	13.6	3,592	16.1
of which:						
Agricultural products	1,407	10.3	1,474	9.1	1,825	8.2
Energy	106	0.8	382	2.4	1,002	4.5
Manufactured products	11,702	86.0	13,970	86.1	18,607	83.2
of which:						
Machinery	935	6.9	1,246	7.7	1,761	7.9
Transport equipment	440	3.2	890	5.5	1,012	4.5
of which:						
Automotive products	258	1.9	616	3.8	696	3.1
Chemicals	1,316	9.7	1,591	9.8	2,319	10.4
Textiles and clothing	4,574	33.6	4,760	29.3	6,261	28.0

Source: Eurostat (2007).

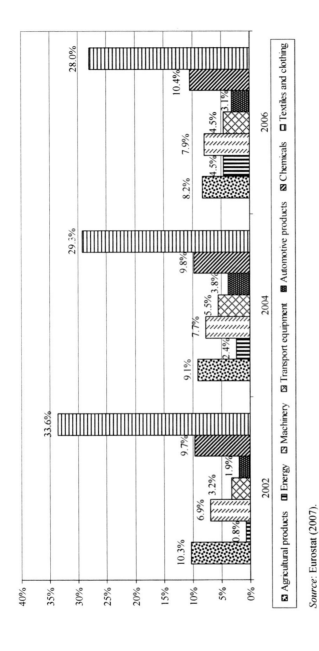

Source: Eurostat (2007).

Figure 4.4 Primary composition of EU exports to India, 2002–06 (%)

59

Table 4.3 *EU exports to India, 2002–06*

SITC Rev.3 Product Groups	2002 (€ 000,000s)	%	2004 (€ 000,000s)	%	2006 (€ 000,000s)	%
TOTAL	14,271	100.0	17,031	100.0	24,061	100
Primary products *of which:*	879	6.2	1,088	6.4	1,593	6.6
Agricultural products	204	1.4	179	1.1	347	1.4
Energy	67	0.5	78	0.5	165	0.7
Manufactured products *of which:*	11,926	83.6	15,444	90.7	21,817	90.7
Machinery	3,540	24.8	5,056	29.7	7,755	32.2
Transport equipment	916	6.4	962	5.6	2,157	9.0
Chemicals	1,366	9.6	1,681	9.9	2,175	9.0
Textiles and clothing	158	1.1	162	1.0	188	0.8

Source: Eurostat (2007).

There is reciprocal trade between the EU and India in some merchandise or services sectors. Precious stones, machinery, chemicals, base metals, transport services and business services are examples. The internationalization of supply chain management can provide one reason for this reciprocal trade; for example, European traders export diamonds to India where they are processed and sent back as finished products. Products may also be differentiated on the basis of price, quality or other attributes for which there exists market demand.

Table 4.4 Shares of India's exports relative to production, 2007 (%)

Sectors	India	EU25 (including intra-EU trade)	EU25 (exports outside the EU
Cereals	2.3	23.1	7.6
Other crops	1.5	30.7	4.9
Products from animal origin	0.7	13.4	3.4
Agro-food	5.6	18.1	5.9
Fisheries	0.5	8.3	2.2
Primary products	6.7	31.7	10.0
Textiles, leather and wearing apparel	28.5	45.4	18.8
Other industry and manufactures	13.6	40.5	16.1
Vehicles	6.7	50.1	14.6
All other services	2.6	5.1	2.8
Transportation and trade	2.9	9.1	5.7

Source: Decreux and Mitaritonna (2007, p. 10).

Within the EU, several member states are the primary export markets for India. Figure 4.5 presents the destination of Indian exports to the different EU Member States in 2006–07. The United Kingdom is the most important individual trading partner, absorbing 26 per cent of India's exports to the EU. This strong trading relationship is what one would expect given the long-term commercial relations built up during the colonial period. Germany (19 per cent) and Belgium (16 per cent) are the next most important EU member trading partners.

Table 4.5 Structure of India's exports, 2007 (%)

Sectors	Sectors share of total exports	Exports to the EU25 as share of total exports	Share of EU25 in sectoral Indian exports
Cereals	2.9	1.8	17.3
Other crops	1.1	0.6	15.5
Products from animal origin	0.6	0.2	8.6
Agro-food	4.5	2.3	14.2
Fisheries	0.0	0.0	10.5
Primary products	2.6	1.7	17.6
Textiles, leather and wearing apparel	20.5	27.1	36.1
Other industry and manufactures	48.0	35.2	20.0
Vehicles	1.3	1.3	27.2
All other services	11.1	17.5	43.4
Transportation and trade	7.4	12.2	45.4

Source: Decreux and Mitaritonna (2007, p. 11).

4.3 UNITED KINGDOM–INDIA TRADE PATTERNS

As suggested above, within the EU, the UK is India's most important trading partner. In 2005, trade in goods and services[4] between the United Kingdom and India registered an average annual growth rate of 20 per cent and 10 per cent respectively. The UK was India's fourth largest trading partner in goods, with a total share of 4 per cent of total Indian exports for 2005. Total UK services imports from India were valued at £1 billion, creating a trade deficit as imports exceeded total UK services exports, valued at £888 million,[5] in India's favour for the same period.

Figure 4.6 shows that over the period 1996–97 to 2006–07, total trade between India and the UK grew at an average rate of 8.9 per cent, from US$4,181 million to US$9,785 million. The growth in India's exports to the UK is higher than India's imports from the UK, creating a trade surplus of US$1,442 million with the UK in 2006–07.

Table 4.6 presents the 15 most important products, measured in terms of value, exported by India to the UK in 2006–07 by the Harmonized System (HS) Code. Mineral oils (HS 27) is ranked first, followed by textiles and clothing (HS 62, 61). Textiles and clothing along with leather and footwear (HS 52, 61, 62, 63, 64 and 42 respectively) are a large component of India's exports to the UK, together constituting 26.7 per cent of the total, with a value of over US$2300 million.

Textiles and clothing alone (HS 61, 62, 63), account for 17.2 per cent of total exports. The remaining 8.5 per cent is composed of leather footwear (HS 64) and leather goods/accessories (HS 42). After the elimination of Multi Fibre Agreement (MFA) quantitative restrictions and quotas in 2005, the share of textiles and clothing, as a percentage of India's total exports to the UK, registered a sharp increase, as did their compounded annual growth which increased from 3.7 per cent to 15.2 per cent. Figure 4.7 illustrates how the elimination of the MFA affected India's exports. The UK therefore figures prominently in India's overall European trade, particularly in textiles and clothing, where India enjoys considerable comparative advantage. The situation for leather and footwear is similar.

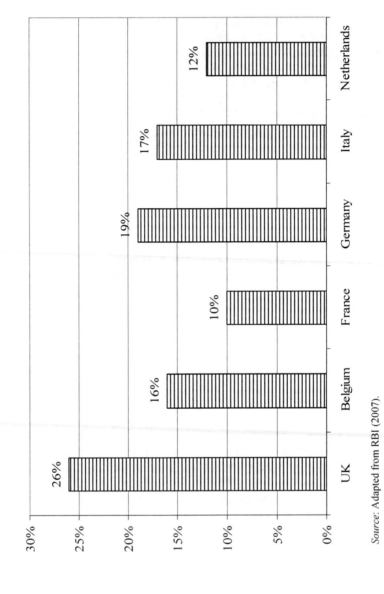

Source: Adapted from RBI (2007).

Figure 4.5 India's primary EU export destinations, 2006–07(%)

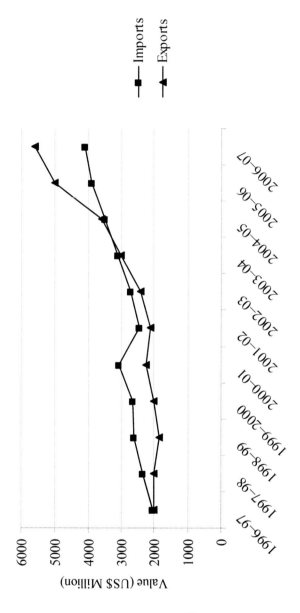

Source: Khorana et al. (2008).

Figure 4.6 Value of trade between India and the UK, 1996–97 to 2006–07

Table 4.6 Profile of India's exports to the UK, 2006–07

HS Code	Top 15 commodities	Export value (US$ millions)	Share in total exports to UK (%)
27	Mineral fuels, mineral oils and products of their distillation; bituminous substances; mineral waxes	818.37	14.58
62	Articles of apparel and clothing accessories not knitted or crocheted	599.35	10.68
61	Articles of apparel and clothing accessories knitted or crocheted	346.16	6.17
84	Nuclear reactors, boilers, machinery and mechanical appliances; parts thereof	335.16	5.97
71	Natural or cultured pearls, precious or semiprecious stones, precious metals, clad with precious metals and articles thereof; imitation jewellery; coins	293.09	5.22
85	Electrical machinery and equipment and parts thereof; sound recorders and reproducers, television image and sound recorders and reproducers, and parts	235.06	4.19
64	Footwear, gaiters and the like; parts of such articles	208.04	3.71
73	Articles of iron or steel	189.67	3.38
63	Other made up textile articles; sets; worn clothing and worn textile articles; rags	179.90	3.20
29	Organic chemicals	168.28	3.00
42	Articles of leather, saddlery and harness; travel goods, handbags and similar articles of animal gut (other than silk-worm)	163.56	2.91
87	Vehicles other than railway or tramway rolling stock, and parts and accessories thereof	145.86	2.60
30	Pharmaceutical products	135.42	2.41
72	Iron and steel	109.67	1.95
39	Plastic and articles thereof	104.55	1.86
	Total exports to the UK	**5,613.63**	**100.00**

Source: Khorana et al. (2008).

4.4 RATIONALE FOR AN INDIA–EU PTA

As discussed in Section 4.1, the motivation behind the India–EU PTA relates to a combination of economic and political factors. The underlying rationale is that, both on a global and bilateral level, India is growing in economic importance and the value of total trade with the EU has increased from €46 billion in 2006 to €55 billion in 2007 (excluding services trade). In 2007, negotiations for an India–EU trade and investment agreement were launched with a target implementation date of 2010–11. Six negotiating rounds have been held so far. The first round of FTA negotiations in Brussels (June 2007) established Working Groups for negotiations. The second round was held in New Delhi (October 2007), the third in Brussels (December 2007), the fourth in New Delhi (July 2008), the fifth in Brussels (December 2008) and the last in New Delhi (March 2009). The negotiating partners exchanged their initial offers in New Delhi in December 2007. The EU suggested that both partners eliminate tariffs on 90 per cent of total tariff lines as well as trade value (imports) within seven years. The remaining 10 per cent of products are included in the Negative List. In total, 446 and 550 products have been included in this list by the EU and India respectively. The coverage of tariff lines has been somewhat of a stumbling block to the progress of the FTA negotiations because India is insisting that the EU eliminate tariffs on 95 per cent of the goods under the FTA instead of the 90 per cent being targeted by the EU–India High Level Trade Group. The proposed India–EU PTA and investment framework aims to address are trade in goods and services, investment, trade facilitation, public procurement, intellectual property rights and geographic indications, competition policy, dispute settlement and regulatory harmonization.

An India–EU agreement in services trade would be GATS compatible. Sensitive sectors will be individually addressed with modalities that include review clauses and partial liberalization. It is claimed that the proposed PTA will lead to 'deeper integration' in trade of goods and services (European Commission, 2006).

The parties have agreed that their PTA will be WTO compatible, building upon the principles and outcomes of the Doha Development Agenda (DDA). For example, both parties support a flexible mediation mechanism to tackle non-tariff barriers. Both parties also share a mutual interest in developing disciplines on transparency in regulation.

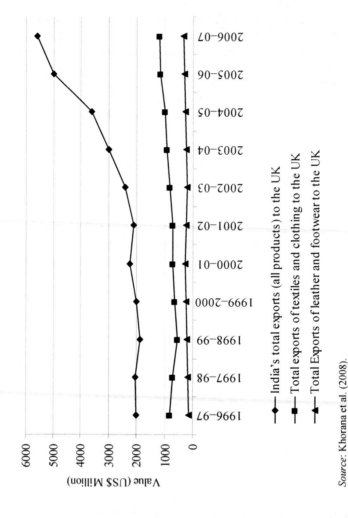

Source: Khorana et al. (2008).

Figure 4.7   Overview of India's exports of textiles and clothing, leather and footwear to the UK

As a result of the acknowledged complementarities between their economies, the contentious issue during the PTA negotiations will not likely be tariffs, but rather non-tariff barriers. Concerns have been expressed, by India as well as by the EU, about the level and extent of the existing non-tariff barriers (NTBs) to trade and their potential to impede the benefits of deep integration for both the partner countries (HLTG Report, 2006; Mohan, 2006). Both parties are convinced that substantial benefits could be achieved through the elimination of non-justified non-tariff obstacles to trade (HLTG Report, 2006). The ability of the parties to effectively address and include the remediation of NTBs in their PTA negotiations will in fact determine the final ability of the agreement to provide welfare gains and trade creation. Conversely, the inability of the parties to effectively address NTBs in the PTA will significantly reduce its potential benefits.

In recognition of the importance of NTBs, the parties established a negotiating framework that includes provisions and guidelines that they specifically seek to address across industries and issues. For example, the EU's High Level Trade Group (HLTG) (2006) reports, that in order to achieve the most effective structure to increase trade, the PTA framework will include:

(a) For services
   • Substantial sectoral coverage, measured in terms of number of sectors, volume of trade and modes of supply[6]
   • No mode of supply should be excluded.
   • Provisions to eliminate substantially all discrimination between the parties.
   • Additional services commitments beyond current levels of openness including:
      • Services liberalization commitments in modes 1, 2, 3 and 4;
      • Exploring areas to facilitate the mutual recognition of professional qualifications in various sectors and related issues;
      • Recognition of sensitivity in certain service sectors;
      • Recognition of the importance of the transparency of regulatory requirements in services.
(b) For investment, improve market access and provide for national treatment to investors:
   • Ensure that host and home states retain their right to regulate;
   • Foster transparency by clarifying the regulatory framework;

- Aim at freeing the flow of payments and investment-related capital movements;
- Facilitate the movement of investment-related natural persons;
- India expressed interest in including provisions on investment protection and promotion in any possible future bilateral trade and investment agreement.

(c) A forum to examine current technical barriers to trade and to exchange general information as well as statutory notifications was established with focus on:
- Ensuring that technical regulations not be more trade restrictive than necessary;
- How to establish mutual recognition for technical regulations and conformity assessment including exploring ways to establish suppliers' declaration of conformity, with a view to increasing bilateral trade.

(d) Pertaining to SPS, enhanced cooperation to promote mutual understanding an trust between the parties was essential:
- Both parties would search for means address SPS in order to facilitate trade;
- Information would be exchanged on good regulatory practices, specific provisions applicable to regionalization, assessment of equivalence.

Given the rapidly rising importance of the EU and India's trade to their respective economies, that complementarities already exist in their economic structures, and that the parties share, inter alia, similar geopolitical motivations, a PTA would further formalize, stabilize and enhance their relationship. The current importance of textiles and clothing, as well as leather and footwear to India as an essential component of its export mix and competitive advantage, implies that these industries must be sufficiently addressed within the framework of the proposed FTA in order to fully realize potential gains.

The textiles, clothing, leather and footwear industries are significant but complex aspects of the Indian economy and exports. Their trade and international commercial relations are fraught with unique characteristics, strengths, weaknesses, barriers and opportunities which merit an in-depth examination. The means by which the India–EU PTA will address trade inhibitors for these sectors, in particular, addressing the limitations that NTBs place upon them, will have a critical impact on these sectors' ability to realize the gains from preferential access to the EU market. The following chapters will examine the textiles and clothing as well as the leather and footwear industries in India in-depth, including an analysis of existing barriers to their export into the EU market. As the UK is the primary European trading partner for these sectors, it is the focus of these industry level case studies and analyses.

NOTES

1. As part of its security strategy 'A secure Europe in a better world' , available at http://ue.eu.int/uedocs/cmsUpload/78367.pdf, which indicates the identification of and cooperation with important strategic partners on the world stage, the EU has been increasingly pursuing bilateral FTAs. Some examples of existing EU FTAs are with Euromed, South Africa, Mexico and Chile. The EU is currently negotiating FTAs with India, South Korea, Andean Community, Association of South East Asian Nations (ASEAN) countries and Central American countries. Negotiations on FTAs have been completed with the Economic Partnership Agreements (EEA) and Gulf Co-operation Council (GCC). Negotiations with Mercosur have been suspended and the possibility of a FTA with China is being debated (DGFT, 2007).

2. Measured as f.o.b.

3. Measured as c.i.f.

4. During 2005, trade in services between the EU and India registered an average annual growth of 10 per cent, with a marginal surplus in the trade of services for India. In the UK, the Trade and Industry Committee Report (2006) also recognized the importance of trade in services in the Third Report of Session (Volume 1) tabled in the House of Commons.

5. Trade and Industry Committee Report (2006).

6. Under the General Agreement on Trade in Services (GATS) services can be classified into four modes of supply. They are: (1) the standard cross-border trade similar to trade in goods where physical interaction of the buyer and seller is not required; (2) consumption abroad where the consumer of the service travels to the service provider (e.g. tourism); (3) commercial presence where the service provider sets up a facility in the home country of the client (e.g. establishing a branch bank); and (4) the temporary cross-border movement of people to provide the service in the importing country (e.g. a repair person dispatched to another country to undertake repairs) (Beaulieu, 2007).

5. The Indian Clothing and Footwear Industries

5.1 TEXTILES AND CLOTHING

The Indian textiles and clothing industry occupies a pivotal role in the economy through its contribution to industrial output, employment generation, and the export earnings of the country. This industry is the Indian manufacturing sector's largest employer, engaging roughly 35 million people (nearly 21 per cent of the total population). In addition, it provides indirect employment to 60 million people or approximately 8.62 per cent of India's total employment. It accounts for 4 per cent of GDP, 14 per cent of industrial production, 27 per cent of India's total foreign exchange and roughly 8 per cent of India's total excise collection.

The textiles and clothing industry is regulated by the Ministry of Textiles, and is comprised of two main divisions. The organized mill sector is characterized by relatively sophisticated technology and integrated composite spinning, weaving and processing mills. In contrast, the decentralized sector, the largest part of the industry, is composed of powerloom units (accounting for 62 per cent of total clothing production), and handloom units (which operate with low levels of technology) as well as hosiery and knitting, readymade, khadi and carpet manufacturing units. The decentralized sector produces nearly 76 per cent of India's total fabric output.

The textile industry consists of readymade garments, cotton textiles, man-made textiles, silk textiles, woollen textiles, handicrafts including carpets; coir and jute. The industry is currently growing at an annual growth rate of 16 per cent in value and is expected to have a total value of US$115 billion (comprised of US$55 billion in exports and a domestic market valued at US$60 billion) by 2012 (Ministry of Textiles, 2007). Overall labour productivity in textiles and clothing appears to be lower than in the remainder of the manufacturing industry.

The critical role that the textiles and clothing industry plays in India's economy is illustrated by the following:

- India is the third largest producer of cotton in the world (after China and the United States) and has the largest area under cotton cultivation. It ranks first in jute, second in silk and fifth in synthetic fibres and yarn.
- India is the world's largest exporter of yarn with an over 25 per cent share of total world cotton yarn exports. Yarn constitutes over 70 per cent of India's total textiles exports. In terms of installed capacity of spinning machinery, it ranks second after China, while in weaving it ranks first in plain looms and fourth in shuttleless looms.
- The apparel and textile industry is India's second largest foreign exchange earner after the information technology industry. The apparel industry accounts for nearly 20 per cent of total industrial output and 26 per cent of India's total exports. This sector is a highly labour-intensive; an investment of Rs. 1 lakh (100,000 rupees) in the apparel sub-sector creates 6–8 jobs.
- It has been estimated that India has approximately 30,000 readymade garment manufacturing units and roughly three million people work in the readymade garments segment.[1]
- India has the highest loom capacity in the world with a share of over 60 per cent of total world tonnage. The power loom capacity is the largest followed by handloom, knitting and hosiery units. Its growth has been stunted by technological obsolescence, fragmented structure, low productivity and low-end quality product.[2] Most of the firms in this segment are small-scale industries (SSIs).[3]
- The handloom sector is the second largest employer in India and accounts for over 15 per cent of employment. Key strengths are flexibility of production in small quantities, openness to innovation, low level of capital investment and immense possibility for designing fabrics.
- The knitting industry is concentrated in Ludhiana (Punjab) and Tirupur (Tamil Nadu), which produces 60 per cent of India's total knitwear exports.

As discussed in Chapter 4, in terms of the United Kingdom's trade, India ranks fifth as a supplier of textiles and clothing with a total share of 4.7 per cent in 2006–07 (Khorana et al., 2008). Table 5.1 shows the value of India's textiles and clothing products exported at a 2-digit Harmonised System (HS) level to the UK over the period 1997–2007. Products that registered an increase during this period are silk, carpets, knitted as well as non-knitted garments and made-ups. Out of these, apparel knitted (HS 61), apparel non-knitted (HS 62) and made-ups (HS 63) accounted for over 80 per cent of India's total textile and clothing exports to the UK in 2006–07.

Table 5.1   Export values of textiles and clothing at HS 2-digit level, 1996–97 to 2006–07

Product		Export value (US$ million)				
HS Code	Description	1996–97	2000–01	2002–03	2004–05	2006–07
50	Silk	15.23	22.28	22.34	29.76	39.26
51	Wool, fine/coarse animal hair, woven fabric	43.84	1.12	1.61	9.75	13.07
52	Cotton	157.97	79.29	52.51	42.13	34.46
53	Other vegetable textile fibres; woven fabrics of paper yarn	12.30	8.53	7.16	6.46	4.84
54	Man-made filaments	38.74	36.83	35.46	40.62	45.07
55	Man-made staple fibre	40.61	23.42	20.88	19.72	18.85
56	Wadding, felt & non woven; special yarns	0.78	1.91	1.94	2.66	5.51
57	Carpets and other textile floor coverings	28.48	32.78	44.65	62.68	91.11
58	Special woven fabric; tufted textiles fabrics	6.10	25.67	14.91	7.74	11.88
59	Impregnated, coated, cover/laminate	5.61	1.73	1.54	2.27	1.96
60	Knitted or crocheted fabrics	8.86	8.50	8.47	6.76	9.97
61	Art of apparel and clothing access, knitted crocheted	85.36	134.86	227.96	277.40	346.16
62	Art of apparel and clothing access, non-knitted-crocheted	271.62	270.75	287.12	380.11	599.35
63	Other made-up textile articles; worn clothing and textile articles	75.20	105.85	104.43	168.20	179.90

Source: Khorana et al. (2008).

Figure 5.1 presents export trends in these products and shows that at present, non-knitted apparel, with a 43 per cent share, constitutes the largest component of India's textiles and clothing exports to the UK. In terms of percentage gain in 2006–07, the share of knitted apparels increased the most, by 14 per cent, followed by non-knitted apparels (8.4 per cent) and made-ups (3.3 per cent) compared to 1996–97 levels.

A total of 1,362 tariff lines have been notified under the EU tariff schedule[4] (Khorana et al., 2008). Table 5.2 presents the export values for the top ten tariff lines within textiles and clothing as well as the percentage change over 2005–06. It also provides the applied MFN and preferential tariff rates that India's exports enjoy under the GSP framework.[5] India's exports to the UK under the primary ten tariff lines in textiles and clothing were US$554 million in 2006–07 which constitutes a share of over 40 per cent in total exports within this product category. Further, 18 per cent of India's textiles and clothing exports are concentrated in two tariff lines: cotton T-shirts (HS 61091000) and blouses, shirts (HS 62063000).

Table 5.2   Applied MFN and preferential tariffs of top ten textile items, India's exports to the UK, 2006–07

HS Code	Commodity	Export value 2006-2007 (US$ millions)	Per cent change (2005-06)	MFN applied tariff rate (%)	Preferential GSP tariff rate (%)
61091000	T-shirts etc. of cotton	127.00	6.15	12.00	9.60
62063000	Blouses, shirts and shirt-blouses of cotton	120.24	(2.58)	12.00	9.60
62052000	Men's or boy's shirts of cotton	57.41	4.94	12.00	9.60
62045200	Skirts and divided skirts of cotton	51.15	(50.42)	12.00	9.60
61112000	Babies' garments etc. of cotton	46.96	30.59	12.00	9.60
62044220	Dresses of cotton	34.99	156.15	12.00	9.60
62034200	Trousers bib and brace overalls breeches and shorts of cotton for men and boys	32.07	43.88	12.00	9.60
62046200	Trousers bib and brace overalls, breeches and shorts of cotton	31.07	25.89	12.00	9.60
50072090	Items other than saris containing >85 per cent by weight of silk	29.55	31.80	7.00	7.00
62064000	Blouses, shirts etc. of man-made fibres	23.26	(12.42)	12.00	9.60

Source: Khorana et al. (2008).

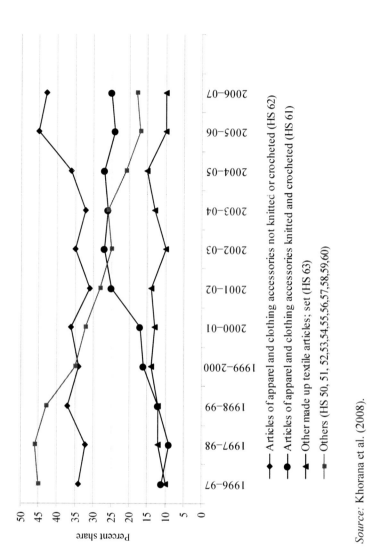

Source: Khorana et al. (2008).

Figure 5.1   India's exports of textiles and clothing to the UK, 1996–97 to 2006–07 (%)

Table 5.2 shows that Indian exporters, who enjoy preferential tariffs for their exports under the present GSP framework, will continue to export at lower tariffs so long as textiles and clothing are classified as sensitive products or have zero tariffs negotiated under the PTA for access to the EU and UK markets.

The benefits of preferential access can, however, be eliminated should the rules of origin (ROOs) requirements be strengthened or stringently applied. In most cases, specific rules of origin are applied for sensitive products, increasing the level of difficulty for suppliers to achieve the specified regional content. This creates an incentive for manufacturers to source inputs from regional suppliers and may act as a trade barrier on its own. By limiting the sourcing of inputs from regional partners, ROOs may encourage vertical integration of the production chain which may not reflect the least cost opportunities to compete effectively in a globalized environment.

5.2   EU REGULATIONS FOR THE IMPORT OF TEXTILES AND CLOTHING

Under its various mandates of protecting consumers, the environment and public health, the EU has legislated restrictions and regulations on the types of compounds and processes utilized in the production of goods and services imported into its jurisdiction. Textiles and clothing imported into the EU are governed by a number of regulations which are directly transposed into the United Kingdom's legislation. Specific requirements that Indian exporters of textiles and clothing are required to comply with prior to exporting their products to the EU and UK have been highlighted in a report for the BHC (Khorana et al., 2008). These are as follows:

- EC Directive 76/769/EEC restricts the use of azo-dyes in textiles and requires that products covered by this legislation may not contain any of the restricted dyes in a concentration above the threshold limit of 30ppm. Examples of products within the scope of this directive are clothing, bedding, towels, hairpieces, wigs, hats, nappies (diapers) and other sanitary items, sleeping bags, textile toys and toys which make use of textile garments, yarn and fabrics intended for use by the final consumer.
- EU Directive 76/769/EEC on flame retardants in textiles restricts the use of tri- (2, 3 dibromopropyl) phosphate (CAS[6] NO 126-72-7) in

textile products like garments, undergarments and linen. This regulation applies primarily to any product that is intended to come into contact with the skin.

- Speciality products for speciality end uses also maintain their own set of quality specifications. For example, defence textiles need rot proofing, children's wear should be colourfast to saliva and garments for Arctic conditions require the ability to withstand extreme cold. Mercury compounds such as substances and constituents of preparations intended for use in the impregnation of heavy-duty industrial textiles and yarn intended for their manufacture are not allowed.

- EU Directive 76/769/EEC establishes guidelines on the use of perfluorooctane sulfonates (PFOS)[7] and related substances. The Directive requires that PFOS must not be made available in semi-finished products or articles, or parts thereof in a concentration equal to or higher than 0.1 per cent by mass calculated for textiles or other coated materials.

- CAS No 87-86-5 EINECS No 201-778-6 states that pentachlorophenol and its salts shall not be used in a concentration equal to or greater than 0.1 per cent by mass in substances or impregnation of fibres and heavy-duty textiles used for decorative furnishings.

- EU Directive 91/338/EC (amends Directive 76/769/EEC) restricts the use of cadmium compounds. It states 'cadmium compounds shall not be used to give colour to finished articles manufactured from the substances and preparations impregnated, coated, covered or laminated textile fabrics'.

- EU Directive 94/27/EEC requires that the rate of nickel[8] release, from products coming into direct and prolonged contact with the skin, must not be greater than 0.5 micrograms/cm2/week.

- Directive 2001/95/EEC on General Product Safety sets provisions for product recall. It states that it is obligation of the producers and distributors to notify the Commission in case of a problem with a product and calls for the creation of a European Product Safety Network.

- EU Directive 2002/371/EC establishes the ecological criteria of the EU eco-label for textile products. It sets limitations on the use of substances that are harmful for the aquatic environment and health; processing additives; restricts the use of chloro-phenols, cerium compounds, halogenated carriers; places limits on heavy metals and formaldehyde, certain auxiliary chemicals, detergents, fabric softeners and compelling agents; and imposes limits on the AOX emissions in bleaching effluents.

- EU Directive 2003/53/EC (amends Directive 76/769/EEC) places restrictions on the use of nonylphenols (NP) and nonylphenol ethoxylates (NPEs)[9] or any of its constituent preparations in concentrations equal to or higher than 0.1 per cent by mass for textile processing. The United Kingdom incorporated Directive 2003/53/EC in its national legislation via Regulation No. 1868 of 2004 on Controls of NP and NPEs.
- Directive 2006/12/EC on waste aims to encourage the recovery of waste and the use of recovered materials as raw materials in order to conserve natural resources, taking into consideration existing or potential market opportunities for recovered waste.
- EU regulation on Registration, Evaluation, Authorisation and Restriction of Chemicals (REACH), entered into force in June 2007. It requires, in addition to other requirements, EU manufacturers and importers of chemical substances (whether on their own, in preparations or in certain articles) to gather comprehensive information on properties of their substances produced or imported in volumes of 1 tonne or more per year, and to register such substances prior to manufacturing in or import into the EU.

The EU has also implemented voluntary regulations for textiles and clothing imported from foreign sources. Examples of voluntary regulations are EC Directive 96/74/EC of 16 December 1996 that lays down requirements on 'care labelling' with recommendations or instructions on how to treat the garment (for example, washing, drying and ironing).

5.3 INDIA'S LEATHER AND FOOTWEAR INDUSTRY

The leather industry in India consists of tanning and finishing, footwear and footwear components, leather garments, leather goods and saddlery and harness products.[10] India is the third largest leather producer in the world, after China and Italy, with over 40,000 SSIs that account for over 75 per cent of total production. The estimated value of leather produced in India is US$4 billion and employs 2.5 million people. Some key indicators of the leather and footwear industry are:

- Most of the leather footwear manufacturing industry is situated in the states of Tamil Nadu, West Bengal and Uttar Pradesh.
- Leather garments are mostly manufactured in Delhi and Chennai. Leather accessories and goods production is concentrated in Kolkata, Chennai and Kanpur.
- The Indian tanning industry is concentrated in Tamil Nadu (60 per cent), Kolkata (20 per cent), Kanpur (13 per cent) and Jalandhar (7 per cent).
- Eighty per cent of the total Indian leather production is sent to three main buying countries: the EU (63 per cent), USA (12 per cent) and Hong Kong (10 per cent).
- India produces 2,065 million pairs of footwear in various categories including leather shoes (909 million pairs), leather shoe uppers (100 million pairs) and non-leather footwear (1,056 million pairs). India exports approximately 115 million pairs of shoes; nearly 95 per cent of its production meets domestic demand.
- Some main brands that buy leather and leather products from India are Pierre Cardin, Versace, Hugo Boss, NEXT, New Look, Tommy Hilfiger, Guess, Brantano, Florsheim, Clarks and DKNY.

India ranks fourth as a supplier of leather and footwear to the UK with a total share of 5.7 per cent in 2006–07. The main product groups exported by India to the UK are leather footwear (HS 64)[11] and leather goods/accessories and garments (HS42); together these constitute 99 per cent of total leather and footwear exported by India to the UK during this period. A complete profile of the UK's imports of leather and leather products can be found in Appendix A. However, within the EU, the UK is the main destination for India's exports of leather and footwear, followed by Germany.

Under HS42, the UK imports suitcases, briefcases (including computer cases), handbags, travel bags and other bags and small leather accessories (including belts, wallets, purses, key pouches) from India. The UK's consumption of luggage and leather accessories was valued at €1,382 million in 2006, an increase of 4.5 per cent per annum on average since 2002, while production fell by an annual average of 7.4 per cent to €207 million. In 2006, the total value of luggage and leather accessories imported by the UK was €1,318 million and more than 58 per cent of imports by value (€769 million) were sourced from developing countries (80 per cent by volume) (Business Wire, 2007).

Figure 5.2 provides the value of India's exports of leather and footwear products to the UK. In terms of value, the fastest growing export segment was leather goods/accessories and garments which increased by 12 per cent followed by leather footwear at 6 per cent. An exception is raw hides and skins (HS 41) that registered a decline of 14.52 per cent during 2001–2007 (Khorana et al., 2008).

Table 5.3 presents the trade patterns of primary leather and footwear items exported to the UK by India. Between 1996–97 and 2006–07, the share of raw hides and skins declined, from 6 per cent to less than one per cent; leather goods/accessories and garments gained in their share of total exports, from 38 per cent in 1996–97 to 44 per cent; while the share of leather footwear remained constant (Khorana et al., 2008).

There are a total of 165 tariff lines in leather and leather products (HS 41, 42 and 63) notified under the EU tariff schedule. Out of this, 136 tariff lines enjoy preferential tariffs (3.5 percentage point reduction at the ad valorem rate) under the GSP scheme. The remaining 29 are non-sensitive meaning that the products come into the EU and UK under zero tariffs. Subsequently, nearly one-fourth of the total tariff lines notified under leather and footwear enjoy duty-free access (Khorana et al., 2008).

Table 5.3 India's exports of leather and footwear to the UK (%)

Product		Share in Leather and Footwear exports (%)				
HS Code	Description	1996- 97	2000- 01	2002- 03	2004- 05	2006- 07
41	Raw hides and skins	6.33	2.17	2.50	1.26	0.73
42	Leather goods/ accessories & garments	38.18	41.74	38.47	39.85	43.69
64	Leather footwear	55.49	56.09	59.03	58.88	55.57
Share of leather and footwear in India's total exports to UK		10.19	12.19	9.90	8.89	6.67

Source: Khorana et al. (2008).

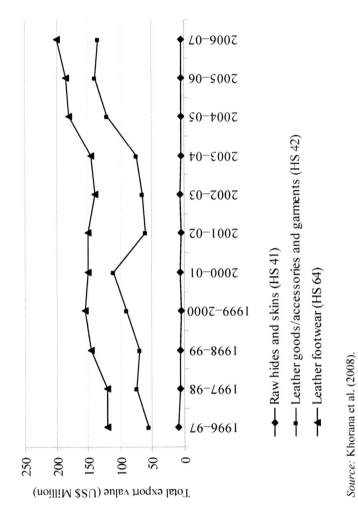

Source: Khorana et al. (2008).

Figure 5.2   India's exports of leather and footwear products to the UK

83

Table 5.4 presents the top ten leather and footwear tariff lines that were exported to the UK in 2006–07; it also shows the percentage change over 2005–06 as well as the applied MFN and preferential tariffs for these products. The total value of exports to the UK under these tariff lines was US$225 million, against total exports of US$374.36 million in this product group. This means that exports under the top ten 8-digit lines constitutes nearly 60 per cent of the total trade in leather and footwear. Out of these, 30 per cent of the total leather and footwear exports qualify under the GSP scheme; the main items are leather shoes (HS 64035111) and accessories (HS 42022190 and HS 42022110).

Table 5.4   Applied MFN and preferential tariffs of top ten footwear items, India's exports to the UK, 2006–07

HS Code	Product	Export value 2006-07 (US$ mill)	Percent change over 2005-06	MFN applied rate (%)	Tariff preference rate (GSP)(%)
64035111	Ankle covered all leather shoes for men	50.59	(0.02)	8.00	4.50
42022190	Other leather handbags	31.45	7.96	3.00	0.00
42022110	Handbags of leather for ladies	27.66	9.33	3.00	0.00
42023120	Wallets and purses of leather	20.66	4.08	3.00	0.00
42031010	Jackets and jerseys	19.50	11.88	4.00	0.00
64031990	Others	17.73	64.62	8.00	4.50
64032029	Other footwear with all leather, open toe	17.56	N.A.	8.00	4.50
64039110	Leather boots and other footwear with rubber sole	16.35	51.25	8.00	4.50
42010000	Saddlery and harness for animals	12.53	(16.02)	2.70	0.00
64039910	Leather sandals with rubber sole	11.25	(10.36)	8.00	4.50

Source: Khorana et al. (2008).

Additionally, 30 per cent of India's total leather and footwear exports to the UK are accessories and garments (HS 42) which are allowed into the EU and the UK at zero tariffs under the existing GSP framework. Therefore, there are no prospects for further tariff reductions within this product group. Within the context of the ongoing PTA negotiations, it is therefore of far greater importance to address the ROO and existing NTBs for these product lines under leather accessories and garments. Tariffs are a non-issue as these products already enjoy duty-free access.

5.4 EU REGULATIONS FOR THE IMPORTATION OF LEATHER AND FOOTWEAR

As with textiles and clothing, the importation of leather and footwear into the EU is governed by a variety of regulations and directives which have also been incorporated into the United Kingdom legislation. Specific requirements that Indian exporters of leather and footwear are required to comply with prior to exporting to the EU and UK, as highlighted in the report by Khorana et al. (2008) are:

- Council Directive 88/378/EEC states the maximum permissible limit of 3.0 mg/kg for Chrome VI in leather footwear and leather products[12] and employs TS 144495 (EN ISO 17075:2008) to test the limit of restricted substance.
- Council Directive 91/338/EEC sets the maximum permissible limit of 100ppm for cadmium in leather and its products; the test procedure to check the permissible limits is microwave digestion and ICP analysis.
- EC Directive 1999/51/EC establishes the mandatory requirements for pentachlorophenol (PCP) of which the content of toxic agents allowed is the maximum of 5 mg/kg (better: < value of detection 0.5 mg/kg).
- Directive 2002/61/EC (amended by 2004/21/EC) restricts the use of azo-dyes and pigments that liberate any of the banned aromatic amines used to produce leather goods, shoes, toys, furniture, decorative articles, jewellery and accessories.
- EC Directive (2002/231/EC) restricts the use of tri- and tetra-chlorophenol- isomers (TECP) and allows a maximum permissible limit of < 0.05ppm in textiles and < 5ppm in leather.
- EU Law EN 71 prohibits the use of lead beyond the permissible limit of 90ppm.

- Arsenic is prohibited under Commission Directive 2003/2/EC of January 2003.
- Commission Directive 2002/62/EC restricts the use of organotin compounds which are tested by ethanol extraction and GC-MS or LS-MS processes.
- EU Directive 2003/11/EC sets the maximum permissible limit (1000ppm) of specific flame retardants.
- EC Regulation 1907/2008 deals with the safe use of chemicals through REACH[13] and seeks to reduce the risks of chemical substances to health, safety and environment through registration of substances manufactured in or imported into the EU market. The registration process requires the industry to take the responsibility to generate the safety data, identify the safety measures needed to manage the risks and to communicate the safety information on the substance to the downstream users throughout the supply chain in both the leather and footwear, and textiles and clothing industries. A recent survey by the Federation of Indian Chambers of Commerce and Industry (FICCI)[14] reports that the one-time compliance cost of REACH could be between 5 and 10 per cent of a manufacturer's turnover in addition to significant recurring costs afterwards.
- There are also mandatory standards on safety footwear in the EU that relate to the tensile strength of leather split, tear strength of leather, water absorption resistance, water vapour permeability as well as abrasion resistance of non-leather outsoles.

The EU maintains additional voluntary requirements affecting leather and footwear imports some of which include:

- The maximum permissible limit for chrome IV (residue products) is 10ppm.
- Energy consumption per pair of footwear (voluntary declaration).
- Recycled PVC is permitted to be used exclusively in out-soles where DEHP (2-ethylexylpythalate) or DBP (butylbenzylphtalate) is not used.
- Packing cardboard boxes should be used for packaging. These are to be made from a minimum of 80 per cent recycled material while plastic bags (mainly used for packing cheaper quality shoes) should be made from 100 per cent recycled material.

Stringent tests on physical characteristics are also required to be undertaken by the leather footwear exporter/manufacturer before the final product is exported to any EU Member State. Some of the main tests conducted on footwear by UK buyers in India are provided in Table 5.5.

Table 5.5 Tests for leather footwear prior to export to the EU and UK

	Required test	Unit of measurement	Testing method used	Specifications
1	Thickness	MM	UNI EN ISO 2589	2.3–2.5 MM
2	Rigidity	Shore	M.I.0002	75±5
3	Resistance to the traction	N/MM	UNI EN ISO 3376 2006	≥2.5
4	Extension at the point of breaking	per cent	UNI EN ISO 3376 2006	40-75
5	Resistance to the pulling	N/MM	UNI EN ISO 3376 2·2006	>4
6	Resistance to the flections–dry	Cycles	UNI EN ISO 5402:2004	100.000
7	Resistance at explosion-pressure	BAR	UNI EN ISO 3379	14–16
8	Solidity of finish to the scratch–at dry 50, 100, 1500, cycle	Note		4–5 According the grey scale
9	Time of water penetration	Dry	UNI EN ISO 5403	≥20 minutes
10	Absorbing water in static conditions	per cent	M.I.0001	≤60
11	PH	per cent	EN ISO 4045	≤3.5
12	Humidity	per cent	UNI EN ISO 4648	16–20
13	Soluble materials inside water	per cent	UNI EN ISO 4096	≤60
14	Ashes	per cent	EN ISO 4047	

Source: Khorana et al. (2008).

The EU also maintains other regulatory parameters that set guidelines on waste treatment and energy consumption. For instance, there are guidelines on the treatment of waste water from leather tanning sites which aim to achieve a reduction of 85 per cent in chemical oxygen demand (COD) content; reduce the use of volatile organic carbons (VOCs) during production of different categories of footwear; and so on. There are also detailed instructions about information on the packaging, modalities for assessment and verification of an Eco-label. In addition, EC Directive 89/686/EEC establishes parameters on occupational and safety footwear.

Beyond the tariffs and regulatory issues discussed in this chapter, substantial barriers impede the trade in textiles and clothing and leather and footwear between India and the EU. NTBs comprise a significant and entrenched challenge impeding trade between India and the UK. Given that a portion of India's exports to the EU enter duty free, tariffs are a far less contentious issue than NTBs. Products on which EU tariffs are high are leather footwear (HS 640420), articles of leather (HS 420321) and footwear with leather straps (HS 640320); tariffs levied are 17, 9 and 8 per cent respectively. The following chapters will discuss the issue of NTBs in detail. Chapter 6 will provide an analysis of NTB's faced by the textiles and clothing industry as well as the leather and footwear industry in both Indian and UK. Chapter 6 will also quantify the perceptions of trade barriers in textiles and clothing as well as in leather and footwear. Chapter 7 will provide an evaluation and recommendations within the context of the preferential trade agreement being negotiated between India and the EU.

NOTES

1. http://apparel.indiamart.com/lib/garments/indian07251998.html.
2. http://apparel.indiamart.com/indian-textile-policy/sectorial-initiative3.html.
3. The definition of SSI is that the investment in fixed assets in plant and machinery whether held on ownership terms on lease or on hire purchase does not exceed Rs. 10 million. (Source: http://exim.indiamart.com/ssi-corner/definition.html#small-scale-industrial-undertakings). Woven apparel and knitted were removed from the SSI sector in 2001 and 2002, respectively.
4. Available at www.europa.eu.
5. The Generalised System of Preferences scheme was adopted through Resolution 21 (II) in 1968 with the objective 'to allow the generalised, non-reciprocal, non-discriminatory system of preferences in favour of developing countries, including special measures for the least advanced among the developing countries to increase their export earnings; promote their industrialisation; and, accelerate their rates of economic growth'. Under the existing GSP scheme, developed countries allow non-reciprocal trade preferences to developing countries and the least developed countries in the form of exemption from and/or a lower duty on notified agricultural and industrial products. The existing EU GSP scheme (Council Regulation No: 980/2005 of 27th June 2005) provides that most eligible products will continue to attract a reduction of 3.5 percentage points in the full ad valorem rate of customs duty payable. Textiles and clothing products eligible for preferential treatment under the existing GSP scheme are tariff lines notified under HS chapters 61–63 of the Tariff Schedule, which attract a 20 per cent reduction in the full rate of duty payable; exceptions are HS chapters 50–60, that have been graduated out from the GSP scheme. Leather and footwear products (HS Chapters 42, 43 and 64) are also eligible for preferential tariffs under the GSP. Footwear (HS 64) and raw hides (HS 43) enjoy reduction in tariffs (of 3.5 percentage points on an ad valorem basis) while accessories (HS 42) come into the EU at zero tariffs under the GSP scheme.
6. CAS numbers are internationally recognized unique identification numbers assigned to chemical substances
7. These substances provide the necessary grease, oil and water resistance to textile, carpets, upholstery, leather, apparel, paper and packaging and in general coating products.
8. Nickel is a metal that is sometimes contained in alloys used in clothing accessories (such as rivet buttons, tighteners, rivets, zippers and metal marks).
9. Nonylphenols (NP) and nonylphenol ethoxylates (NPEs) are persistent and bio-accumulative chemicals suspected to have endocrine effects.

10. Leather production consists of the following main processes. These are:
    (a). Beamhouse process in which salt, dirt and hair are removed. The process involves the following:
        i.   De-salting and soaking the hides to remove salt (which is used to preserve skins). The process uses a large amount of water (up to 20 cubic metres of water per ton of hide. The most significant of the pollutants produced by the soaking process include salt, hide surface impurities, dirt and globular protein substances dissolved in water.
        ii. Liming: Conventionally, unhairing is done by treating soaked hides in a bath containing sodium sulphide/hydro-sulphide and lime. The effluent from this process is the most polluted effluent of the tanning process. The pollutants include suspended solids, sulphides and nitrogenous material.
        iii. De-liming and Baiting: In this pelt is processed in a bath of ammonium salt and proteolytic enzymes. The pollutants from the process include calcium salts, sulphide residues, degraded proteins and residual proteolytic enzymatic agents.
    (b). Tanning under which the hide is treated with chemicals to produce leather. Chrome is the most common tanning agent used in the world. Conventionally, chrome tanning consists of pickling, tanning and basifying. The main pollutants of the tanning process are: chrome, chlorides and sulphates.
    (c). Post tanning (wet finishing): This includes neutralization, retanning, dying and fat liquoring. The pollutants from the process include chrome, salt, dyestuff residues, fat liquoring agents and vegetable tannins.
    (d). Finishing: The leather is given desired properties. The main pollutants produced during finishing are suspended solids and chrome.
11. This consists of leather footwear, leather shoe uppers and non–leather footwear.
12. Chrome VI is a residue in leather. This is used to make the leather more supple and pliable than vegetable-tanned leather so that it does not discolour or lose shape as drastically in water as vegetable-tanned. It is also known as wet-blue for its colour derived from the chromium.
13. The new regulation entered into force on 1 June 2007 and will be implemented in phases within the next ten years.
14. Please see http://www.ficci.com/press/443/95.doc.

6. Non-Tariff Barriers

6.1 WHAT IS A NON-TARIFF BARRIER?

Non-tariff barriers (NTBs)[1] are measures other than tariffs, which have the potential to distort trade (Baldwin 1970; OECD, 2005b; Business Dictionary, 2009), that are connected with state (administrative) activity and influence prices, quantity, structure, and/or the direction of international flows of goods and services as well as the resources used to produce these goods and services (UNCTAD, 2005). The primary motives for using NTBs are to promote economic, industrial and regional development as well as protect specified sectors from imports or from dumped or unfairly subsidized imports. NTBs often serve legitimate purposes in their domestic market, but become barriers in international markets. For example, a country may legitimately act to increase safety standards for motorized vehicles within its jurisdiction. The regulations adopted to accomplish this legitimate domestic objective however, can act as NTBs for a foreign supplier who must now adjust their production process to meet the new regulations. Also unlike tariffs, NTBs are not subject to reporting to the WTO. Common measures of NTBs include tariff-equivalents of the NTB and its frequency measures. These NTB measures are used in various trade models, including gravity equations, to assess trade and/or welfare effects of the measured NTBs (Beghin, 2006).

Several studies have attempted to classify and highlight the growing importance of NTBs in world trade, however a broad consensus on their typology is lacking at the international level (Donnelly and Manifold, 2005; OECD, 2005b). Trade measures or barriers (including tariffs) with discretionary or variable components according to the measure and related activity have been classified by UNCTAD[2] (1995) and Non Agricultural Market Access (NAMA).[3] Table 6.1 presents an inventory of the major categories of NTBs classified in the economic literature.

Table 6.1 Classification of non-tariff barriers

Type of NTB	Implementation of the NTB
Quantitative restrictions and similar specific limitations	Examples of quantitative restrictions are import quotas, export quotas, licensing requirements for imports and exports, voluntary export restraints, prohibitions, foreign exchange allocation restrictions, surrender requirements, import monitoring, temporary bans aimed at balancing trade, discriminatory bilateral agreements, counter trade, domestic content and mixing requirements, mandatory certification and allocation processes for quantitative restrictions.
Customs procedures and administrative practices	Customs procedures and administrative practices, such as customs surcharges, customs valuation, minimum import prices, customs classification procedures, customs clearance procedures, minimum customs value, excise and special formalities create barriers to trade.
Non-tariff charges and related policies affecting imports	Imports may also be affected by various policies and non-tariff charges, such as special sales taxes, variable levies, border tax adjustment, value added tax, anti-dumping and countervailing measures, cash margin requirements and rules of origin.
Government participation in trade, restrictive practices and more general policies	Governments often provide subsidies and other aids and allow for State trading. In addition, there are State procurement policies, tax exemptions for critical imports, and single or limited number of channels for imports of food and agricultural products.
Technical barriers to trade	Governments often set standards on the basis of health and sanitary regulations and quality standards, safety and industrial standards and regulations, packaging and labelling regulations, advertising and media regulations which act as non-tariff barriers to trade.

Source: Khorana et al. (2008).

A survey of the existing literature on global NTBs suggests that the utilization of certain NTBs, such as quantitative restrictions, decreased in the post Uruguay Round (Amjadi and Yeats, 1995; Stephenson, 1999; Estevadeoral and Devlin, 2001; McGuire et al., 2002). Earlier studies found that historically, common NTBs in use were import licensing systems; variable levies in production and export subsidies (agricultural products); import/export quotas in textiles and clothing; local content (automotive industry); and state trading operations (Laird and Vossenaar, 1991; Laird, 1999). Recent studies, however, confirm that the use of NTBs has since evolved from quantitative to other trade–distorting measures. Non-tariff barriers are most common in textiles, agricultural goods, fuels and iron and steel. The NTBs which most severely affect developing countries' exports are quantitative restrictions and voluntary export restraints. Another study by the OECD (2005b) analysed the incidence of NTBs and concluded that technical barriers to trade (TBT) comprised nearly half of the total NTBs faced by developing countries' exporters. Customs and administrative procedures and sanitary and phyto-sanitary (SPS) measures follow in the order of importance. Quantitative restrictions, trade remedies, government participation in trade, and charges on imports are other NTBs that are less prevalent and account for less than 5 per cent of total NTBs.

It has been shown that technical regulations, standards and conformity assessment procedures can act as border-protection instruments (Wilson, 1999, 2000, 2002; Stephenson, 1997; Michalopoulos, 1999). There are also animal health and plant protection measures that appear to be driven by protectionist interests; these are mainly applied in the case of agricultural imports (Zarrilli and Musselli, 2004; OECD, 2005b). In addition, there are growing concerns regarding regulations related to environment and labour standards which impacts trade between developing and developed countries (Michalapoulos, 1999; Bhattacharya, 1999; Bhattacharya and Mukhopadyaha, 2002; Chaturvedi and Nagpal, 2002). Market failures in developing countries also inhibit trade as a result of domestic exporters facing cumbersome and inefficient customs procedures within their own countries (Daly and Kuwahara, 1998).

Regional differences exist in NTBs, therefore these barriers have the potential to have geographically diverse impacts. For instance, in Latin America and the Caribbean, sanitary and phyto-sanitary barriers and agricultural export subsidies of importing developed countries have been identified as the main NTBs that impede market access in the major OECD markets (ECLAC, 2003). Similar studies on Africa and the Middle East suggest that the previous Multi-Fibre Agreement (MFA) quotas and voluntary export restraints (VERs) were important NTBs faced under the MFA regime (Yeats, 1994; Amjadi and Yeats, 1995; Gugerty and Stern, 1996). In Asia, the incidence of NTBs is mainly concentrated mainly in textiles and clothing; NTBs in this sector are usually imposed by developed countries in the form of technical regulations and labelling rules (Bhattacharya, 1999; Bhattacharya and Mukhopadhaya, 2002).

NTBs are usually quantified based on the intent or immediate impact of a measure (Laird and Yeats, 1990). Francois and Reinhardt (1997) review various econometric modelling approaches in their study. Deardorff and Stern (1998) as well as Dee and Ferrantino (2005) evaluate different methods to measure NTBs and suggest that most NTB measures and analysis focus on the increase in the price of imports resulting from NTBs, the resulting import reduction, the change in price responsiveness of the demand for imports, the variability of the effects of NTBs, and the welfare cost of NTBs. Nerb (1987) uses perception surveys, case studies and economic models to quantify the potential size of gains suggested from the elimination of NTBs in the European Community. Emerson et al. (1988) suggest that the removal of internal market barriers would result in economic gains. OECD surveys on the perception of exporters regarding the incidence of NTBs in developing countries use qualitative methods, that is, surveys and questionnaires (OECD, 2002; 2005b). These studies have had their advantages and shortcomings documented; see for example OECD (1997), Deardorff and Stern (1998), Michalopoulos (1999), Bora et al. (2002), McGuire et al. (2002), Dean et al. (2003), and Andriamananjara et al. (2004).Studies conclude that measuring NTBs and their effects is a challenge, because of the heterogeneity of policy instruments and lack of systematic data (Beghin, 2006).

6.2 NON-TARIFF BARRIERS AND INDIA

The major NTBs imposed by developed countries faced by Indian exporters are standards, testing, labelling and certification requirements (Khorana et al., 2008). The Indian government compiled an inventory of NTBs that have the potential to impede exports and includes complicated health regulations, labour standards, unfair customs procedures, trade defence measures such as anti-dumping duties and also licencing systems (Arun, 2008). Another recent study by FICCI (2008), reported that the Registration, Evaluation, Authorization and Restriction of Chemical Substances (REACH) regulation of EU requires extensive testing and imposes high compliance costs on

Indian exporters. The study estimated that the one-time cost of complying with REACH ranges between 5 to 10 per cent of a manufacturer's turnover, in addition to significant subsequently recurring costs.[4] The OECD conducted a survey of Indian firms exporting to the EU and identified the main NTBs faced by them as being labelling requirements (fabrics, apparel, textiles); technical standards (leather goods, coffee, tea, pharmaceuticals and electrical machinery); anti-dumping measures (chemicals, man-made staple fibres, iron and steel bars); and child labour laws (carpets and floor covering). High port fees and taxes can also significantly add to the cost of exports. Fees for the authentication of export documents by the consulates of importing countries also add to the total exporters' costs (Mehta, 2005). Strict rules of origin (ROO) are often cited as an important NTB faced by Indian exporters in textiles and clothing. Non-recognition of processes conferring origin to the final product as well as discriminatory and unilateral changes in rules by the importing countries and the methods often used (WTO, 2003, 2004,, 2006). In leather and footwear, the most common NTBs faced by India's exporters relate to animal health, product safety concerns and unethical treatment of animals (WTO, 2003, 2004, 2006).

For instance, the NTBs faced by Indian exporters in the US and Japan are mainly SPS measures on agricultural products. In the EU, NTBs are imposed through a variety of measures including but are not restricted to, firstly, SPS measures such as restrictions on the presence of chemicals or antibiotics; second, strict ROO requirements on textiles and clothing exported under GSP preferential tariffs; third, barriers imposed for environmental reasons. Austria, Germany and the Netherlands are examples of developed countries that impose limits on chemical residues in leather and textiles exported from developing countries, including India.

Foreign countries exporting to India also face NTBs. Prior to the liberalization of the Indian economy in the 1990s,[5] the most common NTBs were import licensing and quantitative restrictions. Table 6.2 presents an inventory NTBs faced by foreign exporters to India by sector for manufacturing. Hasheem (2001), Das (2003), Aksoy (1991), Mehta (1997, 2005), Pandey and Gang (1998) and Mehta and Mohanty (1999) use frequency ratios to calculate the degree of import coverage in manufacturing to analyse the incidence of NTBs. These show that there has been an overall decrease in the incidence of NTB usage in India. A recent study of leather and footwear shows that the coverage of NTBs declined, from 45 per cent of the manufacturing sector in 1991–92 to 33 per cent in 1999–2000 (Das, 2003).

Table 6.2 An overview of NTBs in the Indian manufacturing sector

Authors	Sectoral Coverage	Findings
Aksoy (1991)	All input-ouput sectors	Quantitative restrictions employed
Mehta (1997)	All the manufacturing sectors included	Quantitative restrictions imposed on 55 per cent tariff lines
Pandey and Gang (1998)	97 input-output sectors were covered	NTBs decline from 94 per cent in 1988-89 to 24 per cent in 1999-2000
Mehta (1997)	HS chapters (various)	Decline in NTBs
Hasheem (2001)	Input-output sectors	Decline in NTBs
Das (2001)	75 NIC industries	NTBs declined from near 100 per cent to 40 per cent from 1980s to 1990-95
Das (2003)	Leather and textiles sectors	NTBs decline in the manufacturing sector from 98 per cent (1980-85), 87 per cent (1986-90), 45 per cent (1991-92), 33 per cent (1999-2000)

Source: Das (2001, 2003) and Khorana et al. (2008).

6.3 THE SELECTION OF TRADE BARRIERS FOR ANALYSIS

The selection of NTBs and other potential trade barriers for more in-depth examination in this book is based on the existing literature that analyses barriers faced by developing countries' exporters in developed countries' markets. For instance, an OECD (2005b) study shows that technical regulations and standards as well as testing and certification arrangements are the main problems reported regarding TBTs, while customs valuation is the predominant problem reported in customs and administrative procedures. Wonnacott and Wonnacott (1995) argue that transport costs drive a wedge between prices paid by consumers in importing countries and the price received by the producers in exporting countries. Limao and Venables (2001) show that infrastructure quality determines transport costs, which in turn affect trade volumes between countries. Similarly, Fink and Smarzynska (2002) show anti-competitive practices in ports and other transport services increase the unit shipping cost which hampers trade between trading partners. Sadikov (2007) analyses the impact of business registration procedures and export signatures and suggests that these reduce overall exports and increase transaction costs. Moenius (2002) finds that the lack of comparable standards is a barrier to trade.

The results of the surveys conducted by Khorana et al. (2008) to assess the perceptions of textiles and clothing, leather and footwear exporters regarding the NTBs they faced in trade between India and the UK, mirror the literature listed above. This study finds that technical barriers to trade contribute substantially to NTBs, as do domestic barriers. The remainder of this chapter draws heavily from the report by Khorana et al. (2008).

6.4 TECHNICAL BARRIERS TO TRADE BETWEEN INDIA AND THE UK

6.4.1 Regulations and Standards

Regulations and standards establish specific characteristics of a product (that is, size, shape, design, functions and performance). Regulations and standards are often designed to affect the product's production and processing methods and not its characteristics per se. The main difference between a standard and a technical regulation lies in compliance. While conformity with standards is voluntary, regulations are by nature mandatory. Regulations and standards substantially affect the textiles and clothing, leather and footwear trade between the India and the UK specifically, and the EU generally.

The most commonly cited examples of EU and UK regulations requiring compliance from Indian exporters in the leather and footwear, textiles and clothing sectors are the restrictions and minimum limits imposed on the use of chemicals. Such requirements include limits on the use of azodyes (these are prohibited beyond the limit of 30ppm by EC Directive 2004/21/EC); chrome IV (prohibited beyond the 3ppm limit by EC Directive 2004/96/EC 4); cadmium (permitted up to 100ppm by Directive 91/338/EEC); as well as polychlorinated biphenyls (PCBs) and polychlorinated terphenyls (Directive 85/467/EEC). The REACH programme also has far reaching implications which impede Indian chemical exports and increases the cost of compliance by £85,000 to £325,000 per chemical. In textiles and clothing, there are specific regulations pertaining to safety of children's clothing and Directive 2001/95/EC[6] sets specific guidelines regarding the use of cords in the head and neck areas for children and young persons aged 7–14 . India's exports of textiles and clothing and/or leather and footwear to the EU and UK must also comply with specific standards such as International Standards Organisation (ISO) 9001-2000,[7] Social Accountability – 8000 (SA)[8] and

Worldwide Responsible Accredited Production (WRAP).[9] There are, however, instances when EU or UK importers require compliance to additional regulations beyond the minimum regulations which increases total production costs and results in the Indian exporters perceiving European regulations as NTBs. A recent survey undertaken by FICCI (2008), found that Indian exporters of textiles are required to have a number of certificates including OEKOTEX, ISO9001, ISO14001, Certification for Fumigation (ISPM), Certification for Social Accountability Standards for Working Conditions (SA8000), Fair Trade Certifications (for Social & Environmental Standards) all of which increase the cost disadvantage of Indian exporters.

To determine the Indian perceptions of EU/UK NTBs, a survey of knowledgeable individuals in India was undertaken. The survey was conducted amongst a broad selection of private firms across India, but focussed primarily in existing production hubs for the leather and textiles industry. The sample included firms that export a variety of different product groups to multiple destinations, and exhibited different levels of experience and turnover. In addition, relevant industry associations, trade associations, export councils and policy planners at various levels of government were consulted. In total, 60 interviews were conducted in India. Appendix B provides greater details regarding the modalities of the survey.

Figure 6.1 presents the perceptions of exporters interviewed in India regarding the incidence of standards and regulations as inhibiting their exports to the UK.

Of the textiles and clothing exporters interviewed in India, 53 per cent perceive regulations and standards as barriers to trade; of these, 10 per cent suggest that they are a significant barrier. There are two main reasons behind this perception. Firstly, most textiles and clothing industries are comprised of small-scale firms and the expense of azodye-free dyeing increases their production costs by over two and a half times. Since small exporting firms have limited access to credit and financing, upgrading production technology in order to accommodate azodye-free production is difficult. Hence, exporters perceive this regulation on the use of dyes as a potential barrier to trade. Secondly, exports are driven by the purchaser, who often is the most important, and at times the sole, source of information regarding product compliance, factory and labour standards.

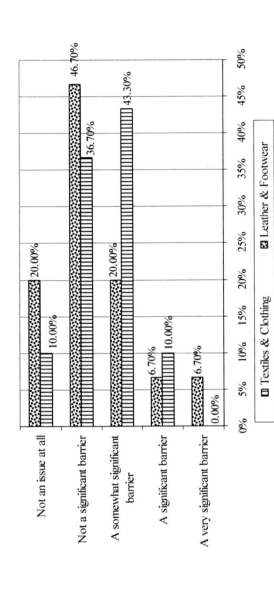

Source: Adapted from Khorana et al. (2008).

Figure 6.1 Perceptions of India's exporters regarding standards and regulations as barriers to trade with the UK

Purchasers often demand compliance in excess of the regulations and exporters have no means of verifying whether the purchaser's requirements reflect the regulatory requirements. The demand of EU or UK purchasers for excess compliance is also perceived as an important NTB by textile and clothing exporters from India.

Of India's leather and footwear exporters, particularly those involved in manufacturing footwear and accessories, 47 per cent do not perceive regulations and standards to be a significant barrier as most exporters have developed the necessary expertise to comply with the required regulations and standards. The existing Indian legislation on tanneries effluent and wastes is stringent and requires all leather product manufacturers to comply as a matter of law. As a result, India's existing rules on environmental norms are sufficient to support the perception of the leather and footwear exporters interviewed that UK and EU regulations are not a significant barrier to their exports. They did however indicate a concern regarding the EU's new REACH[10] regulation on chemical substances.

NTBs can take diverse and imaginative forms but can also have varying degrees of legitimacy as contributors to health, social or developmental objectives. Responses to the survey highlighted the range and variance of NTBs as perceived by India's exporters of textiles and clothing and leather and footwear. India's exporters in these two industries are often required to implement Western social and health norms in their factories. Participating exporters of leather and footwear in Chennai and textiles and clothing exporters in Bangalore indicated that UK-based and other foreign buyers regularly fail to take into account existing Indian socio-economic conditions when implementing regulations and standards that must be met by their Indian suppliers. A particular example was the specific health standard requirement imposed by the UK (and EU) on India's exporters to provide Western-style toilets with toilet paper in India. The exporters perceived this health standard as an NTB as such health requirements may not be hygienically feasible or socially possible given that local workers are used to Indian-style toilets.

In order to ensure compliance with the established regulations and standards, some means of audit and enforcement is necessary. Depending upon how onerous the method and process may be, audits and enforcement can act as an NTB. For example, an exporter from India reported that his manufacturing firm was required to furnish dental x-rays of the workers to the social audit team of the European purchaser. This was to support the claim that child labour was not employed in the production process. Getting x-rays of all workers imposed a significant additional cost for the exporter.

Another exporter in the south supplying footwear to a major shoe chain in the UK commented on the periodic (every six months) social audit visits by external consultants. These visits were to ensure that the exporter continued to follow the code of conduct designed by the importer. Consultants, therefore, visit the factory and socially audit the exporters' premises. This leads to an increase in the total costs of the exporters.

Indian exporters must comply with India's legislation on occupational health and safety, however, there have been instances when they have been required to comply with additional regulations and standards imposed by the importers, over and above India's legislation. An example from the leather and footwear industry shows that EU and UK importers required Indian exporters to implement specific requirements on good plant design, operational control and measures targeted at preventing hazards. Therefore, the importer required all the exporting firms' employees to be aware of the possible origin of accidents on the factory's premises. The exporter explained that the implementation of this specific measure to provide information to all employees was not always possible as the firm's labour force was employed on a daily contract basis through labour contractors. In this case, the contracted employees were not the responsibility of the manufacturer and the requirement of imparting training on health and safety issues raised costs, reduced profits and were perceived as a barrier.

There are also additional regulations requiring the fumigation of containers for shipping export consignments. A recent survey by FICCI (2008) found that a fumigation certificate for an exporter costs roughly €50 per container, adding to their total costs, and reduces the competitiveness of Indian exporters in the EU market.

6.4.2 Testing and Certification

Regarding testing and certification, Article 2.2 of the Agreement on Technical Barriers to Trade (TBT)[11] of the WTO states that an importing country can apply measures to the extent necessary to protect human, animal or plant life or health and that this should be based on scientific principles that are backed by sufficient scientific and technical evidence. This implies that importing countries can require exporters to conduct relevant testing and certification to authenticate the use of chemicals in manufactured products. The leather and footwear sector is subject to multiple tests and certification requirements. Tannery waste must be tested to ensure that it contains less than 5mp chromium post treatment (tested in accordance with ISO 9174 or EN 1233 or EN ISO 11885). Safety footwear

must be self-certified by testing in accordance with CEN TC 309 WI 065 –
4.9. Regulations restrict and control the use of azo-colorants[12] in dyed
leathers (tests are done according to CEN ISO/TS 17234:2003) and textiles
(tested under EN 14362-1:2003). Buyers often enforce regulations in excess
of the minimum requirements and most small exporters face difficulties in
meeting the additional requirements. Figure 6.2 reports the interview results
of the perceptions of Indian exporters to testing and certification acting as
barriers to their exports entering the UK market.

Of the participating textiles and clothing exporters, nearly 57 per cent do
not perceive testing and certification as an issue or as a significant barrier
because testing and certification is already mandatory for exports. In leather
and footwear, 66 per cent of India's exporters do not perceive testing and
certifications to be a potential barrier; of this, 33 per cent perceive it to be
not significant while the remaining perceive it as not being a barrier at all
(not an issue). However, 7 per cent of all exporters interviewed perceive
testing and certification requirements to be a very significant barrier and 3
per cent perceive it as a significant barrier.

Respondents in India's leather and footwear industry provided detailed
examples of how testing and certification can affect their ability to export,
increase their costs and/or reduce their profitability. A footwear exporter in
Delhi reported that extensive physical and chemical tests are carried out by
EU buyers before the product is placed in the EU market. These tests are
generally done in the EU within six to eight weeks of the goods being
shipped by the exporter. During this period, storage conditions (moisture,
temperature) can cause chemical reactions in residues left by tanning leather
which can cause changes in the physical appearance of leather footwear. As
a result, the sample fails quality tests, leading to the rejection of the entire
consignment and significant losses for the exporter. The respondent
indicated that the footwear manufacturer is usually unable to trace the
details of the tannery that processed the leather yet chemical treatments
used in the tanning process can lead to changes in the appearance of
footwear even months after its production. As a result, tracing the origin of
chemical residues in the final product is difficult. Hence, should the
footwear fail the chemical restrictions test, the exporters must bear heavy
losses through no fault of their own. The majority of Indian leather
tanneries have limited in-house technical capabilities.

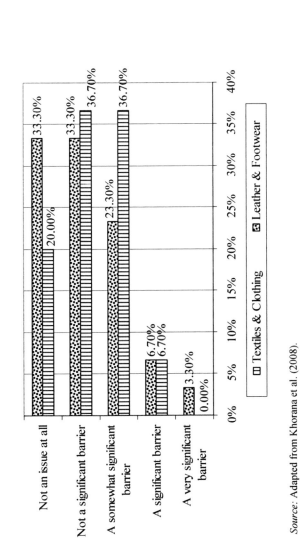

Source: Adapted from Khorana et al. (2008).

Figure 6.2 Perceptions of India's exporters regarding testing and certification as barriers to trade with the UK

Even in the case of large tanneries, technical capability is largely restricted to rudimentary testing facilities; very little research and development is carried out. These firms depend on outside sources for testing and certification of the leather produced from raw hides. As most in-house tests and results are not recognized by European importers, testing and certification must be completed by foreign testing agencies nominated by the importers, or in nominated laboratories in the importing country. Given the large cost difference between domestic and foreign testing agencies, this translates into higher per unit costs for small export values. The European buyers nominate agencies such as SGS Testing[13] and Specialised Technology Resources Inc[14] to undertake the tests. There is often a delay of several weeks before the necessary tests and certification can be completed by the international agencies, therefore placing the Indian exporters at a comparative cost disadvantage. An exporter of textiles and clothing, who had been exporting for nearly two decades to the UK, confirmed that requests for higher than the minimum testing and certification requirements were becoming increasingly common, incurring higher testing costs, lower profit margins and leading to an increased cost disadvantage to the producer when export volumes are low.

6.4.3 Labelling and Packaging

Eco-labels are normally issued either by government supported or private enterprises once a product has met the criteria for the eco-label. One such criterion is based on life cycle analysis (LCA); for instance in textiles and clothing, the LCA includes the entire value chain from fibre to spinning, weaving, processing and stitching. A common eco-label strategy arising from LCA is the so-called cradle-to-grave approach which, when applied to textiles and clothing, involves making an assessment of the products' impact on the environment during its life-cycle from the processing of raw materials through production, distribution, consumption (maintenance, i.e. washing, ironing, dry-cleaning) to the final disposal of the product. In this manner, an eco-labelling scheme informs consumers of that product's environmental attributes, permitting the consumer to make a more informed purchase decision. These labelled environmental attributes may cause the consumer to consider that particular product as being environmentally superior to other products in the same category.

The EU maintains a variety of eco-label programmes applicable to textiles and clothing and leather and footwear exports from India. EU members may also use individual national labels. For textiles and clothing, these include programmes that indicate reduced water and air pollution during fibre production, limited use of substances harmful to the environment and in particular the aquatic environment and health, guarantee of shrink resistance during washing and drying, guarantee of colour resistance to perspiration, washing, wet and dry rubbing and light exposure as well as those that cover the entire production chain. The EU eco-labels are valid in the 27 Member States, but national labels are normally valid only in one country.[15] There are both government and private labelling schemes. Examples of government-sponsored schemes include Blue Angel (Germany), Ecomark (Japan), Environmental Choice (Canada), White Swan (Nordic Countries), Eco-Mark (India), Green Label (Singapore). Similarly, examples of private labelling schemes are Öko-Tex (Germany), Green Seal (USA), Bra Miljöval (Sweden) and Britta Steilmann Collection (Germany). The FICCI (2008) survey reported that the OEKOTEX Certificate cost approximately £1600, which translates into roughly 2 per cent of the value of an average sale for an exporter.

Additionally, European importers often maintain private environmental labels that Indian suppliers are required to meet. Examples of voluntary environmental labels by EU Member States are the Markenzeichen Schastoffgeprufth Textilien (MST) label, which indicates a lower level of pollutants in consumer goods and the Markenzeichen Unweltschonende Textilien (MUT) label which indicates analyses of air, water and soil pollution in all production processes. Another private label example is Ökotex, developed by Ostereichisches Textil-Forschungsinstitut, which sets norms for both raw materials and final products (Chaturvedi and Nagpal, 2002).

Beyond eco-labels pertaining to production processes, packaging norms require exporters to initiate measures that reduce wastage at source, eliminate harmful materials in packaging waste, maximize the recovery of packaging waste for re-use, recycling, composting or to generate energy, thereby minimizing the quantity of packaging waste requiring final disposal. For instance, EU Directive (94/62/EC) imposes the limit of 100ppm by weight for concentration levels of lead, cadmium, mercury and hexavalent chromium in packaging for leather and footwear, textiles and clothing products. Similarly, the EU Directive (96/74/EC) on textiles establishes labelling requirements such that the final product is exclusively composed of textile fibres containing at least 80 per cent (by weight) textile fibres and textiles incorporated into other products. In addition, Member States may demand that their national language to be used for labelling forcing exporters to develop and seek approval for appropriate labels. These are perceived by the exporters as being a common form of NTB. Figure 6.3 illustrates the degree to which labelling and packaging requirements are perceived as potential barriers to market access to the UK by India's textiles and clothing, leather and footwear exporters.

In textiles and clothing, 33 per cent of India's exporters perceive packaging and labelling requirements as a potential barrier, of which 10 per cent consider them a significant barrier. The percentage of India's leather and footwear exporters that believe packaging and labelling acts as a barrier to trade is lower — 27 per cent, of which 17 per cent and 10 per cent perceive this requirement to be a somewhat significant and significant barrier, respectively. Labelling and packaging requirements perceived to be NTBs can be EU-based, member country-specific, applied across multiple countries or buyer-specific.

The EU maintains a mandatory Conformité Européenne (CE) Marking Programme which indicates that the product bearing the CE mark meets all relevant EC directives, usually in terms of health and safety. CE marking is required before any product can be placed in the European market, regardless of origin. Some Indian exporters of textiles and clothing, leather and footwear indicated that they believed the CE mark to be an NTB, particularly given their lower technical capabilities and scarce in-house expertise relative to their EU competitors.

The interviews of textiles and clothing, leather and footwear exporters from India revealed that stringent environmental rules in countries such as Germany impact India's ability to export. The multiplicity of labels is a potential problem as Indian producers, who are mainly small-scale industries, must incur additional costs to apply for individual eco-labels specific to each EU country. A further concern that was raised is that the criteria for individual eco-label schemes do not take into account India's unique environmental and labour conditions.

Meeting standards set by labelling requirements can present a formidable challenge to most small-scale Indian firms attempting to export to the EU and UK. An example is compliance with Öko-Tex 1000, which necessitates demonstrating environmentally-sound techniques for the entire production process of textiles and clothing. In contrast, Öko-Tex 100 requires specific limits for only the final product. Additional investment by exporters is needed in order to meet the Öko-Tex 1000 voluntary label, adding to overall costs and lowering profit margins. A fundamental problem for India's exporters in textiles and clothing, leather and footwear is a lack of input traceability in the supply chain such that the manner by which an input was made or provided is often impossible to determine.

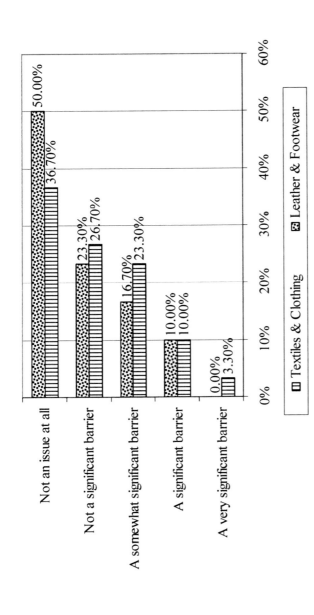

Source: Adapted from Khorana et al. (2008).

Figure 6.3 Perceptions of India's exporters regarding labelling and packaging as barriers to trade with the UK

Confusion regarding EU and UK labelling requirements is a very common, as the frequency of the questions raised by interviewees illustrates. A footwear exporter in Delhi was unsure whether the manufacturer is responsible for all components of the footwear. Is the component producer or the shoe assembler held responsible if the shoe is rejected as not being eco-friendly?

The packaging of leather shoes is also complicated by individual country labelling requirements. Leather shoes for export are usually packed in individual boxes with 12–18 pairs in a carton. European importers have specific requirements about the type and form of information provided on the packaging. For example, some require information about the order to be printed on the boxes (order number, box number, name department or contact person etc.) or the inclusion of specific promotion details on the package. This adds to the production cost and is a cost barrier for the exporter.

Buyer-specific labelling or packaging requirements places India's small exporters at distinct cost disadvantages in a number of ways. European importers source their products through buying agents/houses. These agencies/houses require Indian exporters to meet buyer-specific requirements on packaging or labelling for like products and may or may not provide the requisite label or packaging, or the Indian exporter may be forced to acquire the necessary items from buyer-specific suppliers in another country.

Mumbai- and Bangalore-based exporters of textiles and clothing provided the example where the European importer required the Indian supplier to procure the packing material from a specific Hong Kong-based agency. A Delhi-based leather and footwear exporter was forced by their European buyer to procure the product's bar-codes from another country despite being available locally. Printing labels in languages other than English, or requiring multiple languages on labels, is also a common complaint. Indian exporters have experienced European buyers specifying that packaging materials must be lower than the permissible concentration levels of lead, cadmium, mercury and hexavalent chromium. Buyer-specific packaging is often not available on short notice and procurements are made from the nearby Asian countries, adding to Indian producers' costs. Generally, European buyers' requirements are often perceived as too complicated to satisfy and are applied to similar domestic products in an inconsistent and discriminatory manner.

6.4.4 Environmental Issues

Specific EU environmental requirements currently apply to India–EU and India–UK trade. Indian exporters must show compliance on discharge of industrial waste that is certified by the government as well as private agencies. Under the environmental regulations of the EU for textile products (Directive 2002/371/EC), there are restrictions on the use of dyes, pigments and finishes, heavy metal impurities, and VOC in printing pastes; prohibitions on the use of chrome mordant dyes, carcinogenic, mutagenic and toxic agents; and limitations on formaldehyde in the final fabric, COD content in waste water from wet-processing sites, the application of halogenated shrink-resistant substances on wool fibres; and others. There are also restrictions on processes and chemicals for specific auxiliary chemicals, detergents, fabric softeners and compelling agents that restrict the use of absorbable organic halogen compounds emissions in bleaching effluent, heavy metals, formaldehyde and chloro-phenols, cerium compounds, and halogenated carriers to a specific limit. Figure 6.4 illustrates the degree to which exporters in India's textiles and clothing, leather and footwear industries perceived environmental regulations as a barrier to trade with the UK.

While over 77 per cent of textiles and clothing exporters do not consider environmental regulations as a barrier when exporting to the UK, the remaining 23 per cent do perceive them as a barrier to UK exports. The majority do not believe environmental regulations are a barrier because nearly all are ISO:9000 certified. Strong environmental laws instituted by the Indian government in major hubs for apparel exports, such as Coimbatore (Tamil Nadu), contribute further to the perception that environmental regulations do not constitute barriers to trade. The remaining 23 per cent that do perceive environmental regulations as a somewhat significant barrier are small firms that must upgrade their production technology to reach the requisite quality. The estimated additional investment of US$13 million for each textiles and clothing manufacturer is perceived as a somewhat significant barrier by the exporters in the sample interviewed.

The small firms in the textiles and clothing industry also use a wide range of chemical agents (such as bleaching agents, sulphur dyes, disperse and colour dyes) for dyeing and printing, which involve extensive use of chemicals including formaldehydes, hydrochloric acid, ammonia, chromium salt, soda ash and caustic soda. If not treated, these can cause significant damage to the environment.

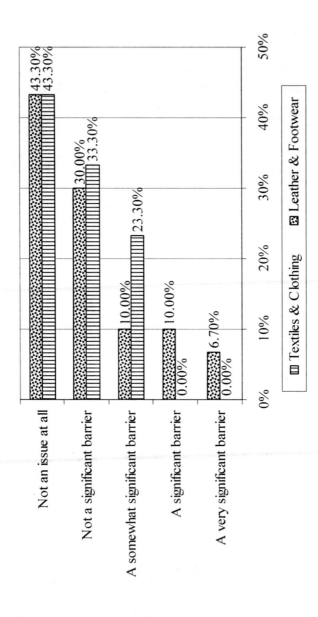

Source: Adapted from Khorana et al. (2008).

Figure 6.4 Perceptions of India's exporters regarding environmental regulations as barriers to trade with the UK

Given India's small and medium- sized exporters' lack of access to credit facilities in order to invest in efficient effluent treatment plants, they perceive environmental regulations as a potential barrier to trade.

The tanning sector of the leather and footwear industry in India is more often impacted by stringent environmental regulations, both domestic and foreign. The Indian tanning sector is plagued by production processes and practices that inherently conflict with environmental regulations. For example, raw hides and skins are salt preserved in India, causing a serious problem of excess salt discharge in tannery effluent. Leather yield from wet salted stock is lower in India than the international norms, partly due to higher levels of process waste. Chemical consumption in Indian tanneries is roughly 25–30 per cent higher than international norms due to the use of inefficient equipment and processes and the lack of efficient recycling facilities. Water consumption in Indian tanneries is more than double that of tanneries in developed countries. Tanning units in India consume an average of 40 litre/sq.ft of finished leather while tanneries in developed countries consume approximately 12–15 litres/sq ft. A majority of the tanneries in India are old with inefficient designs, leading to bottlenecks for process and material handling, multidirectional material flow and excessive material handling. Most of these tanneries have unhygienic working conditions, inadequate ventilation and lighting (Government of India, 1992).

Therefore, it comes as no surprise that in the leather and footwear industry, the percentage of exporters who do not perceive environmental regulations as a barrier is slightly lower than in textiles and clothing, at 43 per cent, while 17 per cent of respondents perceive environmental regulations as a significant/very significant barrier.

Explanations for these low levels include the fact that compliance with the high standards set by the Indian Pollution Control Board contribute significantly to total production costs. Restrictions on the use of some chemical dyestuffs also affect the perceptions held by Indian leather and footwear exporters. For example, Germany restricts the import of leather products containing benzedrine, PCP and formaldehyde primarily on grounds of consumer health.[16] The EC standards for PCP are at 1000 ppm or 10mg/kg but Germany's standard is even lower at 5 mg/kg. These stringent German environmental standards have been criticized by developing countries (India, Brazil and South Africa) as well as by other EU member states including France and Italy.[17]

Indian exporters also perceived that the regulations on residues in raw hides and wet-blue leather (EU Directive 76/769/EEC of July 1976), commonly associated with the leather tanning industries, manifests as a recurring NTB. Studies show that the total cost for the tanneries to comply with environmental regulations is approximately 5 per cent of the total production cost (Knutsen, 1999). The adoption of cleaner production methods by Indian tanneries is extremely low; the use of efficient de-salting methods, replacement of ammonium salts with substitutes such as carbon dioxide, and the use of enzymes for de-hairing is limited as many tanners are unable to afford the additional costs associated with these technologies. Consequently, environmental compliance is an issue mainly with small and medium-sized tanning firms and, in turn, leather footwear manufacturing firms.

6.4.5 Information Asymmetry

Information asymmetry is an imbalance of information that exists between parties to a transaction where one party has more or better quality information than the other, thereby creating a potential imbalance of power between transaction partners (Hobbs and Kerr, 1999). India's textiles and clothing, leather and footwear exporters tend to suffer information asymmetry over foreign markets and buyers, legislation, standards and regulations. The extent to which Indian exporters believe information asymmetry is an important NTB in their trade with the UK is illustrated in Figure 6.5.

Information asymmetry is clearly an issue facing India's textiles and clothing exporters where 83 per cent perceive information asymmetry as a somewhat significant/significant barrier to their exports. In sharp contrast, only 7 per cent of leather and footwear exporters consider information asymmetry as a significant or very significant barrier to trade. An explanation for the marked difference is the active involvement of the Indian Council for Leather Exports (CLE) in providing information to all its members, thus reducing the issue of information asymmetry being perceived as a barrier to exports.

Approximately 67 per cent of textiles and clothing exporters, and 66 per cent of leather and footwear exporters acquire information about market access primarily through buyers and buying houses. Industry and government sources are less important sources of information on markets. Information asymmetry is perceived as a barrier because of the heavy reliance Indian exporters have upon the buyers, and because they trade directly with the buyers.

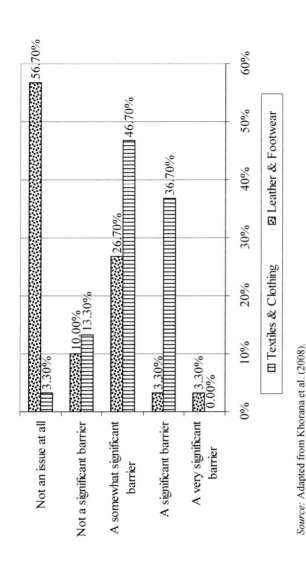

Source: Adapted from Khorana et al. (2008).

Figure 6.5 Perceptions of India's exporters regarding information asymmetry as a barrier to trade with the UK

This is particularly relevant for textiles and clothing as the Apparel Producing and Exporting Council does not play a dynamic role in providing members with information on company-level databases, forcing this sector's exporters to contact the trade section of the embassy/high commissions for information on new, potentially lucrative, overseas markets. The difficulties encountered by textile and clothing exporters are illustrated by their lack of information on changing regulations; for example, on the use of dyestuffs such as cobalt blue and sulphur black which have been banned globally. Despite the availability of easily sourced close substitutes, switching costs to upgrade technology and new treatment facilities will require an estimated investment of over US$13 million. Alternatives such as non-benzidine dyes including 'direct black 38 dyes' and 'direct black 22' are available, priced between US$8–10 per kilogram, but often exporters suffer from a lack of information regarding final costs. As a result, they are deterred from switching to these dyes.

Textiles and clothing exporters also suffer from a lack of information due to the plethora of eco labels found in the EU. Many find the basic concepts and terminology confusing. A common complaint was that no clear definitions of eco-label parameters exist and there are significant differences between various eco-labelling schemes. It is evident that the rapid changes in EU environmental regulation together with new country-specific eco-labelling schemes cause confusion and concern amongst textile and clothing producers and exporters. In this manner asymmetric information acts as an NTB for textiles and clothing exporters

In contrast, the CLE (head and other regional offices) provide regular information updates to India's leather and footwear manufacturers and exporters regarding fairs, exhibitions and potential markets. Similarly, the Central Leather Research Institute provides market development assistance and technical support. As a result, India's leather and footwear exporters do not face the same lack of information and, hence, do not perceive information asymmetry as a potential barrier to the same degree.

6.5 DOMESTIC BARRIERS FACED BY INDIAN EXPORTERS

In addition to the non-tariff barriers that exist in their destination markets, India's textile and clothing, leather and footwear exporters face domestic barriers that can also impede their export activities.

6.5.1 Inadequate Infrastructure

In India, inadequate infrastructure refers to poor road, rail, port and airports networks, electricity and water shortages as well as inadequate technological infrastructure and obsolete machinery. Essential infrastructure deficits affecting the textiles and clothing, leather and footwear industries, would include transportation, power and utilities.

The Indian rail network is the largest in the world but it is a major constraint to export growth. It fails to generate the resources needed to keep up with demand. Existing commercial rates are very high as commercial traffic subsidizes passenger traffic, displacing freight from railways to road transport. The inefficiencies of the rail network and the state of the nation's highway system reduce manufacturers' ability to move goods to ports.

India's electric power sector is characterized by poor reliability, severe capacity shortages, frequent black-outs and low per capita consumption. Disruptions in electricity supplies (including frequent power stoppages, fluctuations and transmission losses) are commonly experienced by exporters in India. High electricity prices increase the total cost for firms in the textiles and clothing, leather and footwear supply chain and undermine their capacity to focus production on the higher value-added segments of demand. A reliable clean water supply is another essential utility for textile and clothing, leather and footwear production. The washing, dyeing, and finishing of fabrics yarns and denim jeans as well as finishing of shoes require reliable supplies of clean water, which is not always available in India.

Telecommunications technology is an essential part of functional infrastructure and includes telecommunications networks, continuous internet and broadband availability, all of which are lacking in India. The result is production and supply chain bottlenecks. Outdated technology prevails in existing production facilities and the lack of financing to upgrade technology places significant limits on export capabilities. India also suffers from a deficit in EU and internationally accredited institutions and agencies for the testing and certification of products. Labour market restrictions and trade union activities in manufacturing are other issues faced by exporters because they hamper their overall efficiency.[18] The absence of basic infrastructure in India and its impact on the ability of textile and clothing, leather and footwear producers to export effectively is corroborated by the interview findings provided in Figure 6.6. The interviews illustrated how India's inadequate infrastructure can impact textile and clothing, leather and footwear exporters in many ways.

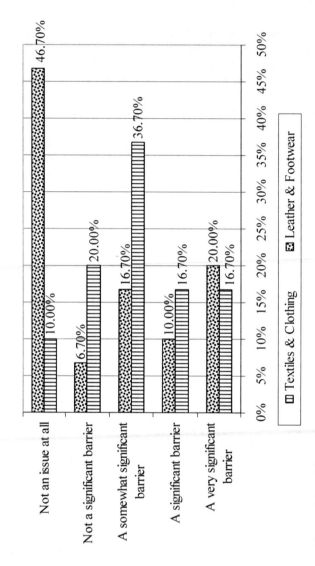

Source: Adapted from Khorana et al. (2008).

Figure 6.6 Perceptions of India's exporters regarding inadequate infrastructure as a barrier to trade with the UK

The dearth of adequate infrastructure is viewed to some degree as a barrier to export growth for roughly 68 per cent of textile and clothing exporters, of which 32 per cent indicate that it is a significant or very significant barrier. In leather and footwear, the percentage of exporters who consider inadequate infrastructure as a barrier to trade to some degree is marginally lower, at 46 per cent, of which 30 per cent view it as a significant or very significant barrier. As a specific example, most textile and clothing, leather and footwear producers in India do not have their own testing and certification facilities, which are required if the firm wishes to export, yet their products must be certified by buyer-approved agencies or institutions. These buyer-approved agencies or institutions can be geographically located in places that disadvantage firms, for example, at a distant location within India, or even in a third country. Hence, additional shipping costs and time delays are imposed on the exporter.

Another example whereby India's inadequate infrastructure affects textiles and clothing, leather and footwear manufacturers, as indicated by interview respondents, is the lack of functioning credit and finance markets. Credit is not available to buy new machinery, adopt new technology or upgrade facilities in order to produce the quality of goods demanded by foreign markets, or to improve efficiency and productivity. Additionally, the high cost of new technology, combined with lack of credit and technical expertise, limits Indian firms' ability to adopt new processes and technology that would enable them to better manage and control their supply chain and the life-cycle of their products.

Transportation problems caused by delays on the roads and congestion at the ports leads to high inventory costs that adversely affects the textiles and clothing, leather and footwear industries' export competitiveness. Domestic transportation difficulties cause delays in shipping the product to international markets, with buyers receiving their shipment later than expected. Foreign buyers may be sufficiently motivated by such delays to seek alternative suppliers.

In Northern India (Agra and Kanpur), manufacturers of leather footwear cited the problem of frequent power cuts and its adverse impact on export competitiveness. Similar instances were reported by exporters in Agra where firms invested in back-up power generation to overcome frequent power cuts and voltage fluctuations. In Southern India, leather and textile exporters based in Chennai and Tirupur did not experience infrastructure-based issues in road networks and port facilities but rather, faced labour unrest and frequent strikes (Chennai, Tuticorin and Cochin port) that impacted adversely on export delivery schedules.

6.5.2 Transport Costs

India's transportation network is a significant component of the country's infrastructure deficiencies. Despite recent efforts to recapitalize and rebuild, India's transportation network still suffers from crumbling railways, primitive roads and highways, and inefficiencies and inadequate capacity at its ports. Of the national road and highway network, only 5 per cent of India's national highways are four-lane roadways, with 80 per cent being two-lane roads and the remaining 15 per cent single lane. India's port system is also inefficient, resulting in long delays and slow turnaround in shipping. Due to the lack of adequate transportation systems, Indian industry suffers a general logistics disadvantage resulting in higher overall transportation costs, which in turn reduce cost competitiveness and raises exporters' per unit costs. Combine the inadequacies of physical infrastructure with transport labour issues, such as frequent strikes on roads and at the ports, which mean exporters' must factor unpredictable delays in shipping and delivery to their already increased transportation costs. Figure 6.7 illustrates the perceptions of exporters' in textiles and clothing, leather and footwear regarding transport costs as a domestic barrier to trade with the UK.

Of textiles and clothing exporters, 70 per cent perceive transport cost as a barrier to their exports, of which 23 per cent indicated that it is a significant or very significant barrier. Leather and footwear exporters show a marked contrast where approximately 21 per cent of respondents consider transport cost as a barrier to trade.

More than 50 per cent of exports are transported over the road network in India. Respondents indicated that common problems with this mode of transportation include inadequate tarmac pucca[19] roads; poor quality of the national highways and roads in rural areas (which lack all-weather connectivity) contributing to wear and tear on vehicles; and congestion on the highways that often leads to additional traffic time. Road safety is an issue as is the inability of outdated vehicle fleets to meet pollution standards. Regionally, the textiles and clothing exporters in Tirupur and the leather and footwear exporters in Chennai expressed less dissatisfaction with their road connectivity to ports. All exporters in both the textiles and clothing, leather and footwear industries were unanimous in the belief that the Indian government must increase its expenditures on infrastructure. Deficiencies in transport infrastructure extend beyond India's road network, affecting ports and shipping.

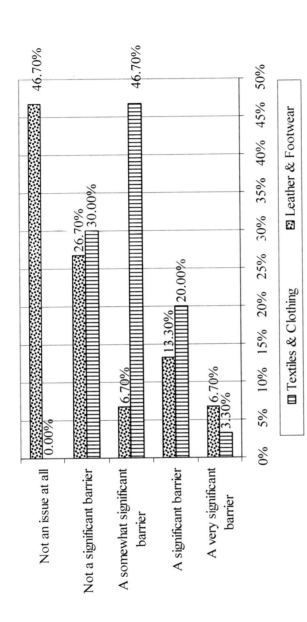

Source: Adapted from Khorana et al. (2008).

Figure 6.7 Perceptions of India's exporters regarding transportation costs as a barrier to trade with the UK

119

The ports of Nava Sheva and Tuticorin, located in India's west and south respectively, enjoy geographical proximity to the EU and are the main shipping points for exports to the UK. Therefore, textiles and clothing, leather and footwear exporters in the north (Agra, Kanpur and the NC Region) and east (Kolkata) of India face a cost disadvantage due to additional transportation costs to ship their products to the two main ports in the west and south. Given that there are few air cargo providers and the monopoly status of Indian Railways, rates for rail and air freight are uncompetitive. Using the road network requires additional transportation time. For all exporters, there are frequent strikes at India's ports resulting in delays in loading containers, contributing to additional warehousing costs and the missing of shipment deadlines.

6.5.3 Corruption and Theft

As discussed above, corruption is an economically important issue in India. The exporting of goods provides multiple opportunities for rent extraction by those administrators and bureaucrats overseeing the export process. The textiles and clothing, leather and footwear sectors are not immune to corruption; the exporters interviewed expressed dissatisfaction with the degree of corruption in sanctioning and certifying documents including the issuing of licences and permits, and inspection of factories to ensure regulatory compliance as well as the processes for accessing government-sponsored schemes providing funds for technological upgrading and modernization. Regulation and oversight issues related to social norms including child labour as well as labour laws also provide opportunities for rent extraction. Figure 6.8 shows the perceptions of textiles and clothing, leather and footwear exporters regarding corruption as a domestic barrier to trade with the UK.

Generally, exporters in both textiles and clothing, leather and footwear industries did not perceive corruption and theft as being an issue. Sixty per cent of textiles and clothing and 70 per cent of leather and footwear exporters do not perceive corruption and theft as a significant trade barrier.

Corruption is a commonly cited problem but exporters refrained from providing any specific examples beyond the unanimous issue of speed money which was cited by all respondents regardless of industry. Speed money reduces the time required for bureaucratic processing of approvals – something that is particularly important for exporters attempting to meet the delivery expectation of customers in importing countries.

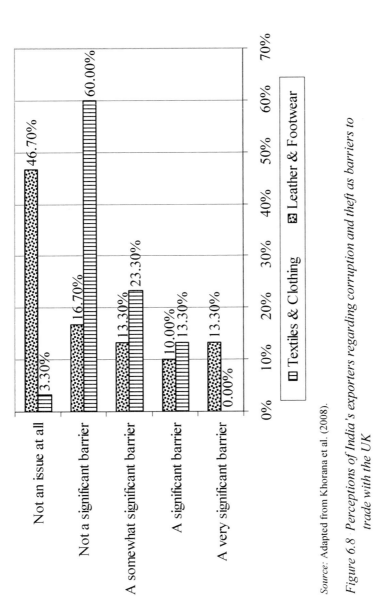

Source: Adapted from Khorana et al. (2008).

Figure 6.8 Perceptions of India's exporters regarding corruption and theft as barriers to trade with the UK

One exporter mentioned that there were more than 35 approvals required prior to establishing a production unit. An objection at any stage by a single inspector can cause unnecessary delays. To counteract their vulnerability to this type of bureaucratic harassment, exporters resort to speed money to expedite the approval process. Of course, the availability of corruption income from bureaucratic delay provides and incentive for officials to invent new approvals.

Exporters also reduce exposure to corruption pertaining to labour laws and regulations by establishing several facilities in different locations rather than a single factory. This strategy, while reducing the disruptive potential of corruption – by effectively elimination it monopoly elements (Schleifer and Vishney, 1993) – reduces economies of scale. Pilferage at Indian ports was an issue that exporters regularly face. While insurance claims could be made, the time, effort and transactions costs in filing such claims often outweighed the value of goods lost.

6.5.4 Legal Differences

International trade involves firms entering into contractual and therefore legal obligations such as delivery dates, financial commitments and payment modes amongst others. By its nature, international trade is conducted over different legal jurisdictions. Hence, differences in the interpretation of the law occur and can affect the flow of goods between countries (Kerr and Perdikis, 2003; Bessel et al., 2006). Legal frameworks for the implementation of the regulatory regimes vary between the EU, UK and India. The perception of India's textiles and clothing, leather and footwear exporters regarding legal differences acting as a barrier to trade is provided in Figure 6.9.

The interview results indicate that differences in legal frameworks are not perceived as a major barrier to trade. Only 3 per cent of both products – leather and footwear, textiles and clothing–exporters perceived legal differences between India and the UK as a significant barrier to their exports. In part, this could be explained by the previous colonial connection between India and the UK that provided a common law basis for the legal systems. In other countries in the EU where, for example, civil law applies, the differences in legal systems could be expected to be a more important barrier to international commercial transactions. The few exporters from the sample who perceived legal difference to be a barrier suggest that this is because of changing regulations.

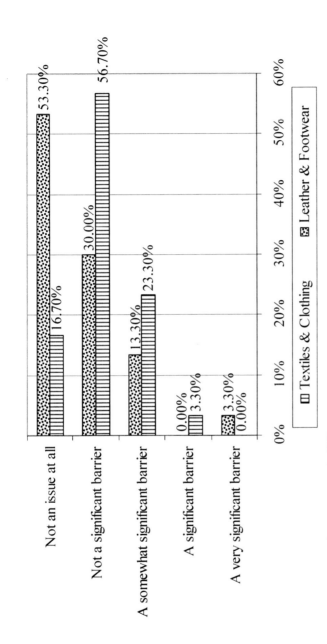

Source: Adapted from Khorana et al. (2008).

Figure 6.9 Perceptions of India's exporters regarding differences in legal frameworks as barriers to trade with the UK

For instance, EC Regulation (3030/93) is the basis of all regulations regarding imports of textiles into the EU and contains country-specific information. Since 1993, the regulation and its annexes have been amended 79 times. These frequent revisions can lead to confusion amongst exporters and costly errors in production.

6.6 TRADE FACILITATION BARRIERS

An additional barrier faced by Indian manufacturing firms exporting their products relates to customs procedures[20] including customs valuation, customs clearance and documentation formalities. Interstate barriers within India, octroi (a local entry tax) and checkpoints – of course a source of corruption income – add to the barriers faced by textiles and clothing, leather and footwear exporters. They believe that substantial barriers exist pertaining to customs clearance and documentation formalities in India as well as in the EU and UK. Seventy-three per cent of India's exporting textiles and clothing manufacturers perceive custom procedures as a barrier to exporting from India; in the UK, each sub-category of customs barrier was perceived as being at a different level of importance. Fewer respondents in the leather and footwear industry (57 per cent) than in textiles and clothing perceive customs procedures as barriers to their exports; of this, 7 per cent viewed them as a significant barrier.

6.6.1 Custom Valuation

Custom valuation is the process whereby an exported good is assessed a value upon which the subsequent customs duty – usually an ad valorem tax calculated as a percentage of the value of the product – is imposed at the importing destination. Generally, customs value is the price actually paid or payable for the goods. In terms of process, the Indian exporter provides an indicative transaction value of the shipment. Should the goods be cleared by the buyers' agents, they will provide a lower transaction value for the goods; subsequently EU or UK customs officials must assess a value for the goods not based on the market price. There is often a discrepancy between the value declared by the exporter and the value assessed in the UK. UK customs may reject the declared transaction value of an imported shipment when the value is deemed to be discounted from market prices. This results in the belief of Indian exporters that prices of their shipments have been over estimated for customs purpose. A common complaint from exporters is that customs valuation methodologies do not reflect actual transaction values. If the importing country's customs officials assign a higher value to the goods than the exporter, this raises the cost of the tariff paid. Exporters see this as a disguised trade barrier. Over one-third of total exporters interviewed perceived that customs valuation is a significant trade barrier. Of course, exporters have an incentive to under-invoice the value of their products because it reduces the tariffs they pay – a percentage calculated on a smaller value. This is the reason why importing countries independently assign value to imports. Disputes over the true value of imports are one of the most longstanding issues in international trade (Kerr, 2001).

Of the 60 per cent of textiles and clothing exporters that perceive customs valuation as a potential barrier to their exports, nearly 27 per cent consider it as a significant barrier to trade. In contrast, 33 per cent of leather and footwear exporters perceive that customs valuation acts a barrier to trade; of which roughly 7 per cent perceive it as a very significant barrier. Figure 6.10 presents the exporters' perceptions regarding customs valuation as an NTB in current trade between India and the UK.

6.6.2 Customs Clearance

Customs clearance is a formality that must be completed for all goods being exported from India. Clearing customs involves a number of procedures and documents to be obtained or signed including an invoice declaration, a value declaration, certificates of origin, certificate of authority for preferential duties, cargo handling, port procedures and a pre-shipment inspection. Formalities involve using official customs warehouses, inward processing, processing under customs control, temporary importation and outward processing, warehouse-bonding and redistribution – all to be provided by the exporter. The process is time-consuming and increases the total administrative costs of exports as well as overall transaction costs. Of course, these are prime areas for corruption rents to be extracted, and in particular speed money. Figure 6.11 shows the perceptions of exporters in both the textiles and clothing, leather and footwear sectors regarding customs clearance acting as an NTB to their exports destined for the UK. Nearly 57 per cent of textiles and clothing exporters perceive customs clearance as a barrier to their exports to the UK; of this, 20 per cent and 37 per cent of the exporters in the sample perceive customs clearance in India as very significant and significant barrier, respectively. Fewer leather and footwear exporters, at 33 per cent, believe Indian customs clearance is a significant barrier while 7 per cent view it as a very significant barrier.

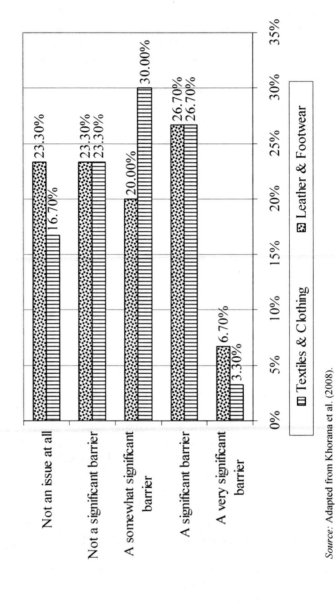

Source: Adapted from Khorana et al. (2008).

Figure 6.10 Perceptions of India's exporters regarding customs valuation as a barrier to trade with the UK

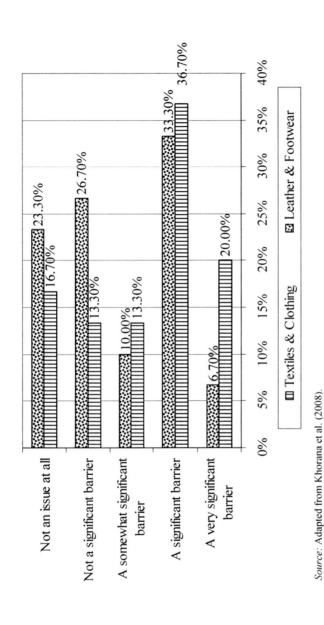

Source: Adapted from Khorana et al. (2008).

Figure 6.11 Perceptions of India's exporters regarding customs clearance as a barrier to trade with the UK

127

One explanation for the view that customs clearance acts as an NTB is the foreign buyers' practice of designating clearing agents to be used by Indian exporters to carry out customs clearance. Textiles and clothing exporters in Bangalore and footwear manufacturers in Chennai stated that the using buyer-nominated agents imposes a higher cost structure upon them as charges are often non-negotiable, leaving exporters little flexibility in negotiating the delivery schedule. The nominated agents often leave exporters with incomplete information or incorrect shipping information which complicates customs clearance. Additionally, the agents do not provide adequate information on rules of origin to the exporters, resulting in their inability to claim any preferential duty rate that their goods may qualify for.

Another group of interviewed exporters had a markedly different view of using buyer-nominated clearing agents. The practice was believed to be a competitive advantage for the exporters as any responsibility for the shipment devolved to the agents immediately upon departure from the production facility. Other exporters indicated that using buyer-nominated agents did not constitute a barrier when the value of exports is very large; the exporters reaped benefits in terms of economies of scale and specialization by focusing upon production and allowing the agents to focus upon clearing customs. When export volume is sufficiently large, the per unit transactions costs associated with the buyer-nominated agents decreases.

6.6.3 Administrative and Documentation Formalities

Administrative and documentation formalities must also be completed for all goods exported from India and consists of registration for the exporter's code, business identification number, sales tax registration, registration with export promotion councils, clearance by excise authorities, quality control, pre-shipment inspections, and clearing and forwarding by agents with documents such as commercial invoice, export order, original copy of the pre-shipment financing letter of credit, excise gate pass, certificate of inspection, certificate of origin and all other banking formalities. There are 18 steps in the administrative and documentation formalities that an Indian exporter has to fulfil in order to export (provided in Appendix C). Documentation formalities contribute substantially to additional time and overhead expenses and the delayed delivery of the requisite documents accompanying the exports can be sufficient to delay the shipment itself. The perceptions of Indian exporters in the textiles and clothing, leather and footwear industries of administrative and documentation formalities as NTBs in their exports destined for the UK are reported in Figure 6.12.

A greater percentage of exporters from the textiles and clothing industry believe that administrative and documentation formalities act as an NTB than exporters in leather and footwear, at 70 per cent and 27 per cent respectively. Of the 70 per cent of textiles and clothing exporters, 36 per cent perceive these formalities as very significant barriers. In sharp contrast, only 7 per cent of leather and footwear exporters believe these formalities are very significant. It was also noted that experienced, larger-scale leather and footwear exporters perceive administrative and documentation formalities as less of a problem as they benefited from economies of scale.

The potentially high transactions costs that can be imposed by India's administrative and documentation formalities were illustrated by the responses of a textile exporter in Erode. Exporters are required to prepare a bank draft to apply for an ROO certificate from the textile committee in Mumbai. This formality can be made less cumbersome if a direct debit facility is made available. It was pointed out that administrative procedures for registration and certification often lead to rent-seeking by the various authorities involved in issuing certificates to exporters.

Thus far, the discussion has focused qualitatively on the perceptions of industry members regarding the incidence and impact of NTBs on their exports. Section 6.7 quantifies these perceptions of trade barriers using a multinomial regression model.

6.7 QUANTITATIVE ANALYSIS OF BARRIERS

Quantitative work completed by Khorana et al. (2008) further explores whether small or large Indian firms face the greatest obstacles exporting to the UK; which set of barriers are more important for different sized firms and whether export experience has a role to play in affecting perceptions. Khorana et al. (2008), in using a multinomial logit regression (MLR) model,[21] attempted to analyse Indian exporters' perceptions of NTBs and other domestic/trade facilitation barriers that impede trade between India and the UK. A set of dependent variables was identified and included the response or outcome variables, that is, those that depict changes in the perception of exporters of the barriers faced if there is a change in any of the independent variables. The main dependent variables were grouped as:

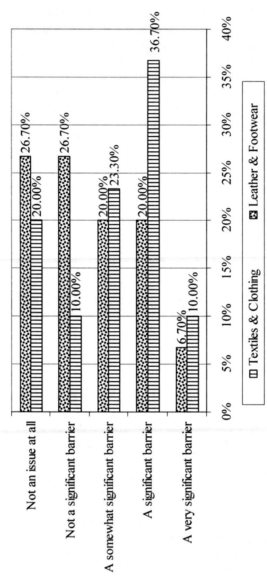

Figure 6.12 Perceptions of India's exporters regarding administrative and documentation formalities as barriers to trade with the UK

- NTBs: regulations and standards, testing and certification, labelling and packaging, environmental measures, and information asymmetry.
- Domestic barriers: transport costs, corruption and theft, inadequate infrastructure, and legal differences.
- Trade facilitation barriers: customs valuation, custom clearance and documentation formalities.

To account for the dependent variables, exporters were asked to rate their perception of the incidence of the various existing NTBs, domestic and trade facilitation barriers based on a Likert scale. This scale ranks the perceptions of exporters from 5 to 1 where:

- 5 = a very significant barrier;
- 4 = a significant barrier;
- 3 = a somewhat significant barrier (that is, this barrier is considered important within the business environment but the firms are able to overcome it);
- 2 = not a significant barrier (as interpreted by the firm on its own behalf) and,
- 1 = not an issue at all (that is, not perceived as a barrier as the respondents did not encounter it).

The independent variables in this regression were firm size and export experience. These independent variables were controlled and their presence determined the change in the perceptions of exporters regarding the severity and incidence of the barriers faced at the time of exporting. To account for the independent variables, the first part of the questionnaire addressed issues relating to exporters' characteristics such as the firms' main sector of activity, turnover, total years of production and export experience and information used to determine the independent variables. Size/turnover was classified on the basis of groups of firms with total turnover ranging from Rs.1[22] to Rs. 5 crores,[23] Rs. 5 to 10 crores; and more than Rs. 10 crores. For export experience, firms were classified into groups of firms with export experience ranging from 1 to 10 years; between 10 to 20 years; and more than 20 years.

6.7.1 Hypotheses

Khorana et al. (2008) formulated two sets of hypotheses to assess the relationship between firm size, export experience and the dependent variables. These are:

6.7.1.a Hypothesis I
Exporting firms' perceptions of NTBs as well as domestic and trade facilitation barriers, are negatively related with the firm size.

The underlying assumption of this hypothesis is that large firms find it easier to respond quickly and efficiently to changes in the international trading environment as compared to small and medium-sized firms. Therefore, large exporters will be able to meet the challenges presented to them by the new business environment created under the EU–India FTA scenario. Existing literature suggests that total output affects export performance with larger firms able to increase exports and absorb more risks compared to smaller firms (Erramilli and Rao, 1993). Moini (1995) also shows that the size of an exporting firm is correlated positively with the size of its total exports. Calof (1994) suggests that internationalization requires appropriate resources and concludes that the size of the exporting firm is an important predictor of its export performance. This suggests that larger exporters (in terms of turnover) might be able to respond better to the challenges of NTBs and other barriers.

6.7.1.b Hypothesis II
There is a negative relation between experience and the perception of exporters towards NTBs, domestic and trade facilitation barriers faced in Indo–UK trade.

In this model, the export experience is measured by the number of years firms have been involved in exporting. The rationale behind the assumption that export experience is an important variable is that firms require specific knowledge to enter foreign markets successfully. Davidson (1990) and Erramilli (1991) suggest prior export experience is a crucial variable that influences any firm's ability to export. Moini (1995) suggests that export activity levels are directly linked with exporting success. De Chiara and Minguzzi (2002) and Majocchi and Zucchella (2003) report that exporting to foreign markets allows firms to become familiar with different national market rules (institutional knowledge) and helps them to acquire business knowledge (information about their clients' different tastes and preferences) as well as internationalization knowledge (to develop internal resources and routines dedicated to servicing international markets). Applying this to the Indian context, the export experience variable is, however, not restricted to experience specific to the UK. This is because it was assumed that experience gained in exporting to any foreign market is transferable. This implies that exporters with previous experience were able to handle the existing NTBs in leather and footwear, textiles and clothing trade with the UK.

6.8 REGRESSION RESULTS FOR TEXTILES AND CLOTHING

The regression results of Khorana et al. (2008) for the textiles and clothing sector in India are presented in Table 6.3 and illustrate the significant barriers faced by Indian exporters to the UK market.

The parameter estimates suggest that Indian textile and clothing exporters, regardless of size or experience, perceive testing and certification as a barrier; Table 6.3 demonstrates the significance level of this NTB. For each unit increase in firms' exports, the probability of inclusion in the group of respondents perceiving testing and certification as a 'somewhat significant' barrier increases by 18 per cent (1.181 − 1 = 0.181). Similarly, for each additional year of export experience, the likelihood of inclusion in the group of respondents that believe that testing is a 'somewhat significant' barrier increases by 44 per cent (1.441 − 1 = 0.441). The increasing trends to protect consumer health (from potentially harmful substances, e.g. allergenic, carcinogenic or poisonous) and the environment (in terms of air pollution, the generation of waste and the contamination of water and soil) means that testing and certification requirements are also becoming increasingly prevalent and may contribute to the perception that they are a somewhat significant barrier.

The results also indicated that export experience and testing are positively correlated, where firms with greater experience believe that product testing and certification are a somewhat significant barrier. Over time, firms with greater exporting experience move up the value chain to become suppliers to speciality stores that specialize in women's and men's fashion apparel as well as fashion accessories. These stores impose specific testing and certification requirements, which often exceed previous minimum specifications.

Table 6.3 *Do textile and clothing firms' perceptions regarding NTBs and other barriers vary by firm size and export experience?*

Dependent Variable	Model fit x^2			Coefficient β Significant categories only		SE β Significant categories only	
	Final	Firm size	Export experience	Firm size	Export experience	Firm size	Export experience
Non-tariff barriers							
Regulations & standards	6.752	*6.265	1.686	–	–	–	–
Testing & certification	*13.814	*9.118	*11.125	(3.984) (6.219)	*2.564(2) *3.054(3)	*1.163(2) *1.181(3)	*1.422(2) *1.441(3)
Labelling & packaging	5.281	2.192	1.898	–	–	–	–
Environmental measures	0.567	0.498	0.207	–	–	–	–
Information asymmetry	3.861	1.061	1.704	–	–	–	–
Domestic barriers							
Transport costs	*11.205	*8.436	*6.383	–	*32.035(2) *32.247(3)	–	*0.868(2) *0.704(3)
Corruption and theft	6.240	1.795	4.624	–	–	–	–
Inadequate infrastructure	8.951	7.012	4.239	–	–	–	–
Legal differences	9.931	*7.435	5.465	–	–	–	–
Trade facilitation barriers							
Customs valuation	7.041	5.374	0.955	–	–	–	–
Clearance issues	*13.330	7.391	6.320	0.626 (5.268)	–	–	*1.367(2)
Documentation formalities	8.648	4.132	4.429	–	–	–	–

Note: * Values are significant at p<0.1, i.e. at the 10 per cent level of significance. Reference category is (1), other categories are (2, 3, 4, 5).

Source: Khorana et al. (2008).

As an example, one speciality store that markets an extensive range of fashion apparel and accessories for women, men, teens, children and infants required its Indian supplier to improve collaboration along the entire supply chain to take account of the product life cycle. The supplier managed to achieve this by allowing the buyer to control access to product data and imagery though a web-based product data management. Most small-scale manufacturers in India are unable to accommodate such sophisticated testing requirements. As a result, this higher degree of testing translates into a somewhat significant barrier in the textiles and clothing sector.

The perception of being a somewhat significant barrier and the positive relationship between the variables signifies that with higher output (or exports), the perception of testing as a barrier increases. That is, larger firms find it to be a more important barrier. For example, in response to EU policy guidelines, the Government of India has banned the use of 112 harmful azodyes. As a result, small-sized firms are more vulnerable than larger firms because of the large firms' existing investments in costly technology and equipment using azodyes. Switching costs to adapt to new non-azodye technology and equipment is high for smaller firms and they are therefore unable to meet testing and certification requirements, resulting in the perception of it being a somewhat significant barrier.

In contrast, larger firms exporting to higher end UK buyers have already switched to alternates like natural dyes, therefore the azodye ban imposed minimal switching costs. Industry sources indicated that substantially greater volumes of natural dyes are required to achieve the same colour as synthetics. As a result, natural dyes are less cost-effective and commercially viable than synthetics and are generally used for niche market products only. Larger firms, while capable of investing in sophisticated technology to utilize natural dyes, are subject to far more stringent and exacting testing and certification requirements from those UK buyers that do not want synthetic dyes. This explains why larger firms might also perceive testing requirements as a somewhat significant barrier.

In terms of inadequate infrastructure resulting in high transport costs, which then adversely affects overall export competitiveness, the parameter estimates suggest that this variable is significant for export experience but not for firm size. For every additional year of export experience, the probability that transport costs are a somewhat significant barrier and a significant barrier falls by 30 per cent and 14 per cent respectively. The negative correlation indicates that firms with greater export experience perceive transport costs as less of a barrier over time as they to learn how best to deal with the specific obstacles facing their business. Exporters with past experience are able to overcome logistic disadvantages through effective supply chain management that assists in reducing transportation costs. In this manner, they benefit from economies of scale and learning as well as lower costs, which explain why experienced firms might perceive transport costs as a lesser obstacle than less inexperienced firms.

Regarding customs clearance issues, the regression analysis suggests that with each additional year of export experience, customs clearance becomes a less important a barrier for firms. The likelihood of the exporter perceiving customs clearance as not a significant barrier increases by 73 per cent $(1.367 - 1 = 0.73)$. The interview results confirm these findings as, over time, exporters have made arrangements to cope with customs clearance, thus reducing its perception as a barrier. The results suggest that as the total years of export experience increases, clearance charges as a percentage of total costs decrease, as does the perception of customs clearance being a barrier to exports.

6.9 REGRESSION RESULTS FOR LEATHER AND FOOTWEAR INDUSTRY

Table 6.4 presents the regression results from Khorana et al., (2008) for the leather and footwear sector.

In the leather and footwear industry, the results show that the more experience firms have in exporting, the greater they perceive regulations and standards to be a barrier. The model shows that the probability of regulations and standards being a significant and very significant barrier increases by 37 per cent and 42 per cent respectively. The WTO Agreement on TBT requires that regulations, standards, testing and certification procedures do not create unnecessary obstacles but at the same time recognizes the rights of the Member Countries to adopt appropriate standards. India's leather and footwear exporters perceive regulations and standards as a significant barrier because UK importers require compliance with specifications that exceed the minimum required regulations and standards.

The interview findings confirmed that as consumer groups exert pressure on retailers for the advancement of consumer and social agendas, retailers in turn ask their suppliers to ensure conformity with the standards. Several large retail groups are integrating social requirements in their private codes of conduct that impose stringent standards on their suppliers.

Table 6.4 Do leather and footwear firms' perceptions regarding NTBs and other barriers vary by firm size and export experience?

Dependent Variable	Model Fit x^2			Coefficient β Significant categories only		SE β Significant categories only	
	Final	F_S	E_P	F_S	E_P	F_S	E_P
Non-tariff barriers							
Regulations & standards	*14.691	6.772	*8.460	—	*(2) 2.049 *(3) 3.070 *(4) 2.708 *(5) 2.673	—	*(2)1.223 *(3)1.352 *(4)1.631 *(5)1.583
Testing & certification	10.542	5.834	4.560	—	—	—	—
Labelling & packaging	6.368	2.231	4.902	—	—	—	—
Environmental measures	7.265	0.370	7.111	—	—	—	—
Information asymmetry	*17.269	*9.636	4.983	—	(95.535)	—	*(5)0.012
Domestic barriers							
Transport costs	*17.866	*12.879	5.649	(3.69)	—	0.910*(2)	—
Corruption and theft	*13.661	6.333	*7.666	(4.55)	—	1.210*(2)	—
Inadequate infrastructure	*15.235	*8.540	7.215	(6.49)	—	1.190*(3)	—
Legal differences	*12.816	2.213	*11.183	—	*(3) 2.713	—	*(3)1.289
Trade facilitation barriers							
Customs valuation	12.859	5.064	7.854*	—	1.598*(3)	—	0.929*(3)
Clearance issues	6.191	0.76	5.723	—	—	—	—
Documentation formalities	11.338	1.61	10.107*	—	2.172*(2) 2.692*(3) 2.302*(5)	—	1.015*(2) 1.083*(3) 1.389*(5)

Note: F_S represents firm size, E_P represents export experience.
* Values are significant at p<0.1, i.e. at the 10per cent level of significance. Reference category is (1), other categories are (2, 3, 4, 5)

Source: Khorana et al. (2008).

137

This means that noncost factors are becoming increasingly important within the supply chain, and buying decisions are not based exclusively on price competitiveness. This is particularly the case for brand name and eco-labelled products. As a result, regulations and standards are perceived to be a significant and very significant barrier as the total years of export experience increases.

The regression results suggest that the less the export experience of the firm, the more significantly information asymmetry is perceived as a barrier. Existing exporters with relatively fewer years of exporting experience find it time-consuming and costly to collect information, understand and comply with administrative requirements. New exporters informed us that export/trade organizations do not support new exporters with branding, image building and information on potential market access opportunities. While there is information on business promotion opportunities at international exhibitions and fairs, participation is expensive. As a result, information asymmetry persists.

The empirical results indicate that as firms gain experience exporting, the perception that customs valuation is a somewhat significant barrier falls. The presence of external third party logistics suppliers (3PLs) in the supply chain that can perform all or part of logistics activities on behalf of UK importers, provides the importers with benefits such as lower costs, improved quality and better integration of logistics activities. Often these 3PLs are freight forwarders who organize the dispatch of cargo by road, rail, ship or sea. Apart from securing cargo space on the relevant mode of transport, these freight forwarders may also deal with customs valuation formalities. Given that these agents have specialized knowledge, their ability to provide appropriately assessed declarations reduces problems of customs valuation in the importing country. As a result, Indian exporters with more experience do not perceive that customs valuation as a somewhat significant barrier to trade as they have been able to delegate these activities to the 3PLs nominated by their UK buyers.

The same is true for documentation formalities and legal formalities. As firms gain experience exporting, the perception of documentation as well as the EU legal environment being a somewhat significant barrier declines. The interviews revealed that exporters must complete a minimum of 18 documents for customs documentation. In addition, rules and procedures for pre-shipment inspection are lengthy and it often takes a few days before the inspection can be carried out. With experience, the transactions costs involved in completing the process decline, reducing documentation's impact as a barrier. Similarly, firms with more experience and exposure to

EU banking regulations, disclosure requirements, bankruptcy laws and accountancy norms view the EU legal operating environment as less of a barrier.

As firms increase in size, the significance of transportation costs as a barrier declines. Transportation is the backbone of the supply chain. For larger firms, export consignments are increasingly handled by specialized agencies. For instance, one agency is responsible for haulage; another for marketing. Additional agents and brokers take on storage and delivery functions. This delegation of responsibilities leads to the perception that transport costs decline in significance as a barrier.

In contrast, there exists a positive correlation between the size of firms and the perception of corruption and theft as a barrier to trade. Small firms may face both market- and bureaucracy-related obstacles. A market-based obstacle for a small firm may be difficulty in gaining access to financing because of proportionally higher fixed costs associated with a loan review as compared to a larger firm. Bureaucratic obstacles relate to administrative discretion and negatively affect small firms that are often unable to sufficiently bribe the appropriate officials, either due to lack of resources or lack of access to higher levels of administration. Large firms are not immune as they may be more vulnerable to the rent extraction associated with corruption. Due to a larger presence, greater visibility and assumed higher profits, large firms can become desirable targets for extracting speed money and kickbacks.

The regression results show that as leather and footwear firms' size increases, the perception that inadequate infrastructure is a somewhat significant barrier increases but the overall findings of the interviews reported in the previous section suggest that infrastructure as a vital and important component of the total domestic business environment for all firms, regardless of size.

In the leather and footwear industry, in most cases, the size of the exporting firm matters. Smaller exporting firms generally report significantly more problems with inadequate infrastructure than larger exporting firms. However, firms with larger export volumes face greater frequency of issues due to inadequate infrastructure than those with a smaller export volume. There exists a direct correlation as export volume increases, the frequency of encountering infrastructure issues also increases. All firms face problems with some aspect of infrastructure.

6.10 CONCLUSIONS ARISING FROM THE EMPIRICAL INVESTIGATION

The regression results for both the textiles and clothing, and leather and footwear industries generally confirm both hypotheses. For the most part, large firms do find it easier to respond quickly and efficiently to changes in the international trading environment as compared to small and medium-sized firms. Larger firms have greater abilities to increase exports and to absorb more risks relative to smaller firms. Larger producers appear to be better able to respond to the challenges of NTBs and other barriers.

Size and experience helps with supply chain logistics and customs formalities. Experience in exporting, regardless of size, reduces issues with inadequate infrastructure to some degree, and transport costs, customs valuation, information asymmetry, documentation and the legal operating environments. Neither size nor experience helps with testing and certification as firms of different size and experience are impacted in a variety of ways by these requirements. Small firms have difficulty meeting minimum testing and certification requirements, perhaps due to lack of capacity, the inability to procure financing or new technologies or any other of the myriad of reasons previously discussed. Large firms that are able to finance or procure technology move up the value chain to supply more sophisticated buyers, but are then subject to equally more sophisticated and stringent regulations or standards, testing and certification. Subcategories of a barrier can also impact different sized firms in different ways. For example, in terms of corruption, a small firm may not be able to access the appropriate official to bribe, or afford the amount of the bribe. In contrast, while larger firms may be able to find the right official and can afford the bribe, their larger presence and status may make them subject to additional incidence of rent extraction.

The regression results indicate that large exporters and those with more exporting experience are well positioned to adapt to, and meet, the challenges that will be presented to them by the new business environment created under the India–EU FTA. Smaller firms with less experience will require assistance in order to capture benefits from the preferential trade agreement. Given the results from the quantitative analysis and the importance of NTBs in the India–EU trade relationship, particularly within the context of textiles and clothing, leather and footwear industries, specific recommendations can be made in order to ensure that these sectors are able to capture the benefits of trade liberalization between India and the EU. These are discussed in Chapter 8.

6.11 IMPEDIMENTS FACED BY UK EXPORTERS OF TEXTILES AND CLOTHING, LEATHER AND FOOTWEAR TO INDIA

We were also interested in the barriers perceived by UK exporters shipping goods to India. In the UK, 25 interviews were conducted amongst trading houses, importers, business councils and trade associations. Consultations were also held with relevant government ministries and organizations. Details regarding the interviews and consultations held in the UK may be found in Appendix B.

Respondents indicated concerns about high existing tariffs,[24] the prevalence of non-tariff barriers as well as India's domestic barriers. Dissatisfaction regarding India's trade policies[25] and the overall business environment was also expressed; which contributed to the overall perception that India is not favourable to foreign companies trading across its boundaries.

6.11.1 Labelling and Certification

UK respondents indicated that India's labelling and marking requirements for textiles, particularly those governed by the Textiles Regulation 1998 (on consumers' protection) were a concern. The regulation requires that yarns and fabrics be marked with product details and its identification information including the marking of words and letters in Hindi and English (in capital letters). The numerals must be marked in conformity to international numerals, with instructions on the height of characters (0.5 cm for yarn and cloth and 0.25 cm for packed yarn and 3 cm on the bale/case) as well as the colour of ink for marking (all allowed except red). The application of marking rules on products exported to India can at times result in delays for EU and UK exporters. UK textiles exporters perceived that this has the potential to impede textiles trade.

High certification costs associated with textiles being shipped to India were another concern of UK textiles exporters. After the phased removal of quotas on textiles, the Indian government insisted on a health certificate regarding azodyes be supplied by foreign firms exporting to India. EURATEX (an organization that promotes the exports of textiles from the EU) indicated that testing fees and procedures particularly hamper UK exporters specializing in small quantities of high quality textiles. These firms must submit a sample for testing per design, with the costs of doing so representing roughly 10 per cent of the product's total c.i.f. value. Other concerns included technical regulations imposed by India that are believed to often lack a science-based justification.

6.11.2 India's Domestic Barriers

High initial costs, delays and procedural complexities are the main issues facing a British entrepreneur attempting to establish a business in India. Some of the obstacles faced include the sheer volume of procedures, the time involved and cost of official fees as well as a required minimum capital deposit prior to initiating the registration process. Entrepreneurs also face high administrative costs, bureaucratic procedures and delays, corruption, paying the necessary speed money as well as a large informal economy – all of which increase the overall administrative and transaction costs of doing business.

According to the respondents, it typically requires 13 procedures and 33 days to establish a business in India. The World Bank (2007) reports it requires 20 procedures and takes 224 days for companies to set up a warehouse to gain access into the Indian market.

The state of India's infrastructure is a sizeable barrier to UK exporters. The UK companies surveyed indicated that the costs of international air and maritime transportation to and within India are high and impede UK exports. The companies unanimously indicated that Indian infrastructure is insufficient for many business operations. The deficiencies and shortcomings in transportation networks, including roads, railroads, ports and shipping as well as urban infrastructure and related services provision presents a formidable challenge to any UK exporter wishing to enter the Indian market. The absence of sufficient and reliable electricity, as well as the general level of technology in many sectors and industries undermines potential opportunities for UK exporters. The lack of a reliable, secure, affordable and environmentally sound electricity system has forced companies to set up captive power generation capacity to escape power failures or fluctuations.

6.11.3 Trade Facilitation Barriers

Those UK exporters surveyed indicated growing concern over the lack of transparency in India's customs procedures and that documentation required to import goods into India, quality assessments and customs valuation are an increasingly important issue. The existing customs procedures are excessively cumbersome. The composition of custom duties is currently, for the most part, non-transparent. The rating and valuation of customs duties is accomplished with a large component of arbitrary decision making. The classification of similar goods in different tariff groups makes it difficult to determine the applicable tariff rate. This is particularly the case where material is imported for further processing in India, particularly in the textile and clothing industry, but also in other industries. In these cases it is almost impossible to calculate the final tariff in advance. At times a customs valuation calculation is based on 'like' products made in India.

Another issue of concern to UK exporters is India's system of additional import duties that roughly double the customs duty at the point of entry. The methodology to calculate import duties and the administration of tariffs through numerous notifications results in a complicated and non-transparent tariff structure.

An examination of India's export and import (EXIM) policy 2008–09 shows prohibitive levels of customs duty. For example, in addition to customs duties, three other duties apply to textiles products including a supplementary tax on additional duty, calculated as a percentage of the base rate of the additional duty. If the base rate of the additional duty is 12 per cent and the supplementary tax is 8 per cent, then the effective rate of the additional duty is 12.95 per cent (12 % x (1 + 0.08)). Second, an additional excise duty for goods is applicable, charged at between five and eight per cent of the landed value. Third, a cess[26] duty of 0.05 per cent is levied on imported products. This cumulative calculation increases the total import duties significantly. In addition to these, individual state governments levy a cess tax on textiles products which varies between the different States. West Bengal and Maharashtra impose a tax that ranges from 4 to 5 per cent while others may charge up to 15 per cent. There are over 50,000 cases of customs valuation pending with the Indian customs.

UK exporters also expressed concern regarding the broad degree of discretion Indian customs officials exercise. Situations have occurred where customs officials have arbitrarily challenged the classification of products such as woven fabrics, children's clothing and lingerie, and sent them for laboratory tests. Indian customs can also reclassify imported products such that the revised classification attracts a higher customs duty. An appeal process is available, however it is lengthy and time consuming. UK exporters indicated that a major benefit they would seek in an India–EU FTA is, should tariffs not be abolished outright, any remaining tariffs must in all cases be applied in a transparent and legally binding way.

UK businesses are also deterred from exporting to India due to the slow and inefficient customs procedures, bureaucracy and excessive documentation formalities. Customs procedures are generally not automated, customs valuations tend not to be based on market prices and the customs clearance process is long and complex, all of which increase transactions costs and opportunity costs. Cumbersome entry procedures were often associated with corruption. The UK companies believe that each step in the process is a point of contact and an opportunity to extract a bribe.

UK exporters also viewed India's burdensome entry regulations for imported goods as having little domestic legitimacy as they did not appear to contribute to enhancing product safety, increasing product quality or pollution reduction. These regulations, however, constrain private investment, push more people into the informal economy, increase consumer prices and fuel corruption. NTBs and other domestic barriers result in high administrative and transaction costs for UK exporters and, therefore, have the potential to be a stumbling block for the trading partners under the proposed FTA.

Figure 6.13 illustrates the main problems of trading with India as indicated by the sample of UK companies.

As illustrated by the discussion in this chapter, the trade between India and the UK in textiles and clothing, leather and footwear is clearly affected by a broad range of NTBs. Technical barriers to trade, customs and administrative procedures and domestic barriers in India figure prominently in the India–UK NTB profile.

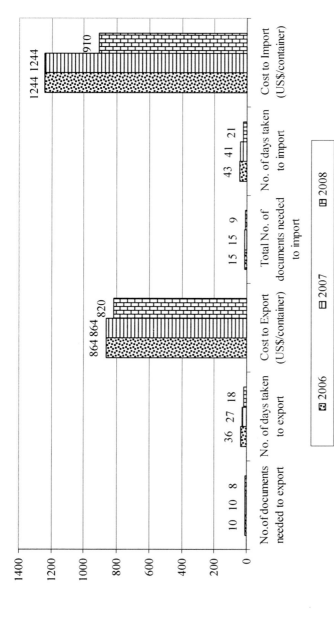

Source: Adapted from World Bank (2007).

Figure 6.13 Main problems of doing business with India as indicated by UK businesses

145

NOTES

1. Measures other than high import duties (tariff) employed to restrict imports. Two such measures are: (1) direct price influencers, such as export subsidies or drawbacks, exchange rate manipulations, methods of imports valuation, customs surcharges, lengthy customs procedures, establishment of minimum import prices, unreasonable standards and inspection procedures; and (2) indirect price influencers, such as import licensing and import.
2. The UNCTAD Coding System of Trade Control Measures (CSTCM) established in 1994 provides classification together with a corresponding tariff number. There are six core categories according to the nature of the measure, these are the following:
   (a)   Price control measures
   (b)   Finance measures
   (c)   Automatic licensing measures
   (d)   Quantity control measures
   (e)   Monopolistic measures, and
   (f)   Technical measures.
   These are further sub-categorized in accordance with the type of measure. Only sensitive product categories and technical regulations are further subcategorized according to objectives of the measure (for example, protection of safety, human health, animal health and life, plant health, environment, and wildlife).
3. NAMA negotiations categorize NTBs as those related to: government participation in trade and restrictive practices tolerated by governments; customs and administrative entry procedures; technical barriers to trade; sanitary and phyto-sanitary measures; specific limitation; charges on imports; and others.
4. http://www.ficci.com/press/443/95.doc.
5. From the 1980s, based on the recommendations of Government of India official committees, India's trade regime was liberalized mainly in intermediate and capital goods by moving items to the Open General Licensing system (OGL). The NTBs faced by foreign exporters in India, however, remained unchanged until 1990.
6. The use of cords in the head and neck areas for children and young persons aged 7–14 is restricted. Restrictions apply mainly to the length of the cords, use of elastic cords and the characteristics of toggles.
7. ISO 9001:2000 is based on eight quality management principles which are customer focus; leadership; involvement of people; process approach; systems approach; continual improvement; fact-based decision making; and mutually beneficial supplier relationships.
8. SA8000 is an internationally accepted instrument for implementing social accountability for a social management system. It is based on the internationally accepted ILO labour standards, but includes tools to implement social standards through the entire system of a company. SA8000 is gaining ground in many industries worldwide because it is the only internationally accepted management system for implementing and monitoring social standards for labour conditions.
9. WRAP monitors factories for compliance with detailed practices and procedures implied by adherence to the following standards: compliance with laws and workplace regulations; prohibition of forced labour; prohibition of child labour; prohibition of harassment or abuse; compensation and benefits; prohibition of discrimination; hours of work; health and safety; freedom of association and collective bargaining; environment; customs compliance; and security.
10. Details of this regulation can be found at: http://www.hse.gov.uk/reach/resources/importe rs.pdf.
11. The Agreement on Technical Barriers to Trade (TBT) attempts to ensure that regulations, standards, testing and certification procedures do not create unnecessary obstacles to trade. However, the agreement also recognizes countries' rights to adopt the standards

they consider appropriate – for example for human, animal or plant life or health, for the protection of the environment or to meet other consumer interests. For details see http://www.wto.org/English/tratop_e/tbt_e/tbtagre_e.html.

12. Azocolorants are the most important class of synthetic dyes and pigments, representing 60–80per cent of all organic colourants. They are used widely in substrates such as textile fibres, leather, plastics, papers, hair, mineral oils, waxes, foodstuffs and cosmetics.

13. SGS industrial services carries out testing for yarn and fabrics; functional garments; uniforms; upholstery materials; home furnishings and made-ups; carpets and rugs; and industrial fabrics. Testing standards undertaken are ASTM and AATCC for the US; BS for the United Kingdom; CAN for Canada; DIN for Germany; EN for the EEC; JIS for Japan; AS for Australia; and BIS – Bureau of Indian standards.

14. STR is a premier international provider of testing and quality assurance services to manufacturers, distributors and retailers of soft lines products. Specific services include testing to AATCC, ASTM, and CPSC protocols for products that will be sold in the US and applying ISO and other appropriate international standards to products that will be sold in Europe and elsewhere. Tests include colour fastness, strength tests, chemical analytical tests, aging tests, flammability, fibre analysis, construction, fabric performance, hosiery testing, and defect investigation, azo dye and ecological analysis to German and European standards; technical support for product development, including care label verification, fibre identification and analysis, garment construction analysis, inspection services including initial factory capabilities audit, fair labour and social compliance monitoring programmes, and in-line and final inspections.

15. The exception to this rule is Nordic Swan, which is valid in all Nordic countries.

16. These are carcinogenic chemicals and medical evidence suggests use of these products might lead to incidence of cancer.

17. While Italy is a major leather producer, thus sharing a common agenda with India's leather and footwear exporters, the motivation behind France's criticisms are likely driven more by its status as a major producer of PCP.

18. The government is aware of this constraint and the Committee on Infrastructure has estimated that an investment of Rs. 2,620 billion over the next 5–7 years is needed to improve ports, national highways and airports (ADB, 2006).

19. Pucca is a blacktop asphalt, all-weather road.

20. The documents to accompany the customs declaration generally include the following: the commercial invoice; the value declaration, where the customs value is to be established; a certificate of origin or invoice declaration where the application for a preferential tariff treatment is requested; an authorization or certificate of authenticity where a favourable tariff treatment is requested; an import authorization or licence where this is stipulated in EU or national law.

21. SPSS (Version 14) software was used to carry out the regressions needed for the analysis.

22. Rupees.

23. A crores is a unit of ten million.

24. The average tariffs in India are high. The average applied MFN rate is 12.8 per cent; industrial products are an exception with low MFN tariffs. Concerns regarding the issue of complex duties of export interest to the EU like wines and spirits and textiles were voiced by many interviewees.

25. Some business associations expressed concerns regarding import restrictions still present in select EU priority items such as marble, granite and glazed newsprint. Other market access barriers faced by EU firms were sanitary and technical standards – shelf life requirements, mandatory certification of products, discrimination and lack of transparency.

26. In India, a cess is a term used for any general tax, usually applied as local taxation, and can be attached to a descriptive prefix, that is, import-cess, irrigation-cess.

7. Preparing for an India–EU Trade Agreement

As indicated by the results of the surveys presented in Chapter 6, NTBs are a prevalent feature of current India–EU trade relations. Barriers to trade arise in multiple forms and venues including different national product standards, testing and certification requirements as well as packaging and labelling specifications. Given that NTBs evolve primarily from differences in regulatory regimes in the EU and India, the importance of identifying and addressing existing NTBs assumes an important role in any potential preferential trade agreement. This chapter also draws on the report by Khorana et al. (2008).

7.1 ECONOMIC ISSUES FOR THE PROPOSED INDIA–EU PTA

A preferential trade agreement (PTA) between India and the EU should lead to an increase in bilateral trade but would not necessarily lead to an automatic increase in economic welfare. The increase in bilateral trade could occur as a result of more efficiently produced imported goods replacing less efficiently produced domestically produced goods. Trade creation as well as allocative and productive efficiency gains follow. In turn, incentives for Indian, EU and UK producers to invest in product and process innovations would increase, thereby improving the dynamic efficiency of the trading partners and subsequently resulting in greater competition amongst firms located within the agreement's partners. The resulting increased competitive pressures may encourage firms to modify their strategies in order to restore their profit margins by either reducing production costs, which can be achieved by concentrating on the activities where their competitive position is strongest (core business), or by garnering market power though increased product differentiation.

Figure 7.1 presents the integration effects of removing NTBs and domestic barriers, showing that removal of barriers would lead to lower costs. Lower prices for consumers would result on one hand and reduce profit margins for producers on the other. These changes would lead to increased demand from consumers and force producers to rationalize their production processes. Hence, overall competitive effects and efficiency in allocation effects may arise when barriers to trade are reduced or eliminated.

Figure 7.2 shows the competition effects on total costs arising from barrier removal under a proposed preferential trade agreement. Prior to the implementation of the PTA, domestic (India) supplier's price is P1, comprized of economic rent in the form of excess profits, x-inefficiencies costs such as excess inventories and potential unexploited economies of scale.

Trade liberalization under the EU–India PTA will increase pressure on exporting firms to adapt their production mix in order to meet changing consumer requirements. These will appear in terms of standards on health, safety and the environment as well as in design, quality and prices. Firms will have to put in place efficient production methods that minimize production costs.

Foreign suppliers face both the direct cost of barriers (such as border delays, technical regulations, etc.) and the indirect cost of market barriers, which when removed, can result in a decrease in prices, from P1 to P2. Opening the economy to competition will force Indian producers to address their X-inefficiencies and to restructure their firms by eliminating inefficient productive capacity and investing in new technologies, thus allowing better exploitation of economies of scale. Consumers will gain due to the price reduction, from P1D1 to P2D2. Domestic producers will initially experience lower profits because of the price decline but the process of restructuring and exploitation of economies of scale would increase their ability to target the larger regional market and thereby increase production and profitability. Similarly, EU producers will gain access to the Indian market after the implementation of the PTA. The resultant effect is that firms both in India and in the EU will improve efficiency and prices will be reduced. The total welfare gain in this case is consumer gain less producers' protected profits. The possibility of trade diversion, however, cannot be ignored.

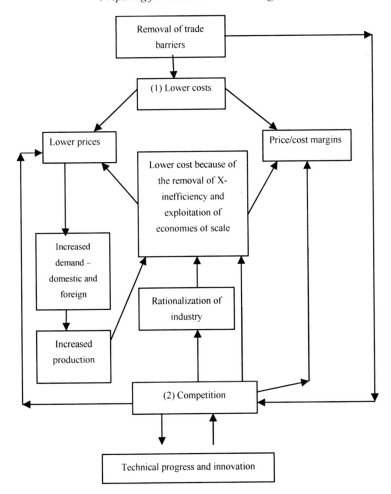

Source: Adapted from Emerson et al. (1988).

Figure 7.1 Integration effects of barrier removal under the PTA

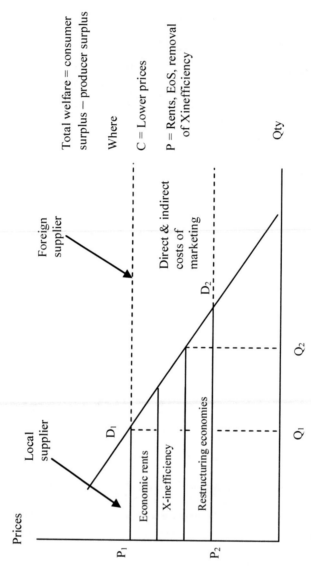

Total welfare = consumer
surplus – producer surplus

Where

C = Lower prices

P = Rents, EoS, removal
of Xinefficiency

Foreign
supplier

Direct & indirect
costs of
marketing

Local
supplier

Prices

Economic rents

X-inefficiency

Restructuring economies

P_1

P_2

D_1

D_2

Q_1

Q_2

Qty

Source: Adapted from Emerson et al. (1988).

Figure 7.2 Competition effects of barrier removal under the PTA

Trade diversion occurs when sources of supply switch away from non-PTA partner suppliers to new PTA partner suppliers (Kerr and Perdikis, 2003). If, prior to the PTA, the MFN levying country (India) chose to import from a non-PTA supplier, this would have occurred because that particular supplier was more efficient (lower priced) than the other trading partner. If post-PTA trade flows move from the old suppliers to the country with which the PTA has been concluded (the EU in this case), it implies that trade moves from the efficient supplier country to the less efficient PTA partner country. Thus, trade diversion leads to a welfare loss brought about by higher costs.

In reality, the PTA is likely to have both trade creation and diversion effects. The question of the overall economic efficiency impact will depend on which effect, that is, trade creation or trade diversion, dominates. In practice, the size of these effects is difficult to measure. In theory, there are several indicators of trade creation and diversion. For example, trade creation is more likely if pre-PTA tariffs of the member countries were higher. India's average MFN tariffs for instance, range between 7 and 10 per cent implying that the EU will be able to supply goods at lower prices thereby leading to higher demand for the EU products in India, that is, trade creating.

The possibility of trade diversion cannot be discounted, however, making the net welfare effect ambiguous. Elasticities of supply and the impact of tariffs on competitiveness are other important issues which need to be considered. Given the existing comparative advantages of both trading partners, the extent of trade creation/diversion must be interpreted cautiously. The greater the difference in comparative advantages, the larger the potential gains from trade creation under the PTA.

An important factor that should also be considered is the existing pattern of trade between India and the EU such that any increased trade between them due to the PTA will be welfare enhancing for both partners. In the goods sector, this is more likely to be beneficial for India given that it has a growing consumer base and is, therefore, an important potential market from the perspective of the UK. An examination of India's trade shows that in 2007, nearly one quarter of India's imports were sourced from the EU, implying limited trade creation effects on the consumption side. This may not be the case on the production side as India and the UK have dissimilar production structures and, therefore, some opportunities for trade creation on the production side are likely to exist. Therefore, the overall effect of the PTA in terms of welfare-enhancing trade creation is ambiguous.

Essentially, the India–EU PTA, in addition to removing tariffs, should place considerable emphasis on reducing the prevalence and incidence of NTBs. Failure to do so will reduce the overall effectiveness of the PTA, inflicting costs associated with revenue diversion without providing any of the compensating benefits of competition and economies of scale. The focus of the India–EU PTA should, therefore, be on deep integration. The proposed PTA must encompass regulatory liberalization and/or harmonization, that is, product standards, testing and certification, customs procedures, bureaucracy as well as incorporate an agreement on investment, services, competition policy and intellectual property protection.

7.2 ADDRESSING NTBs WITHIN THE PROPOSED INDIA–EU PTA

As the India–EU PTA proposes to reduce 90 per cent of tariff lines to zero, effectively negating their relevance as a trade barrier outside of agriculture and a few other sectors, the importance of addressing NTBs will assume greater significance in determining the overall success and effectiveness of the PTA. Within the context of current India–EU trade patterns, NTBs arise primarily because of regulatory divergence between India and the EU. The main NTBs identified by this study, affecting India's exports to the UK, are technical regulations, standards, labelling and packaging, and testing and certification requirements. Interviews with stakeholders show that the production processes in the leather and footwear, textiles and clothing industries are chemically intensive and, as a result, the EU and UK impose regulations on these imports in the interests of consumers' health and safety. These regulations are a significant problem, particularly for India's small exporters who are, for the most part, more vulnerable than larger firms to increasing regulatory costs. Meeting buyer-specific requirement in addition to regulatory thresholds may necessitate engineering investments, the purchase of specialized equipment for production and effluent treatment systems, all of which contribute to producers' overall cost structures.

In addition to higher costs of production, Indian exporters may also suffer from the loss of economies of scale when smaller production runs are necessary in order to meet the various national standards in individual EU country markets. The inability to immediately implement mechanisms to facilitate compliance delays exporters' responses to changing consumers' demands and may result in the loss of market share as consumers shift demand to other suppliers. There are also additional domestic and trade facilitation barriers associated with poor infrastructure, high transport costs, corruption, social compliance issues and problems with customs procedures that impede Indian exports of textiles and clothing, leather and footwear to the UK.

Given the findings reported above, a set of recommendations aimed at reducing the incidence of NTBs and other barriers to trade faced by Indian exporters can be suggested. In addition to addressing trade barriers, trade facilitation and capacity building measures will be integral to successful export promotion. In order to increase market access for Indian exporters within the framework of the proposed India–EU FTA, both demand and supply side initiatives are required. Addressing existing NTBs within the context of the ongoing India–EU PTA negotiations is fundamental. Measures to support the development and adoption of internationally harmonized technical regulations in India are essential. The harmonization initiatives will be facilitated through technical and financial support from the EU. Further, discussions between Indian and EU regulatory agencies are required to identify specific areas of regulatory divergence and similarities with a view to harmonization in addition to a joint collaborative review of existing technical regulations and standards. Such an exercise could identify the central issues that need to be addressed to overcome regulatory heterogeneity over the longer term.

7.2.1 Suggestions for the Immediate Short Term

In the immediate short term, harmonization prior to the establishment of set standards is recommended. The first step will involve an identification of the leather and footwear, textiles and clothing products for which minimum, rather than higher, standards and regulations are imposed by UK buyers. Information dissemination amongst Indian exporters is necessary first, on mandatory technical standards, testing and certification, as well as labelling and packaging regulations. Second, notifications on voluntary standards will provide exporters with necessary additional compliance information. A collaborative approach involving the EU, the UK and India is recommended, so that this initial harmonization can be undertaken prior to setting levels for standards. It is important that the information on technical standards, testing and certification, labelling and packaging regulations is continuously updated.

The Indian government should complement this approach with domestic initiatives that improve the capacity of Indian industry to adapt to changing regulations and private sector standards. Incorporating accessible, interactive web sites would contribute towards disseminating this information to all Indian exporters; leather and footwear, textile and clothing exporters must be able to easily acquire compliance information whether via websites or a greater information provision role being shouldered by trade shows or industry associations. The Council for Leather Exports is an example of the latter. In addition, some means by which public comments on these issues can be received and reviewed by the regulatory agencies in India and the EU should be put in place. These measures would help ameliorate the persistent problem of information asymmetry that plagues India's leather and footwear and textile and clothing exporters.

7.2.2 Suggestions for the Medium Term

In the medium term, a three phase approach to regulatory harmonization can be suggested. It includes design, notification and enforcement of regulations and standards. To achieve the objective of regulatory harmonization, particularly in standards, testing and certification, labelling and packaging, consultations with all stakeholders, whether significantly or potentially affected in India, the EU and the UK, should be held. Consultations should occur at the earliest possible stage while reviewing or developing regulations and standards and regularly throughout the process to ensure transparency and a clear understanding amongst exporters of the regulatory environment and compliance requirements. Regular consultations with stakeholders will also help ensure that the design of the harmonization strategy can be achieved on a practical level. In this manner, harmonization would hopefully reduce the sheer multiplicity of standards faced by Indian exporters when shipping to different EU member states.

It is, however, important to ensure that exporters of leather and footwear, textiles and clothing do not bear firm-specific costs in harmonization or information dissemination. Notification of all changes should be made available electronically (or by other means such as mail or fax should electronic distribution prove difficult) as well as through help desks or industry associations in regional leather and footwear, textiles and clothing production clusters. Creating these multiple channels for the consistent dissemination of reliable, accurate information would help address the current problem of poor awareness of legislative procedures, appeals procedures, administrative guidelines and practices, as well as decision making in the different EU member states. Both the EU and Indian governments should provide for institutions to monitor the implementation of regulations and standards as well as to ensure that the institutional framework is accountable and transparent.[1]

The underlying goal of regulatory harmonization is eventual regulatory convergence between India and the EU in the longer term. In order to facilitate convergence and address the existing problems associated with regulatory heterogeneity, transparency, predictability, proportionality and a scientific basis should be substantial principles in the formulation of any policy or regulation.

Harmonization and regulatory convergence can be partially achieved in the longer term through technology transfer. Technical transfer and revitalization of technology in small-scale and medium-sized leather and footwear, textiles and clothing firms will help exporters gain access to new technology, managerial skills, information, marketing channels and equipment. Improvements in technology are critical to enabling small as well as newly exporting firms in the leather and footwear and textiles and clothing industries to implement requisite buyer-specific technical regulations. The Indian government should, in collaboration with the EU, facilitate an overall technical advancement as well as diffusion and modernization of production processes in the leather and footwear, textiles and clothing sectors. Joint India–EU efforts should focus on cleaner processing technologies and reduced effluent release by promoting the use of eco-friendly chemicals and minimizing waste. The suggested modalities to be adopted are discussed under the sector-specific sections which follow.

7.2.3 Policy Recommendations for Testing and Certification

Implementing uniform testing and certification standards, procedures and expectations will help address the problems posed by the current testing and certification environment. Establishing jointly accredited laboratories and testing centres in all regional leather and footwear, textiles and clothing production hubs in India would contribute greatly to reducing transactions costs for firms. The EU can extend support for the Indian government's efforts in this area by establishing joint accreditation bodies in regional clusters and sub-clusters. Specific recommendations to address existing NTBs pertaining to testing and certification in leather and footwear, textiles and clothing industries include:

- Improve mutual understanding amongst officials in the UK and India on testing, certification and accreditation methods to enhance information exchange between the different agencies responsible for establishing standards.

- Disseminate information on national standards, certification and accreditation procedures and establish national and regional contact points.
- Promote simplification and transparency in standards, certification information and compliance procedures.
- Promote and facilitate the alignment of EU, UK and Indian domestic standards with international standards to ensure that internationally aligned standards are embodied in their respective national laws and regulations.
- A transition period must be defined for all new laboratories and inspection bodies deemed competent to undertake specific tests or inspections (scope of accreditation) and are, therefore, accredited to issue certificates of compliance. These should be accredited by the national accreditation authorities in the EU, UK and India.
- Encourage EU, UK and Indian co-operation to promote technical and institutional capacity-building in testing, certification and accreditation in order to provide for the exchange of information on existing programmes and to ensure ease of access. In addition, potential gaps in the regulatory architecture should be highlighted so that future cooperation may be enhanced.
- The Indian government should devise a coherent policy framework that strengthens the capacity of its domestic producers to adapt to growing competition, and simultaneously allows them to capture trade opportunities that are being created through improved market access under the PTA.

7.2.4 Policy Recommendations for Labelling and Packaging

In the short term, it is suggested that the Indian government compile and provide detailed information on EU labelling and packaging requirements to its exporters. This could be accomplished by launching a network of regional/local enquiry points and help desks for exporters on a nationwide basis. In the longer term, harmonization of regulations on labelling and packaging is a means to address the problem of Indian exporters' inability to comply with disparate regulations under the existing India–UK trade environment. The Indian government could also support the development of domestic capacity in local firms to access, assess and comply with required regulations. EU importers and institutions can be encouraged to support this type of capacity building in India. The relevant EU and UK agencies could provide information and/or training to Indian exporters through the web, industry associations, trade shows, conferences and through trade consulates in India.

7.2.5 Policy Recommendations for Improved Environmental Stewardship

Concerns regarding the degradation of the environment need to be examined with a sense of urgency. Environmental stewardship has become a major issue in international trade and, while there has been little progress at the WTO, environmental provisions are increasingly being incorporated into PTAs. The Indian government and private sector leather and footwear, textiles and clothing firms, as well as other forms of manufacturing must be more pro-active in this area. The Indian government needs to correct the existing situation of non-compliance by domestic firms and also play a role in supporting exporters in meeting EU environmental requirements. India, the EU and the UK could develop the means to foster the provision of access to environmentally sound technology to Indian exporters.

Sector-specific incidence of environmental requirements that impact adversely on leather and footwear, textiles and clothing exports first need to be identified. Next, the Indian government could work strengthen domestic exporters' capacities, especially small exporters, to adopt environment-friendly technology in order to alleviate existing supply side constraints. Third, EU buyers and importers could transfer environmentally sound technology to India's exporters, particularly those buyers that have been consistently importing from specific Indian suppliers over an extended time period. The EU would thereby provide Indian leather and footwear, textile and clothing exporters with technical assistance, helping to address the issues of non-compliance with environmental regulations and overall, reducing cross-border environmental externalities. Suggested measures by which to achieve this include:

- Initiate joint programmes stressing the importance of environmentally sustainable development in the leather and footwear, textiles and clothing sectors. An initial step would be to support firms in these sectors in curbing emissions. An example of this type of effort, proposed for the leather and footwear industry, is the provision of technical support that would enable its exporters to use package scrubbers and air pollutant treatments to reduce H2S and CS2 emissions into the air.

- Provide assistance to exporting companies to upgrade manufacturing facilities and adopt environmentally-friendly technologies. Partnership programmes can be started between the EU and India to reduce pollution generation at source since end-of-pipe pollution control can only be a short-term approach to industrial environmental management. For instance, EU agencies can assist in the provision of environmental monitoring/testing equipment and services, solid waste removal technology and wastewater disposal systems.
- Conduct national and regional workshops on environmental regulations. The EU REACH Directive has generated considerable debate in India. REACH replaces 40 existing EU directives regulating chemicals used in the production of products with a single directive on all aspects of EU chemicals policy. This directive has broad application and is currently confusing for Indian exporters. Given the importance of this directive, bilateral government assistance for industry in understanding and achieving compliance should be an imperative.

7.2.6 Policy Recommendations for Information Management and Dissemination

Gathering information about new and emerging environmental and health requirements as well as effective management and dissemination of technical requirements is a critical element of any proactive adjustment strategy. Hence, it is important to address the NTB of information asymmetry. To overcome this barrier, it is important that the leather and footwear, textiles and clothing sectors in India gather information on the relevant regulations that affect them in the EU market. Measures to assist them in doing so could include:

- Establish national and regional information exchanges. At present India's exporters face major knowledge gaps, particularly on the listing of voluntary standards, buyer-specific requirements and eco-labelling schemes. These gaps can be overcome by coordinated public and private sector information-gathering initiatives. Small exporters face particular difficulties in gathering sufficient timely information and correctly interpreting it. The EU and Indian governments' efforts could, therefore, be geared towards addressing their needs.

- Early notification systems would be an effective mechanism whereby Indian exporters could obtain information on new and emerging standards and regulations in the UK and EU markets. These could include institutionalized feedback by which Indian exporters/producers can alert the government about potential difficulties they may encounter in meeting requirements.
- European buyers could provide support on REACH by providing all relevant information to their suppliers. The need for a buyer–supplier dialogue is imperative to help exporters comply with REACH.
- Participation in international fairs and exhibitions is very important. Indian leather and footwear, textiles and clothing exporters should participate in international fairs and exhibitions. In addition to serving as a means to showcase their products, vital information exchanges occur amongst industry members at such fairs.

7.2.7 Policy Recommendations for Inadequate Infrastructure

It is generally recognized that India needs to improve its existing infrastructure. An essential requirement for business development in India is the provision of efficient, reliable and affordable infrastructure services such as electrical power and water supply; road, rail and air transport and telecommunications networks. From a trade policy (NTB) perspective, efficiency in transportation, telecommunications and electricity provision are important determinants of an exporters' ability to overcome barriers to trade. High quality infrastructure will lead to a positive multiplier effect on the entire economy.

Firstly, it will reduce overall transit time, reducing overall production and logistics lags for textiles and clothing, leather and footwear exporters. Secondly, an efficient infrastructure framework would help exporters to exercise more effective control over all elements of their supply chain. Reliable infrastructure would therefore allow Indian textiles and clothing, leather and footwear exporters to better capture their competitive edge, which is currently marginalized by infrastructure deficiencies. It is important that the Indian government plays a pro-active role in the development and support of domestic infrastructure including, for example, the establishment of sustainable infrastructure linkages between modes of transport.

Suggested measures include upgrading road networks and connectivity as well as the introduction of competitive pricing for rail and air freight. Similarly, reliable transportation from production hubs to ports to minimize transit time for shipments is vital. Given the size of the investment required in order to upgrade, expand and maintain India's infrastructure, private sector involvement is critical. Public–Private partnerships (PPPs) are a potential strategy given their inherent ability to reduce corruption, increase accountability in both the public and private sectors, and promote investment in infrastructure at a reasonable cost.

The Indian government has initiated PPPs for some infrastructure development in roads, ports and airports, in part to foster a more competitive business environment. Far more, however, needs to be done. For example, port privatization has been initiated but is limited. Privatization of ports and the introduction of competition in various port services such as pilotage, towing, loading, handling and other ancillary services will increase overall efficiency. Reducing power outages is another critical aspect of infrastructure improvement. Existing textiles and clothing, leather and footwear exporters would benefit as their efforts to focus production on the higher value-added segments of the supply chain is highly dependent on uninterrupted power supplies.

The creation of more regional or sector-specific production clusters (in addition to the existing ones) might allow small and medium exporters to benefit from the rise of a common pool of resources such as technology parks, training and design institutes and common effluent management facilities. Sector-specific measures for textiles and clothing, leather and footwear are discussed in detail in the following sections.

Diffusion of new technology will also be essential in ameliorating India's overall infrastructure deficiencies. The Indian government could facilitate the acquisition and use of new technology via financial, training and technological support. This includes providing leather and footwear, textiles and clothing exporters with financial incentives to purchase new and quality used machinery that would mesh with more high technology infrastructure. Financial incentives could encompass simplifying loan disbursement procedures, providing working capital financing and technological training support.

7.2.8 Policy Recommendations for Trade Facilitation

Improvements in trade facilitation in export, import and transit procedures would facilitate export growth. Proposed measures to promote trade facilitation between the EU, UK and India include:
- Accelerated and simplified procedures for the release and customs clearance of goods;
- Promotion of standardized and simplified customs and export documentation, including, if possible, paperless systems;
- Promotion of transparency in customs regulations and procedures;
- Establishing single enquiry points to provide information on customs issues;
- Promotion of regular interaction with traders and trade representatives for better communications and interactions, particularly regarding new initiatives;
- Collection and dissemination of information on the trading partners' respective rules of origin;
- Transparent procedures for legal recourse and appeals, complaints or mediation services in the case of disputes with customs;
- Formulating a time frame for the establishment of a single window system for the clearance of products at all the major Indian ports;
- Periodic updating of customs procedures manuals, including all recent supplementary notifications and making these available on the web portal of relevant government ministries;
- Use of advanced electronic information and electronic risk analysis systems that will enable EU and Indian Customs departments to identify high-risk cargo at the initial stage of shipping and take action to control such shipments;
- Enhancing cooperation between EU and Indian customs to introduce advanced customs control equipment (non-intrusive inspection equipment, using x-ray, gamma ray and radiation scanning technologies).

7.2.9 Policy Recommendations to Address Corruption

Complicated and non-transparent labour laws in India are one reason for the perception of pervasive corruption amongst textiles and clothing, leather and footwear exporters. Therefore, active labour market programmes (ALMPs) and policies[2] that reform and strengthen existing social laws are necessary. India's restrictive labour regulations must be re-engineered to facilitate the movement and specialization of labour between and amongst firms. The provision of additional technical and vocational education programmes would contribute towards a more dynamic labour market and functional employment exchanges. Liberalization and re-design of labour regulations at the individual state level in India would also provide an opportunity for textiles and clothing, leather and footwear manufacturers to have improved access to a flexible labour resource.

Addressing the broader question of bureaucratic corruption is an extremely complex issue. Given the degree of dependence on corruption income in the public service, reforms are likely to be fiercely resisted. Of course, reform must involve public officials who clearly have a conflict between the public interest and their own welfare. One major problem is the absence in competition in the provision of government services such as approvals and inspections – each official has a local monopoly. Finding ways to provide firms with alternative suppliers of government services will likely yield considerable results. Competition will lead to reductions in the bribe price. Alternatives such as anti-corruption ministries and campaigns seldom work.

Take the example of speed money. If there were ten potential suppliers of a required signature, they could be forced to bid to provide the service to a firm requiring approval. The service provider that could provide the most expeditious approval at the lowers cost would be the only one to get paid. Competition would both lower the price and increase the speed of service. Without competition, bureaucrats can extract monopoly rents. The reality is that there is no magic formula for eliminating corruption. It will require inventive solutions. If there were a policy formula for getting rid of corruption, a wide range of countries would have used it. Corruption is, however, endemic in developing and transition economies. India's regulatory raj is legendary for the degree and sophistication of its corruption (Wade, 1985). It is unlikely that a PTA can have any real influence on a problem of this magnitude.

7.2.10 Policy Recommendations for Rules of Origin

Rules of Origin (ROO) are the criteria by which the nationality of goods (i.e. where they were produced) and subsequently, the applicable set of trade preferences are determined. ROO are crucial in any PTA to prevent trade deflection (that is, to ensure nations not party to the PTA do not route their goods through a partner nation to gain the preferential access given by the PTA to its members). The rigour of the ROO implemented by the PTA would depend upon the differential between the MFN or preferential GSP rates of duty and those conferred by the PTA; the greater the differential, the greater the perceived risk of trade deflection, the more rigorous the ROO. Methods used by ROO in granting originating status to goods include value-added criteria, change in tariff classification and process definition.

A variety of ROO could be applied to different products within the India–EU PTA framework. In general, the best guidelines for India–EU ROO would be simplicity and transparency, allowing goods of Indian origin to benefit from tariff liberalization. For Indian products manufactured with imported inputs, implementing the import value requirement, based on the relative value of domestic (Indian) to imported inputs, is advised. The import value requirement can be determined with relative ease using suppliers' invoices to support the value of the imported inputs.

In the longer term, the import value requirement on content can be replaced with the value-added tariffs approach where the preferential component is excluded from tariffs and MFN duties should be paid on the non-preferential component of the product. This would simplify the administration of the ROO requirement and support a gradual transition to zero tariffs between the PTA partners. However, merely simplifying ROO requirements may not be sufficient to meaningfully increase bilateral trade between the EU, UK and India. Capacity building could be initiated by the EU in India to address its institutional and regulatory weaknesses as well as existing supply-side production constraints.

7.3 SECTOR SPECIFIC RECOMMENDATIONS

Within the context of present EU, UK and India trade flows, the primary issues manifesting as potential barriers to trade (both NTBs and domestic barriers) are regulations and standards; inability to fulfil testing and certification requirements; labelling and packaging; environmental requirements; lack of adequate infrastructure and high transport costs; obsolete technology; and lack of information on possible market opportunities.

These issues compound existing supply-side constraints which include the predominance of small-scale operations and lack of integrated supply chains. As a result, products fail the life-cycle requirements. Other constraints include a lack of modern machinery due to poor availability of credit; overall low-skilled labour (meaning export orders cannot be produced to international norms); infrastructural bottlenecks such as poor roads, port congestion and inadequate electrical power supplies. Beyond these barriers, which could be applicable to any aspect of Indian manufacturing, there are specific issues facing the textiles and clothing, leather and footwear industries.

7.3.1 Textiles and Clothing

The principal demand side constraints faced by Indian textiles and clothing industries are competition on non-price factors and the need to upgrade the poor quality of technology to improve the quality of exports. Several initiatives are proposed to address the NTBs and other domestic barriers impeding textiles and clothing exporters. It must be noted that the success of any measures, existing or proposed, to increase the competitiveness of the textiles and clothing industry, is also predicated upon improvements in India's general infrastructure and infrastructure linkages. The absence of such improvements will greatly undermine the effectiveness of any other measures.

7.3.1.a Existing policy initiatives – textiles and clothing

The Indian government has recognized the need to improve the textiles and clothing industry and created an integrated industry approach to upgrade production technology. To improve the industry's global competitiveness, the government has removed and streamlined the restrictions on small-scale garment industries. The Indian government has already invested Rs. 60,000 crore in the textiles and clothing industry, and acknowledges that an additional minimum investment of Rs. 150,600 crore is needed during the Eleventh Plan period.[3]

Recent initiatives taken by the government to address the existing domestic barriers and the overall business environment in the textiles and clothing sector include:

- Creation of the Technology Upgrade Fund Scheme (TUFS) is the principal government initiative and includes the provision of over US$650 million for technology improvements. The scheme provides for reimbursement of 5 per cent interest paid on term loans for technological upgrades of machinery and equipment. The TUFS can be used until the final year of the 11th Five-Year Plan. There have been mixed responses to this scheme.
- A PPP-based Scheme for Integrated Textile Parks[4] was introduced to support the textile industry with infrastructure facilities for

establishing textile units that meet international environmental and social standards.

- Focus Market Scheme[5] was created to offset high freight costs.
- Other government initiatives to enhance the overall competitiveness of the apparel sector include Apparel Parks for Exports, a Textiles Centre Infrastructure Development Scheme[6] and a Technology Mission on Cotton.[7] The Indian Government has waived import duties on raw cotton, rationalized excise duty structure, reduced the customs duty on machinery and removed the duty drawback on raw cotton exports.[8] These measures are expected to boost overall competitiveness. The government has developed handloom clusters and has put in place guidelines on corporate and depreciation tax to foster the overall competitiveness of the textiles and clothing sector.

7.3.1.b Proposed policy initiatives – textiles and clothing

The government of India has also proposed new policy measures and strategies to address specific NTBs, domestic barriers and the more general problems of the textiles and clothing industry. These include:

- Develop capacity to comply with technical regulations and standards, testing and certification as well as labelling and packaging requirements. The first step is to support new investments in machinery. New machinery will enable small exporting units, in particular, to address their inability to comply. Specific modalities that have been suggested are:
    - Provision of concessional financial support to exporters for the acquisition of new and used textile machinery in order to produce higher quality textiles and garments for export. Improved machinery and equipment should enable exporters to meet technical regulations and standards at competitive prices.
    - Provision of technological support for pre-weaving machinery, yarn dyeing facilities and post-weaving processing to enable small-scale exporters to meet testing and certification requirements, as well as significantly enhancing the productive and processing capacity of the textiles sector. This will, in turn, support increased production of home textiles and garments, which comprise 80 per cent of total Indian exports to the UK.
    - Initiate measures to strengthen testing labs and assist textile facilities in securing ISO 14000 certification.

- Establish neighbourhood apparel and textiles training institutes and marketing complexes in all major textiles and clothing production clusters and sub-clusters.
- Ensure uninterrupted power supply and improve its quality. Occasional power outages adversely impacts the hosiery production industry in Tirupur which, when combined with voltage variations and the high cost of power,[9] renders such production unviable.
- Provide adequate water supply to meet the need for effluent treatment plants along with special industrial estates for power looms.
- The government should create an infrastructure blue print that identifies large clusters of industries in the existing textile and clothing production hubs and sub-hubs.

In addition to government initiatives, it is imperative that the textiles and clothing industry actively addresses the strategic linkage of exports with infrastructure and assists small exporting firms in overcoming their existing constraints. Industry-oriented recommendations to increase competitiveness include:

- A proactive role for textile and clothing associations to create common infrastructure pools that would foster the development of quality checks; extend assistance in processing, finishing and certification and taking steps to reduce overall administrative and transactions costs.
- An industry role in the provision of market information on new markets and policy guidelines. Industry associations can support small and new exporters by providing them with market information about the market demand for textiles and recent policy initiatives of the government.[10] Specialized institutions for compilation and dissemination of marketing information should be created.
- The industry should place emphasis on design and technology, quality and innovation and economies of scale. Skill development for workers engaged in the sector is vital for enhancing its export potential.

At the micro level, individual firms can contribute towards the creation of an enabling domestic environment through the identification and capitalizing upon its core strength and competencies. The small average size of Indian textiles and clothing firms is often a challenge. It limits the ability of such firms to respond to the demands of UK buyers. Individual firms should invest in information technology and communications to proactively keep themselves informed of latest sector level developments in the EU and the UK.

7.3.2 Leather and Footwear

Although it shares similar barriers as the textile and clothing industry in terms of inadequate infrastructure and the nature of most barriers to trade, the Indian leather and footwear industry also faces its own industry-specific challenges. The Indian government has implemented several initiatives to assist the industry, with several others proposed.

7.3.2.a Existing policy initiatives – leather and footwear

In recognition of the export and employment generation potential of the industry and the need to modernize and upgrade production and processing facilities, the Union government increased the financial allocation for the leather sector in the 11th Plan to Rs.1,300 crore.[11] The Indian government introduced a scheme to upgrade technology in existing tanneries, footwear, footwear components and leather product production facilities. Under the Integrated Leather Development Programme (ILDP) all leather tanning and product facilities are eligible for modernization assistance.[12] The ILDP consists of two sub-programmes, the Integrated Development of Leather Sector[13] and the Infrastructure Strengthening of Leather Sector.[14] Some other initiatives include the creation of leather parks[15] – two in Chennai and one each in Nellore, Agra and Kolkata. In addition, Kolkata and Rohtak will have government-sponsored development institutes for the industry. Design centres have also been established to improve the design capabilities of the Indian leather and footwear industry; an example is the Kolkata Leather Complex. Other steps taken to address the existing trade facilitation barriers are the free import and export of raw hides and skins, semi-finished and finished leather; de-licensing of integrated tanneries to convert raw hides and skins into finished leather; and de-reservation of some leather goods from the small-scale sector.

7.3.2.b Proposed policy initiatives – leather and footwear

The leather and footwear industry could also benefit from a number of proposed initiatives which include:

- Export cluster[16] mapping that could offer a common pool of expertise through technology parks and other common infrastructure resources to exporting SMEs in leather and footwear. This will provide the exporters access to common facilities such as testing labs, processes and footwear/garments designing, alternate power generation, consultancy services and common effluent control (for effluent from tanneries and associated footwear manufacturing industries).
- The establishment of Common Processing Zones in export clusters, which in addition to offering shared facilities, will further function as a composite unit for sales, repairs, servicing and training for leather tanning and finishing machinery, as well as machinery for leather footwear, garments and products. These would enhance exporters' ability to address NTBs and other domestic barriers as well as enhance their export competitiveness.
- The Indian government can develop additional infrastructure to help firms overcome existing domestic constraints. Exclusive leather complexes, on the lines of Calcutta Leather Complex, could be developed in other major production centres. Improvements in efficiency of ports, internal transport, customs procedures and supply chain management are also necessary for augmenting exports and overall productivity.
- The creation of a Research and Development Centre to promote research related to leather technology and technology transfer. Such a centre will enable firms to comply with health and safety, quality and environment requirements. It will also support the introduction of clean technologies at the level of exporting firms and help them meet the EU environmental requirements. The centre should aim at promoting technologies for reduction and treatment of effluents and tannery-generated wastes. In addition, these should address existing concerns about quality management, technical upgrading and productivity improvements.
- Establish training institutes to hold regular basic and refresher training along with vocational training for skilled and semi-skilled workers primarily in the leather sector. The segments covered should include tanning, leather finishing, value added, leather chemicals, components, machinery and basic effluent treatment. It is suggested that seminars and updated information be made available on standardization and total quality management, packaging for exports (training programme), quality and environmental certification (ISO 9000, ISO 14000, CE Marking etc.) as well as barcoding technology.

- The development of horizontal and vertical linkages with research laboratories, industry and user agencies through a multiplicity of programmes including electronic data processing and consultancy. It is imperative that Indian exporters participate in trade fairs, conferences and exhibitions organized in the international market. Beyond showcasing Indian leather and footwear products, such events allow exporters to acquire more knowledge regarding their industry and potential markets.

7.4 CONCLUSIONS

The detailed examination of two labour-intensive Indian manufacturing sectors provided in this chapter, as well as Chapter 6, supports the supposition that in any PTA, the devil will be in the details. Beyond the general problems related to inadequate infrastructure and endemic corruption, the trade barriers are likely to be sector-specific. Hence, it is not possible to provide a comprehensive evaluation of a PTA in any single book or study. What the results of this investigation suggest is that micro level knowledge is important. Thus, every sector of the Indian economy would be well advised to undertake a similar exercise. Firms need to be surveyed. Firms engage in trade, not governments. They deal with NTBs first hand. They need to inform governments of their concerns. Only then can trade negotiators know where they should concentrate their energies.

It is also clear that to fully reap the potential benefits of the proposed India–EU PTA, a great deal of bilateral cooperation will be required. In part, this is because the agreement will be between a modern market economy and a developing one. The technically advanced EU will have to share its knowledge with its Indian partner. Differences in levels of development are, however, only part of the story. The complexity of markets requires a cooperative approach to managing and disseminating information. Information asymmetry, as illustrated in the case of textiles and clothing, leather and footwear, can be a major barrier to trade. It cannot be corrected unilaterally. Firms and governments in both countries need to tackle the problem. Table 7.1 summarizes the areas that should be addressed by the various stakeholders in order to facilitate the EU–India PTA.

In the final chapter, the broader theme of the proposed India–EU PTA is taken up again. It is important, however, to keep in mind the lessons that have been learned in the sector level case studies. No matter how grand the vision, trade is only the sum of individual international transactions undertaken by firms that operate in business environments unique to individual industries.

Table 7.1 Issues to be addressed in order to facilitate the EU–India PTA

Areas to be addressed to facilitate the ongoing negotiations	Indian Gov't	EU	Ass'ns	Exporters L&F	Exporters T&C
Joint collaborative review to identify specific areas of regulatory divergence and similarities between the EU and India	×	×			
Support the development and adoption of internationally harmonized technical regulations	×	Support advised			
Information dissemination on standards and regulations	×	×	×		
Consultations on existing regulatory framework	×	×	×	×	×
Promote simplification and transparency in information and procedures, proportionate and science-based regulation	×	×			
Promote and facilitate the alignment of domestic standards of the EU, UK and India with international standards	×	×			
Develop capacity to comply with technical regulations and standards, testing and certification as well as labelling and packaging requirements.	×	Support advised	×		
Promote technical and institutional capacity-building in testing, certification and joint accreditation	×	×			
Harmonization and regulatory convergence	×	×			
Undertake capacity-building measures and technical assistance	×	×			
Address the existing problems in trade facilitation issues	×				
Address the issue of rules of origin under the FTA negotiations	×	×			
Develop domestic infrastructure in India, e.g. transport infrastructure, set up technology parks and Common Export Zones, infrastructural blueprints, upgrade technology, provide concessional finance, power and water supply to the exporters	×		Assist using PPP		
Promote research related to leather and textile technology and technology transfer to enable firms to comply with health & safety as well as quality requirements.	×	×	×	×	×
Emphasize the importance of environmental compliance	×		×		
Impart education, training and conduct research	×		×		
Focus on export promotion through participation in international fairs and exhibitions	×		×	×	×
Provide regular and updated market information on new markets	×		×	×	×
Set up technology parks, Common Export Zones, infrastructural blueprints	×		Promote		

NOTES

1. In OECD (2001), the elements of regulatory transparency included items such as:

    *   Consultation with interested parties.
    *   Plain language drafting of laws and regulations.
    *   Legislative simplification and codification.
    *   Registers of existing and proposed regulation.
    *   Electronic dissemination of regulatory material.
    *   Controls on regulatory discretion established through standardized, transparent procedures for making, implementing and changing regulations.
    *   Appeals processes that are clear, predictable and consistent.

2. ALMP was recommended by the International Labour Organization (ILO). ALMPs have been sub-divided broadly into three categories: direct job creation, labour market training and job brokerage (improving the match between job seekers and vacancies).
3. For details see http://sify.com/finance/fullstory.php?id=14569626.
4. This was approved in July 2005 to create new textile parks of international standards at potential growth centres.
5. The Focus Market scheme was introduced to offset high freight costs and other barriers faced by exporters in accessing select international markets with a view to enhance India's export competitiveness to these markets. This scheme allows a duty credit facility of 2.5 per cent of f.o.b rates. Sixteen additional countries including ten Commonwealth of Independent States (CIS) members have been included under the Focus Market Scheme, to complement the 57 countries notified earlier. The 16 new countries are: Armenia, Azerbaijan, Belarus, Georgia, Kazakhstan, Kyrgyzstan, Tajikistan, Turkmenistan, Ukraine, Uzbekistan, El Salvador, Dominican Republic, Guatemala, Trinidad and Tobago, Serbia Montenegro and Uruguay.
6. TCIDS Scheme came into operation effective 3 August, 2002 and is meant to upgrade infrastructure facilities of textile centres such as Tirupur, Coimbatore, Karur, Bangalore, Delhi–Noida–Gurgaon, Panipat, Ludhiana, Ahmedabad, Mumbai, Bhiwandi, Ichalkaranjee, Burhanpur, Salem–Erode, Varanasi– Mau, Meerut–Pilakhua, Surat, Sholapur, Calcutta, Chennai, Cannannor, Amritsar, Baddi, Malegaon and Bhilwara.
7. This has been launched to improve productivity and quality of cotton for manufacture and exports of competitive downstream textile products.
8. Details are available on http://www.aepcindia.com/portal/newsfull.asp?newsid=4963&catid=8.
9. The rate of power in Tamil Nadu is Rs. 3.20/unit for up to 10 KVA and the remaining power is at a higher rate, Rs. 5/unit KVA. In other Southern states, the average power cost is less – in Karnataka the costs is Rs. 3.45/unit, Kerala is Rs. 2.39/unit.
10. Small power-loom weavers were not aware of the subsidy to upgrade to semi-automatic looms by adding warp and weft stop mechanisms or about the TUF scheme. This highlights the importance of information dissemination as well as the creation of awareness on the schemes offered by the State government for the development of the textiles and clothing sector in India.
11. Out of this, Rs.300 crore is to set up leather complexes and parks; Rs. 353 crore for upgrading and establishing the institutional facilities, design and training centres; Rs. 240 crore for upgrading and installating infrastructure for environmental protection; Rs. 25 crore for the development of leather and leather goods under mission mode; and Rs. 917 crore for foreign and domestic investment promotion, research evaluation and consultancy services.

12. The assistance allowed was up to 30 per cent of the total project cost for SSI units and 20 per cent for non-SSI units; this was subject to a maximum of US$110,000 per unit.

13. The IDLS aims at technology upgrades and modernization in all segments of the leather industry, that is, tanneries, footwear components, saddlery, leather goods and garments.

14. The aim of the ISLS Scheme is to provide infrastructure facilities and capacity building in the leather and footwear sector and has 11 sub-programmes including leather complex (tannery); footwear complex; footwear component park; INTECHMART; saddlery development; human resource development; non-leather footwear; support to rural artisans; leather goods park; global benchmarking and the establishment of National Institute of Footwear Design and Technology.

15. Under this scheme, 25 per cent of the project cost is provided to units under the market access initiative scheme of the Ministry of Commerce and Industry. As a result of this scheme, several individual units have come forward to establish their own design centres.

16. A cluster may be defined as a local agglomeration of enterprises (mainly SMEs, but often also including some large enterprises), which are producing and selling a range of related and complementary products and services. A typical leather cluster includes leather tanning units, leather finishing units, leather goods producers, leather garment manufacturers, designers, sub-contractors, merchant buyers and exporters. For instance, the leather cluster in Ambur is composed of three segments. These are: integrated export-oriented leather and shoe units, job-working small tanneries and micro enterprises producing shoes for the local market. 'Footwear Design & Development Centres' have been established at Noida, Agra, Madras and Kanpur where the footwear clusters exist. These centres provide consultancy services for factory set-up, lay-outs, technology, trouble-shooting, cost reduction and productivity improvement.

8. Oh East is East, and West is West, but What if the Twain Shall Meet?

When Rudyard Kipling wrote his poem entitled The Ballad of East and West[1] over a hundred years ago he probably would have expressed considerable disbelief in what is being contemplated for the economies of India and Europe – a broad-based melding of an eastern and a western market. For many, his sentiment would hold true today. Given the hurdles one can imagine, even contemplating an India–European Union trade agreement may seem like folly. In this book, however, we have attempted to answer the question posed in our chapter title's mangling of Kipling's words; but What If the twain shall meet? What if it could be agreed that the largest developed country market will be joined to the second largest developing country market? The answer is germane not only to India and the European Union, but the rest of the world as well. When preferential trade agreements were sanctioned in the GATT[2], it was never contemplated that an entity with the trade diversion potential of and India–EU agreement would be created – or one that could garner efficiencies in economies of scale that might well prove unassailable over the long run. In some ways, an India–EU agreement is a good substitute for what could be achieved by global liberalization of trade. Given the transaction costs and vested interests associated with the WTO's 150-plus members negotiating, meaningful multilateral liberalization looks increasingly like an impossible task. Even if the Doha Round can be concluded, its ambition will be too modest to significantly enhance global market integration.

Of course, an India–EU agreement will not lead to free trade – trade will still be managed. A free trade result will not be perceived as optimal by either India or the EU. According to Gaisford and Hester (2007, p. 68):

it is important ... to acknowledge that, while free trade would allocate world resources efficiently, at least in a competitive market setting, it is seldom a reasonable policy objective for a country. Moreover, in a world of imperfect competition, where countries are asymmetric in size and power, and governments must be cognizant of a variety of conflicting interests, achieving free trade is a virtual impossibility.

The central question is what can realistically be achieved?

One reason to be optimistic about what could be achieved in an India–EU trade agreement is that neither party is particularly interested in pushing for a significant increase in market access for agricultural products. Both the Indian and the EU markets for agricultural products are heavily protected, both have significant vested interests in retaining the current protected status and both have very effective protectionist agricultural lobbies. In India's case, its defence of barriers to market access has been credited with the collapse of the WTO's Doha Round negotiations in 2008.

One of the options being discussed at the Doha Round negotiations is for a special safeguard for agricultural products that would allow countries to impose additional trade barriers when faced with a surge of imports. This special safeguard would only be available for use by developing countries. The Indian position wanted a formula for allowable increases in trade barriers that could, under certain circumstances, lead to the imposition of higher barriers than existed before Doha Round liberalization – in effect allowing an increase in trade barriers. Developed countries wanted the level of protection provided by the special safeguard capped at pre-Doha Round levels – not going backward on protectionism. India was alone in its unwillingness to compromise – but under the WTO's consensus-based decision making that was enough to suspend the Round. Regardless of the merits of the particular case, it shows the divisiveness of agricultural trade issues and the lengths that countries will go to isolate the agricultural sector from international market forces.

It may well be, however, that the agreement to disagree over special safeguards for agriculture may be symptomatic of India's discomfort with the Doha Round agriculture negotiations. India, along with Brazil and China, were the major players in the G-20 group of developing countries that came together to challenge the hegemony of developed countries – particularly the group known as the Quad (the US, the EU, Japan and Canada) – at WTO negotiations. While united in their ambition to get a better deal for developing countries at the WTO, differences over the question of market access for agricultural products weakened the effectiveness of the G-20 at the negotiations. Brazil, which is a large agricultural exporter, wanted an aggressive stance taken by the G-20 on liberalization of market access. On the other hand, India did not wish to liberalize access to its agricultural markets. As a result, and to Brazil's chagrin, the G-20 focussed its efforts on elimination of the export subsidies on agricultural products of developed countries.

The EU has a long history of protecting its agricultural markets from international competition. Barriers to market access underpin two important pillars of the EU's Common Agricultural Policy (CAP). Barriers to imports are used to protect agricultural producers facing international competition. They are also necessary for the functioning of the CAP's export subsidy regime (Gaisford et al., 2003). While the EU made concessions during the Doha Round regarding its export subsidy regime, meaningful progress on increasing market access has been much more difficult. The agricultural sector has always been treated as being an exceptional sector where government intervention, including protection from imports, was the norm. Of course, this perception of the agricultural sector is widespread among developed countries. According to Skogstad (2008, p. 9):

> The interpretive framework that guided agricultural policies in most industrialized countries – including the United States, Western European nations, Japan and Canada – in the post-Second World War period rested on the belief that agriculture was an exceptional economic sector and without government intervention, agricultural producers, consumers and society at large would be adversely affected.

While problems with competing agricultural exporting countries and the cost of CAP subsidy programmes have led, of necessity, to reforms of the CAP in recent years, the protective market access regime has remained essentially intact – with the exception of the removal of variable levies as a policy option as a result of the Uruguay Round. Market access has remained the most contentious issue for the EU at the Doha Round's agricultural negotiations. Thus, the prospect of having a trade agreement with a country that is undemanding as far as agricultural market access goes has implicit appeal for the EU. Hence, having agricultural market access off the table during the negotiations is desirable from the viewpoint of both India and the EU.

Having liberalization of market access for agricultural products off the table in a potential India–EU PTA might mean that the agreement would not be sanctioned by the WTO. According to Article XXIV.8 (a) (i) and Article XXIV.8 (b) of the GATT, customs unions or free trade areas should encompass substantially all trade. These provisions, however, are seen as weak provisions that have never been fully tested in the WTO (Perdikis, 2007). It seems unlikely that the WTO would raise objections on these grounds to the formation of a PTA between two major economies such as India and the EU.

If agriculture is off the table in the negotiations, then the prospects for what can be achieved in the negotiations are likely to hinge on the next most contentious sector(s). To our mind, and hence why they have been the focus of this book, the textiles and apparel and the footwear industries have this potential. Labour-intensive manufacturing, of which textiles, apparel and footwear are the sectors that show the greatest degree of unrealized comparative advantage (leaving aside transaction cost issues), has been fighting a long rearguard action in developed countries since the inception of the GATT in 1947. While, at times, various versions of the Multi-fibre Agreement and its predecessors may have actually been able to roll back any apparent liberalization gains, these successes were tactical in nature rather than strategic. The pressure to liberalize comes not only from countries with comparative advantages in labour-intensive production but also from some internal constituents in developed countries.

Unlike the agricultural sector, neither the workers in these sectors, nor their employers, have been able to acquire (or generate) the mantle of being considered exceptional. Italy's high end clothiers and cobblers may have come closest by branding themselves as artisans. For the most part, the low-paid, poor working condition jobs in these sectors in developed countries have been perceived as not being the types of jobs that were worth saving. Employers in these sectors were often seen as latter-day Simon Legrees for employing people at such low wages and in such poor working conditions.

As a result, there was little sympathy for the sector – although the plight of workers received sympathy – among the constituency interested in fostering international development in developed countries. They perceived the removal of trade barriers to labour intensive manufactures as an essential prerequisite to industrialization in labour-rich countries. They could be a powerful domestic political presence that had to be taken account of by politicians.

This does not mean that those with vested interests in protection for these sectors have not been strident in their defence of their protection, or ineffective. They have simply not been able to associate themselves with the general good as has been the case with farmers. The closest they have come to being able to make these types of arguments has been a result of the geographic concentration of these industries. The spectre of the closing of a textile mill or shoe manufacturer that was the sole industrial employer in a town – and the commensurate loss of community – has been a powerful image of considerable use to protectionists. For the most part, however, the vested interests have had to forego the cover provided by being able to be associated with the general good and ask that protection be maintained for their interest directly. This is simply a much harder case to make.

In negotiations between India and the EU, the Commission can be expected to fight hard and cunningly to retain as much protection as possible for these sectors. The momentum is, however, with an Indian push for liberalization for these sectors. In particular, India will see these sectors as being areas where they can make gains against their international competitors by obtaining preferred access. EU officials know that this is the area where India can see potential benefits arising from the agreement – and that they will have to give concessions to obtain what they want in terms of access to India's protected sectors in services, infrastructure, capital equipment and technology-intensive manufactures. Hence, the devil will be in the details.

As suggested in the previous chapters, India's negotiators are going to have to be well informed regarding the non-tariff barriers that can restrict imports of textiles, apparel and footwear. While removal of tariffs is important, little market access is likely to be gained if non-tariff barriers are not also addressed in a significant way. The first step is being informed about the non-tariff barriers that exist. The work in the previous chapters provides the first step in this direction. The sectors are complex with a vast array of product lines and where non-tariff barriers may be specific to individual product lines. Governments cannot possible know the scope of non-tariff barriers without the assistance of industry – after all they are the ones that run into non-tariff barriers on a day-in and day-out basis. Of course, when trade does not currently occur due to tariffs or other obvious barriers to trade, firms may not be able to easily discern what lies hidden behind the more transparent barriers. Studies that delve deeply into EU regulations and standards are the only method by which governments, and hence their negotiators, can obtain information on these opaque barriers to trade.

Of course, the EU will have non-tariff barriers in these sectors that they will simply not agree to remove – particularly in the area of standards. Some opaque barriers may not be discovered until the formal barriers are removed. Some barriers to trade – more correctly commerce – may arise from practices or requirements originating in the private sector. The removal of formal barriers and transparent non-tariff barriers will lead to opportunities for Indian firms. Being ready to capitalize on those opportunities is the key to reaping the benefits of the agreement and to being able to realize what India expects from the agreement. Being export-ready, however, is a major challenge.

Firms that have not had access to a foreign market are unlikely to be export ready – why would they? With a trade agreement on the horizon, however, there needs to be a concerted effort by firms to get ready – and governments have a role to play in this process. This is particularly true for the textile, apparel and footwear sectors in India that have remained relatively small-scale and often have little management experience in the international commercial arena. Governments can help bridge that gap. They can foster the development of industry associations that can facilitate the sharing of information on EU standards and other requirements. They can provide funds for short training courses for company officials. They can provide venues in India for local businessmen to interact with Europeans directly or electronically. They can directly provide information on EU standards. It is important that the Indian government understand that its role does not end with the negotiation of the agreement – that is just the beginning.

Firms in the EU will also face non-tariff barriers and transaction-cost-increasing business practices when they attempt to take advantages of the opportunities provided by the removal of barriers to trade in both services and goods arising from the agreement. The Indian regulatory raj is notoriously opaque. Successfully navigating it will require both patience and a considerable investment in human capital. Indian business culture is very sophisticated – but the culture differs considerably from that in the European Union. European business models cannot simply be transferred to the Indian environment. Differences in business culture simply translate into additional transaction costs. Sometimes those transaction costs will be sufficiently high to make what on the surface appears to be a mutually profitable opportunity no longer attractive. Again, while many EU-based firms may be better positioned to make the necessary transaction-cost-reducing investments, particularly in human capital, to have success in the Indian market, there will still be a role for both EU institutions and governments of the member states in getting their firms export-ready. Again, the job is not finished once the agreement is signed.

Over time, as the integration of the Indian and EU economies deepens, business cultures and transaction-cost-increasing aspects of the regulatory regimes will begin to change. As vested interests in the agreement grow, so too will the pressure for transaction-cost-reducing innovations and regulatory reforms. This process is at the heart of the deepening of economic integration. The overwhelming majority of these changes will be the result of altering business practices and lobbying for changes to domestic laws and regulations. The agreement itself, however, may need to be amended. Renegotiation provisions need to be explicitly built into the agreement – and they must be carefully constructed.

One of the major failings of the NAFTA agreement, for example, is that it has no renegotiation mechanism (Kerr, 2006). As a result, the NAFTA looks increasingly like a one shot deal. While there are areas where the agreement is flawed and where opportunities for both the broadening and deepening of North American economic integration could be fostered, there is no mechanism to allow such a progression. While each country has the right to unilaterally leave the NAFTA – and hence attempt to force renegotiation – this would likely be viewed sceptically by the other partner countries. As a result, new negotiations may not be agreed – meaning the countries revert to WTO rules including the re-imposition of tariffs – or that the negotiations would be conducted with a considerable degree of acrimony. The alternative would be mutually agreed renegotiation. Opening the entire agreement for renegotiation, however, would lead to considerable pressure by protectionist interests to roll back provisions of the agreement that they considered not to have been in their interest. Given the unequal bargaining power of the US in any future negotiations, Canada and Mexico both worry about US attempts to roll back aspects of the agreement. As a result, they will not agree to a full-scale renegotiation of the agreement. Further progress on economic integration is effectively blocked.

In the WTO, however, there is a mechanism to move the process forward. WTO members can agree to launch a new Round of negotiations. Implicit in this process is that there can be no retreat from what has already been achieved. For example, tariffs are bound and a new round of negotiations cannot raise them – hence the principled objection to India's position on the special safeguard for agricultural products in the Doha Round negotiations. Further, an agenda on what aspects of the WTO agreements will be opened for negotiations must be agreed by the members – for example, the WTO's Agreement on the Application Sanitary and Phytosanitary Measures was not opened for renegotiation in the Doha Round. Hence, it is possible to move forward at the WTO without providing an opportunity for protectionists to have existing provisions reversed. The proposed India–EU agreement should have an explicit renegotiation clause that includes: (1) a no roll-back clause; (2) a mutual agreement on re-opening the agreement: (3) and a clause allowing for mutual agreement on which aspects of the agreement will be re-opened.

Trade agreements need to be living documents that can be adjusted to enhance the benefits of market integration. Of course, sovereignty is always guaranteed through the ability of parties to give notice of their withdrawal from the agreement.

The NAFTA experience also suggests that for an undertaking of the magnitude of an India–EU trade agreement, an institutional infrastructure needs to be put in place. The NAFTA institutions have proved to be too sparse. The EU model with its Commission and dispute settlement body will better foster integration. Unlike the EU, where the Commission actively promotes the European Union, no institution speaks for North America. The NAFTA institutions, such as they are, consist of individuals representing the interests of the individual governments. EU Commissioners are explicitly expected to take an EU view rather than promote the interests of their governments. The Commission brings forth EU-wide initiatives. Creating such institutions does not mean that a project as ambitious as the EU is being contemplated for the India–EU relationship, but it will help make the trade agreement a living document as opposed to the largely atrophied NAFTA.

The joining of two large economies such as India and the EU needs to be approached from a long-term perspective. Rapid changes in trade rules threaten existing investments in both physical and human capital. Instead of a rapid opening of markets, long phase-ins should be built into the agreement – up to twenty years to allow existing investments to be depreciated and some less malleable human capital to retire. The phase-ins should be gradual and, most importantly, be transparent so that they can be anticipated. East can meet West, but they will need time to get to know each other. In the beginning, exploitable advantages and perceived threats will likely define the commercial environment. The participants must build the trust that allows the joint perception of beneficial opportunities.

NOTES

1.   Kipling's famous poem starts with these four lines:

   Oh East is East, and West is West, and never the twain shall meet,
   Til Earth and Sky stand presently by God's great judgement Seat
   But there is neither East nor West, Border, nor Breed, nor Birth
   When two strong men stand face to face, tho' they come from the ends of the earth!

   An accessible version of Rudyard Kipling's Ballad of East and West can be found at: www.everypoet.com.

2.   Not that there was ever a choice not to sanction preferential trade agreements. They are simply a fact of relations among governments that had to be accommodated in the international trade architecture.

Appendix A

Table A.1 UK imports of leather and leather products, 1996 and 2006

		2006				1996		
Rank	Partner Name	Trade Value (US$ mil)	Share (%)	Rank	Partner Name	Trade Value (US$ mil)	Share (%)
	World	408	100.0		World	404	100.0
1	Italy	127	31.0	1	Italy	139	34.4
2	China	57	14.1	2	United States	22	5.5
3	Germany	23	5.7	3	Germany	20	5.0
4	**India**	**23**	**5.7**	**4**	**India**	**19**	**4.7**
5	Ethiopia	16	3.9	5	France	18	4.5
6	Spain	15	3.6	6	Netherlands	16	3.9
7	Netherlands	14	3.4	7	China	13	3.3
8	United States	13	3.3	8	Hong Kong	13	3.3
9	Austria	12	2.8	9	Brazil	13	3.2
10	Hong Kong	11	2.6	10	Spain	12	3.1
11	Poland	9	2.3	11	Thailand	12	2.9
12	Thailand	9	2.3	12	Belgium	10	2.5
13	France	8	1.9	13	Argentina	7	1.8
14	Belgium	6	1.5	14	Portugal	6	1.6
15	Malaysia	6	1.5	15	Uruguay	6	1.5
16	Taiwan	5	1.2	16	Canada	5	1.2
17	Brazil	4	1.0	17	Nigeria	5	1.1
18	Argentina	4	0.9	18	Ireland	4	1.0
19	Hungary	4	0.9	19	Denmark	4	1.0
20	Turkey	3	0.8	20	Taiwan, China	4	1.0

Note: Leather and Leather Products 61 (Leather Manufactures) SITC Rev.3.

Source: WITS (COMTRADE) and Khorana et al. (2008).

Table A.2 UK imports of textile and textile products, 1996 and 2006

	2006				1996		
Rank	Partner Name	Trade Value (US$ mill)	Share (%)	Rank	Partner Name	Trade Value (US$ mill)	Share (%)
	World	30456	100.0		World	18539	100.0
1	China	6387	21.0	1	Hong Kong	1783	9.6
2	Turkey	2899	9.5	2	Italy	1598	8.6
3	Italy	1844	6.1	3	Germany	1365	7.4
4	Belgium	1815	6.0	4	Belgium	1127	6.1
5	**India**	**1434**	**4.7**	5	France	986	5.3
6	Germany	1425	4.7	**6**	**India**	**839**	**4.5**
7	Bangladesh	1336	4.4	7	United States	779	4.2
8	France	1208	4.0	8	China	778	4.2
9	Hong Kong	1025	3.4	9	Portugal	693	3.7
10	Netherlands	957	3.1	10	Turkey	692	3.7
11	Sri Lanka	774	2.5	11	Netherlands	632	3.4
12	Romania	740	2.4	12	Ireland	612	3.3
13	Pakistan	681	2.2	13	Indonesia	531	2.9
14	Portugal	586	1.9	14	Pakistan	479	2.6
15	Indonesia	518	1.7	15	Bangladesh	369	2.0
16	Morocco	502	1.6	16	Spain	288	1.6
17	Spain	462	1.5	17	Sri Lanka	282	1.5
18	United States	446	1.5	18	Malaysia	276	1.5
19	Thailand	347	1.1	19	Thailand	259	1.4
20	Ireland	299	1.0	20	Israel	254	1.4

Note: Textile & Textile Products: 26+65+84 of SITC Rev.3.

Source: WITS (COMTRADE) and Khorana et al. (2008).

Appendix B: Methodology of the Study Commissioned to Analyse NTBs Faced by Indian Exporters in the UK

B.1 METHODOLOGY

This section draws heavily on the research study 'Convergence Towards Regional Integration between the EU and India: Trade Implications for the UK and India', commissioned by the British High Commission in India, to analyse NTBs that currently impede trade between the UK and India in the leather and footwear, textiles and clothing sectors.[1]

Postal and personal interviews as well as consultations with stakeholders, trade associations, policy makers and academia were conducted throughout India during 2007–08.

The surveys and interviews conducted for this study involved the use of a questionnaire that addressed the following issues:

a) Factual information pertaining to the respondents, that is, turnover of the firm, location, and export/import experience. The main objective was to determine whether the perception of the incidence of NTBs in the present India–UK trade varies according to the respondent firm's size and export experience.
b) Indian exporters perception of the existing NTBs, domestic and trade facilitation barriers in EU–India trade and how this impacts on the existing pattern of trade between the partner countries.
c) The general perception of UK companies of the barriers faced when trading with India.

B.1.1 Modalities Used to Implement the Study in India

B.1.1.a Sample selection A postal survey and personal interviews were conducted. The sample selection for the textiles and clothing sector was based on information available from the Apparel Exports Promotion Council (AEPC) and the Confederation of Textile Industry in New Delhi. Similarly, the sample of firms selected in the leather and footwear sector was based on information provided by the Council for Leather Exports (CLE), Chennai. This sample included firms exporting different product groups to various destinations, with a variety of experience and turnover.

B.1.1.b Geographic distribution The study was conducted across India but was focussed primarily in the production hubs for leather and textiles. The textiles and clothing exporters interviewed were located in the hubs of Tirupur, Bangalore, Mumbai and Delhi. In the South, textiles exporters were interviewed in Tirupur (knitwear cotton), Coimbatore (yarn), Erode (yarn and fabrics) and Bangalore (basic and fashion garments). In the West, the main textiles hubs are Mumbai (for made-ups and fashion garments); Delhi, Noida and Gurgaon (for fashion and basic garments) in the North. The majority of leather and footwear firms are located in Tamil Nadu, West Bengal and Uttar Pradesh; the primary producing areas for leather footwear and accessories production. The main leather and footwear exporters interviewed were located in Chennai, Agra and Kanpur (footwear manufacturing), Delhi and Kolkata (leather accessories).[2]

B.1.1.c Personal interviews A total of 60 interviews were conducted in India by the research teams. Relevant industry associations, trade associations, export councils and policy planners working at various levels in the government were also consulted.

B.1.2 Modalities Used to Implement the Study in the UK

B.1.2.a Sample selection modalities Her Majesty's Revenue & Customs provided the UK with trade statistics and data regarding trading partners in the various product groups. Data was available at the 8-digit level which was then aggregated, providing the main importers in the target product groups of leather and footwear and textiles and clothing. The results show that 22,645 UK firms imported leather and footwear, textiles and clothing products from all over the world. Of these, the top 5 five per cent of importers (679 firms) were selected for the preliminary postal survey. The importers targeted for the postal survey were selected on the basis of the highest import values in each of the product groups, that is, in leather and footwear (HS 41, 42, 64, 67); textiles and clothing (HS 52, 57, 61, 62, 63). Hence, the product groups with the highest import values included the largest number of importers in the sample. Given that some firms imported under both of the product groups, adjustments for the double entries were made which resulted in a final sample of 485 firms. These selected firms were classified into four major categories: hypermarkets/supermarkets; retailers; internet shopping stores and specialty stores. The postal survey was tested on a small sample of firms (at the end of January 2008) and the final survey sent out to 485 firms in February 2008 but resulted in low response rates.

B.1.2.b Interviews and meetings with stakeholders In the UK, the main business houses, importers, business councils and trade associations were contacted in late February/early March 2008. Semi-structured interviews began in April (after most of the interviews had been completed in India) and these continued until late May. A total of 25 importers, business councils and trade associations were interviewed regarding their opinions (of the businesses, trade promotion organizations and business councils) on problems faced in exporting to India. In addition, telephone interviews were conducted with some importers to assess their perception to trading with India after the EU–India FTA has been finalized.

B.1.3 Consultations

B.1.3.a Consultations with the stakeholders, policy planners and academic community are an important and integral part of this study. These consultations were conducted after the end of the first and second phase of the project in India and the UK, respectively. Consultations were held of the basis of continuous feedback from exporters and importers, the different associations and policy planners. Great care was taken to ensure fair representation of stakeholders in textiles and clothing, leather and footwear throughout the course of the study. For instance, all textiles and clothing as well as leather and footwear exporters and importers associations, producer/consumer organizations, regional experts and academics working on India and EU trade issues were consulted. The underlying goal of this exercise was to involve the stakeholders and solicit the opinion of industry associations, policy planners and academics working on similar issues to increase the overall credibility of the project. In addition, dissemination and discussion of the preliminary findings of the study was carried out through organized focus group discussions with the relevant industry organizations and policy planners, both in India and the UK.

B.1.3.b Focus group discussions in the UK The stakeholders' participation session held in London in May included 20 distinguished trade practitioners, academics, trade associations and business councils working on leather and footwear, textiles and clothing as well as policy planners from the UK and Indian governments. The discussions started with an overview on the present state of talks on the EU–India FTA and the preliminary findings of the study. The main issues deliberated upon were the barriers faced by the UK firms trading with India as well as NTBs faced by Indian exporters in the UK.

B.1.3.c Stakeholders' workshop Stakeholders' participation was organized through a workshop in New Delhi in August 2008. The event was attended by officials from the Indian government including the Ministry of Commerce and Industry, the Ministry of Textiles, Export Promotion Councils, business confederations, leading exporters, academia and the media. The main issues addressed were NTBs as well as the domestic and trade facilitation barriers faced by the Indian exporters and how these have the potential to impact adversely on existing UK–India trade.

B.2 Descriptive Statistics

Personal interviews were held with 60 Indian exporters (30 in leather and footwear and 30 in textiles and clothing). The interview questionnaire had two parts: the first part included questions on the exporting firms' characteristics, for example, the firm's main sector of activity, total turnover, total number of employees, total years of production and export experience. In the second part of the questionnaire, the exporters were asked to rank their perception on the incidence of NTBs, domestic and trade facilitation barriers. The questions were scaled on a five-point Likert scale from 5 to 1. The exporters were asked to rate their perception of the incidence of various NTBs, domestic and trade facilitation barriers faced in the current UK–India trade. The scale used was 5 = very significant barrier; 4 = significant barrier; 3 = somewhat significant barrier, that is, this barrier was considered and perceived as important by the exporter but his firm could manage to overcome this barrier; essentially this was interpreted by the firm on behalf of itself; 2 = not a significant barrier; and 1 = not an issue at all, i.e., this was not perceived to be a barrier because the respondents did not face this barrier in trading with the UK.

An assessment of the interview results helped us evaluate the first hand exporter's specific experience. It also gave us insights on how differences in regulatory regimes and asymmetric information have the potential to impede trade between the partner countries. This section classifies three main trade barriers (other than tariffs) faced by leather and footwear, textiles and clothing exporters in India:

(i) NTBs: These barriers relate mainly to the Technical Barriers to Trade Agreement (TBT)[3] of the WTO. Some examples of NTBs faced relate to regulations and standards; testing and certification; labelling and packaging. Other barriers identified were environmental compliance and information asymmetry.

(ii) Domestic barriers: The main barriers identified by the exporters in trading with the EU, the UK and any other country are inadequate infrastructure, high transport costs, corruption and theft, and legal differences, that is, legal procedures between the partner countries.

(iii) Barriers related to trade facilitation: Examples of these barriers were customs procedures which include valuation, clearance, administrative and documentation formalities.

NOTES

1. UK was India's fourth largest trading partner in goods and accounted for 4 per cent of total Indian exports.
2. Regional production statistics provided by the CLE shows that other areas where leather and its products are manufactured are Mumbai, Jalandhar, Hyderabad, Ambala, Gurgaon, Panchkula and Karnal. These are, however, not regional hubs but areas where the manufacturing sector has developed.
3. The Technical Barriers to Trade Agreement (TBT) tries to ensure that regulations, standards, testing and certification procedures do not create unnecessary obstacles. However, the agreement also recognizes countries' rights to adopt the standards they consider appropriate – for example, for human, animal or plant life or health, for the protection of the environment or to meet other consumer interests. For details see http://www.wto.org/english/tratop_e/tbt_e/tbtagr_e.htm. An example of how regulations can potentially impact trade is the REACH legislation of the EU. For details see http://www.wto.org/english/new_s/news07_e/tbt_9nov07_e.htm.

Appendix C: Administrative and Documentation Formalities to be Fulfilled by Indian Exporters

The report by Khorana et al. (2008) highlighted the different administrative and documentation formalities needed to be fulfilled by Indian exporters. These are:

1. Procurement of various multiple registrations including acquiring permanent account number, importer–exporter code number, business identification number, SSI registration (for small units), sales tax registration, opening and maintaining a Running Bond Account with the Maritime Collector of Central Excise, registration with export promotion councils, and so on.
2. Procurement of an export order and its processing which includes terms and conditions of contract, mode of payment, and confirmation of the order by exporter.
3. Procurement/manufacture of goods, as per the specifications of the importer, by securing pre-shipment finance from a bank on the basis of security of letter of credit (L/C) or Confirmed Export Order or Personal bond along with Export Credit Guarantee Corporation (ECGC) policy.
4. Clearance by Excise Authorities from the premise of the exporter after physical verification on payment of duty and subsequent rebate or clearance under bond. The next step includes fulfilling the requirement of quality control and pre-shipment Inspection.

5.   Dispatch of goods to the gateway port for shipment by road or rail, and requisite application to the insurance company to obtain insurance cover for various risks.

6.   Completion of formalities relevant to a member of the export promotion council or floor price regulation, canalization, certificate of origin, ECGC cover, consular invoice, export license, and so on, wherever may be required.

7.   Documents required by Clearing & Forwarding (C&F) agent for processing prior to shipment are the following:

   (a) Commercial invoice
   (b) Original export order
   (c) Original copy of L/C
   (d) Original GR1 or SDF form (this form is now waived by the Reserve Bank of India (RBI) for shipment values less than US$25,000)
   (e) Original AR-4A/AR-4 form with duplicate copies
   (f) Original excise gate pass
   (g) Packing and weight lists
   (h) Certification of inspection
   (i) Declaration form in triplicate
   (j) Consular invoice, where necessary
   (k) Export license, where necessary
   (l) Endorsement regarding floor price, canalization, and so on, where necessary
   (m) Purchase Memo on demand, where necessary
   (n) Railway or lorry receipt
   (o) Certificates of origin

8.   The C&F agent takes delivery of the goods from the rail or road carrier and arranges for storage in a warehouse until a carting order is received from the port authorities. In the meantime the agent prepares the shipping bill with requisite details for customs clearance. The shipping bill along with the other documents listed above is submitted to the export department of the Customs House for examination.

9.   On clearance of the shipping bill by the Customs Authorities, the C&F agent presents the port trust with a copy of the shipping bill to the Shed Superintendent of the port authorities and obtains a Carting order to bring the export consignment into the transit shed for physical examination. Thereafter, a Dock Challan with the requisite details along with an assessment of Dock charges payable is prepared.

10. The Dock Challan and the Shipping Bill are forwarded to the preventive officer for physical examination of the goods and 'Let Ship/Let Export' endorsement.
11. On payment of port charges, the C&F agent obtains the Mate Receipt from the port authorities. It is then presented to the Customs Preventive Officer to certify the fact of shipment on all copies of the Shipping Bill, AR-4A/AR-4 form, and other documents.
12. The Mate Receipt is presented usually to the Agent of the shipping company to obtain the requisite number of originals and copies of the Bill of Lading.
13. The C&F agent then forwards to the exporter the following documents:
    (a) Full set of Bill of Lading
    (b) Export Promotion copy of the shipping bill
    (c) Copies of customs invoice
    (d) Duplicate copy of AR-4A/AR-4 form
    (e) Duplicate copy of GR1/ SDF form, where necessary
    (f) Copies of commercial invoice duly attested by customs
    (g) Original export order
    (h) Original L/C
14. On receipt of these documents, the exporter sends to the importer the shipment advice and forwards the following documents:
    (a) Non-negotiable copy of the Bill of Lading
    (b) Customs invoice
    (c) Commercial invoice
    (d) Packing list
15. He also files a claim with the Maritime Collector of Central excise in the port town for rebate of central excise duty or to get credit in the bond account.
16. The exporter secures payment for the value of the export consignment on presentation and processing of the following documents to the negotiating bank.
    (a) Bill of exchange, first and second exchange
    (b) Full set of Bill of Lading (clean on board), all negotiable copies and one non-negotiable copy
    (c) Original copy of L/C
    (d) Two copies of commercial invoice
    (e) Two copies of customs invoice, if necessary
    (f) Two copies of Certificates of Origin
    (g) Two copies of packing list

     (h) Two copies of Marine Insurance Policy
     (i) Four copies of bank certificate
     (j) Additional copies of commercial invoice to be certified by the bank and returned to the exporter
     (k) Consular invoice, where necessary

17.   The negotiating bank transmits/sends the following documents to the banker of the importer by first class air mail/express courier followed by a second set of these documents by second class air mail/courier to ensure receipt of at least one set, if the other is lost in transit or delayed. (Messages through SWIFT are authorized).
     (a) Bill of exchange
     (b) Negotiable Bill of Lading
     (c) Commercial Invoice
     (d) Customs Invoice
     (e) Insurance Policy
     (f) Certificate of Origin
     (g) Consular invoice, Export certificate, where necessary

18.   Packing list

19.   The negotiating bank transmits/sends the duplicate copy of the GR1/SDF form to the Exchange Control Department of the RBI. The original copy of the bank certificate, along with attested copies of the commercial invoice are returned to the exporter, and the duplicate copy of the bank certificate is forwarded to the Joint Directorate General of Foreign Trade, Import & Exports of the area on repatriation/receipt of the bill payment.

References

Ahluwalia, I.J. (2007), *Indian Economy: Looking Ahead*, Development Centre Seminar, 22 June, Paris: OECD.

Aksoy, A. (1991), The Indian Trade Regime, Policy Research Working Paper # 989, Washington, DC: The World Bank.

Amjadi, A. and A. Yeats (1995), *Non-Tariff Barriers: What Did the Uruguay Round Accomplish and What Remains to be Done?*, World Bank Policy Research Paper No: 1439, Washington, DC: The World Bank.

Andriamananjara, S., J. Dean, M. Ferrantino, M. Feinberg, R. Ludema and M. Tsigas (2004), 'The Effects of Non-Tariff Measures on Prices, Trade, and Welfare: CGE Implementation of Policy-Based Price Comparisons', *Social Science Research Network*; online access at papers.ssrn.com.

Arun, S. (2008), 'Non–Tariff barriers pose hurdle for exporters', *Financial Times*, 3 June, New Delhi, available at: http://www.financialexpress.com/news/nontariff-barriers-pose-hurdles-for-exporters/317727/3 (accessed: 28 May, 2009).

Arun, T.G. and F.I. Nixon (2000), 'Privatisation in India: "….miles to go"?', in N. Perdikis (ed.), *The Indian Economy: Contemporary Issues*, Aldershot: Ashgate.

Asian Development Bank (ADB) (2006), *Asian Development Outlook: 2006*, Manila, Phillippines: Asian Development Bank.

Bakhshi, S. and W.A. Kerr (2008), 'Incorporating Labour Standards in Trade Agreements: Protectionist Ploy or Legitimate Trade Policy Issue?', *International Journal of Trade and Global Markets*, 1(4), 373–391.

Baldwin, R. (1970), *Non-Tariff Distortions in International Trade*, Washington, DC: Brookings Institution.

Beaulieu, E. (2007), 'Trade in Services', in W.A. Kerr and J.D. Gaisford (eds), *Handbook on International Trade Policy*, Cheltenham, UK and Northampton, MA, USA: Edward Elgar, pp. 150–62.

Beghin, J.C. (2006), Non Tariff Barriers, Working Paper 06-WP 438, December, Ames, IA: Center for Agricultural and Rural Development, Iowa State University, available at: http://www.econ.iastate.edu/researc h/webpapers/paper_12703.pdf, (accessed: 26 May, 2009).

Bessel, K.M., J.E. Hobbs and W.A. Kerr (2006), 'Food Safety and Private International Law: Liability, Traceability and Transboundary Marketing', *Journal of International Food and Agribusiness Marketing*, 18(1 and 2), 29–48.

Bhattacharyya, B. (1999), 'Non-Tariff Measures on India's Exports: An Assessment', *Occasional Paper* No. 16, New Delhi: Indian Institute of Foreign Trade.

Bhattacharyya, B. and S. Mukhopadhaya (2002), *Non-Tariff Measures on South Asia's Exports: An Assessment*, Delhi: South Asian Association for Regional Cooperation (SAARC).

Bora, B., A. Kuwahara and S. Laird (2002), 'Quantification of Non-Tariff Measures: Policy Issues in International Trade and Commodities', *Study Series* No. 18., Geneva: UNCTAD.

BusinessDictionary.com (2009), 'non-tariff barrier (NTB)', Web Finance, Inc., available at: http://www.businessdictionary.com/definition/non-tariff-barrier-NTB. html, (accessed: 27 May, 2009).

Calof, J.L. (1994), 'The Relationship Between Firm Size and Export Behaviour Revisited', *Journal of International Business Studies*, 25(2), 367–87.

Cameron, R. and K. Loukine (2001), *Canada–European Union Trade and Investment Relations: The Impact of Tariff Elimination*, Ottawa, ON: Government of Canada, Department of Foreign Affairs and International Trade, Trade and Economic Analysis Division (EET).

Chaturvedi, S. and G. Nagpal (2002), WTO and Product Related Environmental Standards: Emerging Issues and Policy Options Before India, Discussion Paper #36, New Delhi: Research and Information System for Developing Countries (RIS).

Clement, N.C., G. del Castillo Vera, J. Gerber, W.A. Kerr, A.J. MacFadyen, S. Shedd, E. Zepeda and D. Alarcon (1999), *North American Economic Integration – Theory and Practice*, Cheltenham, UK and Northampton, MA, USA: Edward Elgar.

Daly, M. and H. Kuwahara (1998), 'The Impact of the Uruguay Round on Tariff and Non-Tariff Barriers to Trade in the "Quad"', *World Economy*, 21(2), 207–34.

Das, D.K. (2001), 'Some Aspects of Productivity Growth and Trade in Indian Industry', Unpublished Ph.D. dissertation, Delhi: Delhi School of Economics, University of Delhi, November.

Das, D.K. (2003), Quantifying Trade Barriers: Has Protection Declined Substantially in Indian Manufacturing, Working paper #105, New Delhi: Indian Council for Research on International Economic Relations (ICRIER), July.

Davidson, P. (1990), 'A Post Keynesian Positive Contribution to "Theory"', *Journal of Post Keynesian Economics*, 13(2), 298–303.

De Chiara, A. and A. Minguzzi (2002), 'Success Factors in SMEs' Internationalization Processes: An Italian Investigation', *Journal of Small Business Management*, 40(2), 144–53.

Dean, J., R. Feinberg, M. Ferrantino and R. Ludema (2003), Estimating the Tariff-Equivalent of NTMs, Working Paper No. 2003-12-B, Washington, DC: US International Trade Commission, Office of Economics.

Deardorff, A.V. and R.M. Stern (eds) (1998), *Measurement of Non-Tariff Barriers, Studies in International Economics*, Ann Arbor: The University of Michigan Press.

Decreux, Y. and C. Mitaritonna (2007), *Economic Impact of a Potential Free Trade Agreement (FTA) Between the European Union and India*, Paris: Centre D'Etudes Prospectives et D'Informations Internationales (CEPII).

Dee, P. and M. Ferrantino (eds) (2005), *Quantitative Methods for Assessing the Effects of Non-Tariff Measures and Trade Facilitation*, Singapore: APEC Secretariat and World Scientific Publishing Co.

Directorate General of Foreign Trade (DGFT) (2007), New Delhi: Ministry of Commerce and Industry, available at: http://dgft.delhi.nic.in/.

Donnelly, W.A. and D. Manifold (2005), A Compilation of Reported Non-Tariff Measures: Description of Information, Working Paper, No. 2005-05-A, Washington, DC: Office of Economics, US International Trade Commission.

Dougherty, S.M., R. Herd, T. Chalaux and A.A. Erumban (2008), India's Growth Pattern and Obstacles to Higher Growth, OECD Economics Department Working Papers, No. 623, 11 Aug 2008, Paris: OECD.

Economic Commission for Latin America and the Caribbean (ECLAC) (2003), *Barriers to Latin and Caribbean Exports to the U.S. Market 2002–2003*, Washington, DC: ECLAC.

Emerson, M., M. Aujean, M. Catinat, P. Goybet and A. Jacquemin (1988), *The Economics of 1992: The E.C. Commission's Assessment of the Economic Effects of Completing the Internal Market*, London: Oxford University Press.

Erramilli, M.K. (1991), 'The Experience Factor in Foreign Market Entry Behavior of Service Firms', *Journal of International Business Studies*, Third Quarter, 479–501.

Erramilli, M.K. and C.P. Rao (1993), 'Service Firms' International Entry-Mode Choice: A Modified Transaction-Cost Analysis Approach', *Journal of Marketing*, 57(3), 19–38.

Estevadeordal, A. and R. Devlin (eds) (2001), *Las Americas sin barreras*, Washington, DC: Inter-American Development Bank.

European Commisson (2006), *The European Union and India: A Strategic Partnership for the 21st Century*, Brussels: EC Directorate General for External Relations, Unit for Relations with India, available at: http://ec.europa.eu/europeaid/infopoint/publications/external-relations/5d_en.htm.

Eurostat (2007), European Commission Directorate General of Trade, Comext, Statistical Regime 4, available at: http://www.delind.ec.europa.eu/en/political_dialogue/summits/seventh/main_indicators.pdf, (accessed: 28 May, 2009).

Federation of Indian Chambers of Commerce and Industry (FICCI) (2008), Press Release on 26th September 2008, available at: http://www.ficci.com/press/443/95.doc (accessed: 28 May, 2009).

Fink, C. and B. Smarzynska (2002), 'Trademarks, Geographical Indications, and Developing Countries', in B. Hoekman, A. Mattoo and P. English (eds), *Development, Trade, and the WTO: A Handbook*, Washington, DC: The World Bank, pp. 403–41.

Fiorentino, R., L. Verdeja and C. Toqueboeuf (2007), The Changing Landscape of Regional Trade Agreements: 2006 Update, Regional Trade Agreements Section, Trade Policies Review Division, Geneva: World Trade Organization.

Francois, J. and A.K. Reinhardt (1997), 'Applied Methods for Trade Policy Analysis: An Overview', in J.F. Francois and A.K. Reinhardt (eds), *Applied Methods for Trade Policy Analysis: A Handbook*, Cambridge: Cambridge University Press.

Gaisford, J.D. and A. Hester (2007), 'Why are There Trade Agreements?', in W.A. Kerr and J.D. Gaisford (eds) *Handbook on International Trade Policy*, Cheltenham, UK and Northampton, MA, USA: Edward Elgar, pp. 57–70.

Gaisford, J.D. and W.A. Kerr (2001*), Economic Analysis for International Trade Negotiations*, Cheltenham, UK and Northampton, MA, USA: Edward Elgar.

Gaisford, J.D., W.A. Kerr and N. Perdikis (2003), *Economic Analysis for EU Accession Negotiations – Agri-food Issues in the EU's Eastward Expansion*, Cheltenham, UK and Northampton, MA, USA: Edward Elgar.

Gerber, J. and W.A. Kerr (1995), 'Trade as an Agency of Social Policy: NAFTA's Schizophrenic Role in Agriculture', in S.J. Randal and H.W. Konrad (eds), *NAFTA in Transition*, Calgary: University of Calgary Press, pp. 93–111.

Goode, W. (2003), *Dictionary of Trade Policy Terms*: Fourth Edition, Cambridge, UK: Cambridge University Press.

Government of India (1992), *Technology Evaluation and Norms Study in Leather Tanneries*, New Delhi: Department of Scientific and Industrial Research, Ministry of Science and Technology, November.

Government of India, (n.d.), 'Eleventh Five Year Plan (2007–2012)', *Planning Commission*, online access at: http://planningcommission.nic.in/plans/planrel/11thf.htm.

Greenspan, A. (2007), *The Age of Turbulence*, New York: The Penguin Press.

Gugerty, M. and J. Stern (1996), Structural Barriers to Trade in Africa, Development Discussion Paper No. 561, Harvard Institute for International Development.

Hasheem, S.N. (2001), *Protection in Indian Manufacturing: An Empirical Study*, Delhi: Macmillan India Ltd.

High Level Trade Group (HLTG) (2006), Report of the EU–India High Level Trade Group to the EU–India Summit, Brussels.

Hobbs, J.E. and W.A. Kerr (2008), 'Agrifood Supply Chains in the NAFTA Market', in K.M. Huff, K.D. Meilke, R.D. Knutson, R.F. Ochoa and J. Rude (eds), *Contemporary Drivers of Integration*, Guelph, ON: Texas A&M University, University of Guelph, Intituto Interamericano de Cooperacion para la Agricultural-Mexico, pp. 89–112.

Hobbs, J.E. and W.A. Kerr (1999), 'Transaction Costs', in S. Bhagwan Dahiya (ed.), *The Current State of Economic Science, Vol. 4*, Rohtak: Spellbound Publications PVT Ltd, pp. 2111–33.

Kerr, W.A. (2000a), 'A New World Chaos? – International Institutions in the Information Age', *Journal of International Law and Trade Policy*, 1(1), 1–10.

Kerr, W.A. (2000b), 'The Next Step Will be Harder: Issues for the New Round of Agricultural Negotiations at the World Trade Organization', *Journal of World Trade*, 34(1), 123–140.

Kerr, W.A. (2001), 'Dumping – One of Those Economic Myths', *Journal of International Law and Trade Policy*, 2(2), 1–10.

Kerr, W.A. (2005a), 'Special and Differential Treatment: A Mechanism to Promote Development?', *Journal of International Law and Trade Policy*, 6(2), 84–94.

Kerr, W.A. (2005b), 'Vested Interests in Queuing and the Loss of the WTO's Club Good: The Long-Run Costs of US Bilateralism', *Journal of International Law and Trade Policy*, 6(1), 1–10.

Kerr, W.A. (2006), 'NAFTA's Underdeveloped Institutions: Did They Contribute to the BSE Crisis?', in K.M. Huff, K.D. Meilke, R.D. Knutson, R.F. Ochoa and J. Rude (eds), *Agrifood Regulatory and Policy Integration Under Stress*, Guelph, ON: Texas A&M University, University of Guelph, Intituto Interamericano de Cooperacion para la Agricultural-Mexico, pp. 213–26.

Kerr, W.A. and J.E. Hobbs (2006), 'Bilateralism – A Radical Shift in US Trade Policy: What Will it Mean for Agricultural Trade?', *Journal of World Trade*, 40(6), 1049–58.

Kerr, W.A. and N. Perdikis (2003), *The Economics of International Business: A Guide to the Global Commercial Environment*, Saskatoon: Estey Centre for Law and Economics in International Trade.

Kerr, W.A. and R.J. Foregrave (2002), 'The Prophecies of the Naysayers – Assessing the Vision of the Protectionists in the US–Canada Debate on Agricultural Reciprocity, 1846–1854', *Journal of International Law and Trade Policy*, 3(2), 357–408.

Kerr, W.A., N. Perdikis and J.E. Hobbs (2000), 'NAFTA and the "New" India', in N. Perdikis (ed.), *The Indian Economy: Contemporary Issues*, Aldershot: Ashgate.

Keynote Publications Ltd. (2008), Hand Luggage & Leather Goods – Market Report, Hampton, UK: Keynote Publications Ltd.

Khorana, S., N. Perdikis and D.K. Das (2008), *Convergence Towards Regional Integration Between the EU and India: Trade Implications for the UK and India*, New Delhi: British High Commission, Foreign and Commonwealth Office.

Knutsen, H.M. (1999), Leather Tanning, Environmental Regulations and Competitiveness – Final Report, Department of Human Geography, University of Oslo.

Kochhar, K., U. Kumar, R. Rajan, A. Subramanian and I. Tokatlidis (2006), India's Pattern of Development: What Happened, What Follows?, IMF Working Paper, Research Department, Washington, DC: International Monetary Fund.

Laird, S. (1999), Millennium Round Market Access Negotiations in Goods and Services, Paper prepared for a meeting of the International Economics Study Group, Birmingham, September.

Laird, S. and A. Yeats (1990), *Quantitative Methods for Trade-Barrier Analysis*, London: The Macmillan Press.

Laird, S. and R. Vossenaar (1991), Porque nos preocupan las bareras no arancelarias?, Informacion Comercial Espanola, Special Issue on Non-Tariff Barriers, November, pp. 31–54.

Leger, L.A., J.D. Gaisford and W.A. Kerr (1999), 'Labour Market Adjustments to International Trade Shocks', in S. Bhagwan Dahiya (ed.), *The Current State of Economic Science*, 4, Rohtak: Spellbound Publications, pp. 2011–34.

Limao, N. and A.J. Venables (2001), 'Infrastructure, Geographical Disadvantage, Transport Cost and Trade', *World Bank Economic Review*, 15, 451–79.

Lipsey, R.C. (1960), 'The Theory of Customs Unions: A General Theory', *Economic Journal*, 70, 496–513.

Majocchi, A. and A. Zucchella (2003), 'Internationalisation and Performance', *International Small Business Journal*, 21(3), 249–68.

McGuire G., R. Scollay and S. Stephenson (2002), APEC and Non-Tariff Measures, draft.

Mehta, R. (1997), 'Trade Policy Reforms, 1991–92 to 1995–96: Their Impact on External Trade', *Economic and Political Weekly*, 12 April, 779–84.

Mehta, R. (2005), Non-Tariff Barriers Affecting India's Exports, RIS Discussion Paper No. 97, New Delhi: Research and Information System for the Non-Aligned and Other Developing Countries (RIS), June, available at: http://www.ris.org.in/dp97_pap.pdf.

Mehta, R. and S.K. Mohanty (1999), *WTO and Industrial Tariffs: An Empirical Analysis for India*, New Delhi: Research and Information System for the Non-Aligned and Other Developing Countries (RIS).

Michalopoulos, C. (1999), *Trade Policy and Market Access Issues for DCs: Implications for the Millennium Round*, World Bank mimeo, Washington, DC: The World Bank.

Ministry of Textiles (2007), Annual Report, 2006–07, New Delhi: Government of India, available at: www.texmin.nic.in (accessed: 27 May, 2009).

Moenius, J. (2002), Three Essays on Trade Barriers and Trade Volumes, Ph.D. Dissertation, San Diego: University of California.

Mohan, M. (2006), 'EU-India summit: Seeking free trade in Helsinki', *The Hindu Business Line Online* at: http://www.thehindubusinessline.com/2006/10/09/stories/2006100900740900.htm, (accessed on 18/12/2006).

Moini, A. (1995), 'An Inquiry into Successful Exporting: An Empirical Investigation Using a Three-Stage Model', *Journal of Small Business Management*, 33(3), 9–25.

Moodley, R.D., W.A. Kerr and D.V. Gordon (2000), 'Has the Canada–US Trade Agreement Fostered Price Integration?', *Weltwirtschaftliches Archiv*, 136(2), 334–354.

Nataraj, G. (2007), Regional Trade Agreements in the Doha Round: Good for India?,

Asian Development Bank, Discussion Paper No. 67, 7 June 2007.

Nerb, G., (1987), 'The Completion of the Internal Market: A Survey of European Industry's Perception of the Likely Effects', *Research on the Costs of Non-Europe: Basic Findings*, Brussels: European Commission.

OECD (1997), *Indicators of Tariff and Non-Tariff Trade Barriers*, Paris: OECD.

OECD (2001), *Flagship Report on Regulatory Quality*, PUMA/REG, Paris: OECD.

OECD (2002), *Overview of Non-Tariff Barriers: Findings from Existing Business Surveys*, TD/TC/WP(2002)38/FINAL, Paris: OECD.

OECD (2005a), *A New World Map in Textile and Clothing: Adjusting to Change*, Paris: OECD.

OECD (2005b), *Analysis of Non-Tariff Barriers of Concern to Developing Countries*, TD/TC/WP(2004)47/REV1, Paris: OECD.

OECD (2007), 'Economic Survey of India, 2007', *Policy Brief*, available at: www.oecd.org/publications/Policybriefs, (accessed 20 March, 2009).

Panagariya, A. (2004), India in the 1980s and 1990s: A Triumph of Reforms, IMF Working Paper, Research Department.

Pandey, M. and I. Gang (1998), 'What was Protected? Measuring India's Tariff Barriers 1968–1997', *Indian Economic Review*, XXXIII(2), 119–52.

Perdikis, N. (ed.) (2000), *The Indian Economy: Contemporary Issues*, Aldershot: Ashgate.

Perdikis, N. (2007), 'Overview of Trade Agreements: Regional Trade Agreements', in W.A. Kerr and J.D. Gaisford (eds) *Handbook on International Trade Policy*, Cheltenham, UK and Northampton, MA, USA: Edward Elgar, pp. 82–93.

Perdikis, N., S.L. Boyd and W.A. Kerr (2004), 'Multinationals, Biotechnology, Intellectual Property and Developing Countries – Should Developing Countries Seek to Be Exploited?', in D. Meyer-Dinkgrafe (ed.), *European Culture in a Changing World: Between Nationalism and Globalism*, London: Cambridge Scholars Press, pp. 1–10.

Reserve Bank of India (RBI) (2007), *RBI Handbook of India's Statistics*, New Delhi: Government of India.

Sadikov, A. (2007), Border and Behind the Border Trade: Barriers and Country Exports, IMF Working paper No. WP/07/292, Policy Development and Review Department: IMF.

Schleifer, A. and R.W. Vishny (1993), 'Corruption', *Quarterly Journal of Economics*, 108(3), 599–617.

Sidgwick, E. (2004). 'Regionalism, Multilateralism and the Doha Development Agenda', in N. Xuto (ed.), *Brainstorming on Convergence of Preferential Trading Arrangements and the Multilateral Trading System*, Bangkok: International Institute for Trade and Development.

Skogstad, G. (2008), *Internationalization and Canadian Agriculture: Policy and Governing Paradigms*, Toronto: University of Toronto Press.

Stephenson, S. (1997), *Standards and Conformity Assessment as Non-Tariff Barriers to Trade*, World Bank Policy Research Working Paper No. 1826, Washington, DC: The World Bank.

Stephenson, S. (1999), Non-Tariff Barriers within APEC, Paper prepared for the Pacific Economic Cooperation Council (PECC) and presented on behalf of the PECC to the meeting of the APEC Market Access Group on 3 February 1999, Wellington, New Zealand.

Trade and Industry Committee Report (2006), Trade and Investment Opportunities with India, Third Report of Session, Volume 1, 2005–06, London: House of Commons.

UNCTAD (1994), *Directory of Import Regimes, Part I Monitoring Import Regimes (UNCTAD/DMS/2(PART 1)/Rev. 1, Sales No. E.94.II.D.6)*, New York: United Nations.

UNCTAD (2005), Methodologies, Classifications, Quantification and Development Impacts of Non-Tariff Barriers, Note by the UNCTAD Secretariat, available at www.UNCTAD.org., New York: United Nations

Van Grasstek, C. (2004), 'US Policy Towards Free Trade Agreements: Strategic Perspectives and Extrinsic Objectives', in N. Xuto (ed.), *Brainstorming on Convergence of Preferential Trading Arrangements and the Multilateral Trading System*, Bangkok: International Institute for Trade and Development.

Viner, J. (1950), *The Customs Union Issue*, New York: Carnegie Endowment for International Peace.

Wade, R. (1985), 'The Market for Public Office: Why the Indian State is Not Better at Development', *World Development*, 13(4): 467–497.

Wilson, J. (1999), *The Post-Seattle Agenda of the WTO in Standards and Technical Barriers to Trade: Issues for the Developing Countries*, Washington, DC: The World Bank.

Wilson, J. (2000), Technical Barriers to Trade and Standards, Challenges and Opportunities for Developing Countries, Paper Presented by the World Bank to the Technical Barriers to Trade Committee Meeting World Trade Organization, Washington, DC: The World Bank.

Wilson, J.S. (2002), 'Standards, Regulation, and Trade: WTO Rules and Developing Country Concerns', in,B. Hoekman, A. Mattoo and P. English (eds), *Development, Trade and the WTO: A Handbook*, Washington, DC: The World Bank, pp. 428–438.

Wonnacott, P. and R. Wonnacott (1992), 'The Customs Union Issue Reopened', *The Manchester School*, 60(2), 119–35.

World Bank (2007), *Doing Business in South Asia*, Washington, DC: The World Bank, available at: http://siteresources.worldbank.orga/SOUTH ASIAEXT/Resources/Publications/448813-1171300070514/dbindiapr. pdf.

WTO (n.d.a.), Committee of Regional Trade Agreements, RTA Database, available at: http://rtais.wto.org/UI/PublicMaintainRTAHome.aspx, (accessed 15 March, 2009).

WTO (n.d.b.), Legal Texts, available at: http://www.wto.org/english/docs_e
/legal_e/26-gats_01_e.htm#articleV, (accessed 15 March, 2009).

WTO (n.d.c.), Legal Texts, available at: http://www.wto.org/english/docs_e
/legal_e/enabling1979_e.htm, (accessed 15 March, 2009).

WTO (n.d.d.), Statistics Database, Trade Profile for India, available at: http:
//stat.wto.org/CountryProfile/WSDBCountryPFView.aspx?Language=
E&Country=IN, (accessed 3 April, 2009).

WTO (2003), Report of the Committee on Technical Barriers to Trade,
G/L/657, Geneva: WTO Secretariat, November.

WTO (2004), WTO Doha Round Bulletin, Issue 2004/38, Geneva: WTO
Secretariat, November.

WTO (2006), WTO Doha Round Bulletin, February Update, Geneva: WTO
Secretariat, November.

WTO (2007), Trade Policy Review of India, WT/TPR/S/182, Geneva:
WTO Secretariat, 18 April 2007.

Yeats, A. (1994), 'Quantitative Assessment of the Uruguay Round's Effects
and their Implications for Developing Countries', *World Bank PRE
Working Papers Series*, Washington, DC: The World Bank.

Yeung, M. and W.A. Kerr (2004), *Canada and the Australia–US Free
Trade Agreement: Enhanced Opportunities or Loss of Special Status?*,
Saskatoon: Estey Centre for Law and Economics in International
Trade.

Yeung, M. and W.A. Kerr (2002), *A New Trade Relationship: Canada and
the EU – Forestry, Minerals and Metals*, Saskatoon: Estey Centre for
Law and Economics in International Trade.

Yeung, M., L. Loppacher and W.A. Kerr (2004), 'The Short and Long
Term Effects of the US Move to Preferential Trade Agreements', in N.
Xuto (ed.), *Brainstorming on Convergence of Preferential Trading
Arrangements and the Multilateral Trading System*, Bangkok:
International Institute for Trade and Development.

Yeung, M., N. Perdikis and W.A. Kerr (1999), *Regional Trading Blocs in
the Global Economy: The EU and ASEAN*, Cheltenham, UK and
Northampton, MA, USA: Edward Elgar.

Zarrilli S. and I. Musselli (2004), 'The Sanitary and Phyto-sanitary
Agreement, Food Safety Policies and Product Attributes', in M.D.
Ingco and J.D. Nash (eds), *Agriculture and the WTO: Creating a
Trading System for Development*, Washington, DC: The World Bank,
pp. 217–236.

Zoellick, R. (2002), 'Unleashing the Trade Winds', *The Economist*, 7
December, 2002, available at: www.economist.com.

Index

212   *Bilateral Trade Agreements in the Era of Globalization*

5, 25, 28, 30-41, 44-5, 49-52,
67, 91, 104, 114, 147, 155,
158-9, 161-2, 167-71, 174-5,
180, 182
domestic barriers 97, 114, 131, 141-
2, 144, 150, 166-7, 170, 193

EC□Chile Free Trade Agreement 18
EC□India 21, 49
EC□India Cooperation Agreement
on Partnership and
Development 49
eco-friendly 108, 157
economic diversification 37
economic integration agreements,
EIA *xi*, 17-8, 29
economies of scale 1-2, 9-10, 14, 19,
28, 122, 128-9, 136, 150, 154,
168, 177
EFTA□Peru 21
Enabling Clause 17, 29
end-of-pipe pollution control 160
environment 13, 17, 20, 24, 38-9, 41,
50, 52, 78-9, 86, 93, 95, 98,
100, 104-6, 109, 111-2, 114,
131-2, 138-41, 146-7, 150,
156-60, 162, 165-8, 170, 172,
182, 184, 193
environmental regulations 109, 111-
2, 159-60
equilibrium 4
EU25 56, 61
EU□India Free Trade Agreement,
FTA 12, 132, 191-2
EURATEX 141
European Community, EC *xi*, 18, 21,
30, 49, 78-80, 85-7, 94, 97,
105-6, 109, 111, 124
European Community Investment
Partners 49
European Economic Community,
EEC *xi*, 17, 49, 78-80, 85, 87,
97, 111, 147
European Free Trade Association,
EFTA *xi*, 20, 21, 45
Everything But Arms 24
export incentives 33

export subsidies 9, 93, 146, 179

Federation of Indian Chambers of
Commerce, FICCI *xii*, 86
foreign direct investment, FDI *xii*,
15, 32, 34-5, 38, 40, 42, 44, 46
Foreign Investment Implementation
Authority, FIIA *xii*, 46

G□20 *xii*, 45, 48, 178-9
General Agreement on Tariffs and
Trade, GATT *xii*, *xv*, 13, 15,
20, 23, 29, 30, 177, 179-80
Uruguay Round 20, 23, 29-30, 42,
93, 174, 179
General Agreement on Trade in
Services, GATS *xii*, 17, 29, 46,
67, 71
Article V 17, 29
Generalised System of Preferences,
GSP *xii*, 49, 76, 78, 82, 84-5,
88, 95, 165
Germany 61, 81, 95, 105-6, 111, 147
global environment 50
Global System of Trade Preferences
among Developing Countries,
GSTP *xii*, 45
globalization 1
gross domestic product, GDP *xii*, 14,
33-5, 37-9, 44, 48, 73
Growth and Opportunity Act 24
Gulf Cooperation Council, GCC *xii*,
21, 46, 71

Harmonised System (HS) Code *xii*,
75, 82, 84
harmonization initiatives 155

import substitution 9, 31-2, 34, 47,
52
import value requirement 165, 191
India□EU Agreement 3, 8, 11, 67,
177, 183
Indonesia 27, 37, 46
information technology, IT *xii*, 35-6,
43, 51, 56, 74, 169
intellectual property, IP *xii*, *xiii*, 23,
25, 42-3, 51, 67, 154